Other books by Carole Golder

Make the Most of Your Sun Sign

★

The Seductive Art of Astrology

★

Carole Golder's Star Signs

★

Love Lives

*Using Astrology to Build the
Perfect Relationship with Any Star Sign*

Carole Golder

An Owl Book
Henry Holt and Company
New York

Henry Holt and Company, Inc.
Publishers since 1866
115 West 18th Street
New York, New York 10011

Henry Holt® is a registered trademark
of Henry Holt and Company, Inc.

Originally published in Great Britain by
Judy Piatkus (Publishers) Limited in 1989.

Library of Congress Cataloging-in-Publication Data
Golder, Carole.
Love lives : using astrology to build the perfect relationship with
any star sign / Carole Golder.—1st American ed.
p.   cm.
"An Owl book."
1. Astrology.   2. Love—Miscellanea.   3. Interpersonal relations—
Miscellanea.   4. Mate selection—Miscellanea.
I. Title.
BF1729.L6G62   1990
133.5'864677—dc20   89-29855
CIP

ISBN 0-8050-1311-3 (pbk.)

First American Edition—1990

Designed by Nancy Lawrence
Illustrated by Hanife Hassan

Printed in the United States of America
All first editions are printed on acid-free paper.∞

9 10 8

Dedication

I'd like to dedicate this book to a Scorpio – Mark Antrobus; to thank Jayne Cooper of Canon for the use of the great Typestar 90 typewriter; and also to thank Judy, Gill, Tina, Michael and Rita, Gerald, Ingrid, Mark Hayles, Mike and Alice, and all the other wonderful people in my life, from Aries to Pisces, who have always proved beyond any doubt that having good relationships is what life is all about!

Contents

Contents

Introduction

When I wrote *The Seductive Art of Astrology* the idea was to show how astrology could make a dream lover become a reality. But long-term reality involves something more than dreams — for in a serious relationship compatability plays a major part.

It is not simply a question of the compatibility between certain signs being greater than with others. It's that by learning more about our own strengths and weaknesses, and those of the people we choose to be part of our lives, we can make all our relationships work on a higher level. It is possible to achieve a good relationship with anyone, not simply on an emotional level but where family ties, work situations and friendships are also involved.

We all have within us different aspects of the various signs, depending on our own specific horoscopes. To get the right sense of yourself, you will have to respond to what rings true for you and accept other effects such as hereditary influences as also playing an important part in your personality.

One of the greatest values of a relationship can be in the process of self-discovery. By relating to another person we start to learn so much more about ourselves — our needs, desires and innermost feelings — and that can be very exciting too. But people involved in any kind of relationship should be totally honest.

Needless to say, honesty can have both positive and negative connotations. If you're a Sagittarian you can be so brutally honest with your thoughts and assessments that you can hurt someone deeply. Honesty is something which has to be used carefully, which is perhaps why people are often afraid of it, because of its constructive and its destructive powers. Without honesty, however, even the most perfect sounding relationship is sure to contain certain flaws, so its importance can never be understated.

Self-discovery must also never be minimized. And that doesn't mean gazing at one's image in the mirror or staring at one's navel, totally wrapped up in oneself to the exclusion of everyone else. It means just the opposite – to learn more about oneself within the structure of society as a whole and in each relationship in particular. It's important to learn to love oneself more too – for if we don't love ourselves how can we truly expect another person to love us?

Relating to other people begins when you are very young. But if you had a difficult childhood, with parents who found it hard to communicate with themselves, let alone with you, it can be very difficult to imagine being on a perfect wavelength with other people. Yet that cannot be used solely as an excuse. Of course there are situations in people's childhoods which are impossible to forget. But it can be almost too easy to blame one's own difficulty in sustaining well-balanced relationships on what has gone on before.

You don't have to believe that you cannot sustain a positive relationship just because of your past. But learning *more* about your own past *can* be extremely helpful; learning more about your parents too. After all, it isn't only astrological make-up which makes you what you are, but your heredity, too.

I am not telling you to change your own personality to fit in with someone else's, but I *am* suggesting that it can sometimes be very beneficial to modify certain characteristics when you know that they are creating something negative. The components of your personality can be heightened or dulled ... magnified or shrunk ... by deciding to change because something depends upon it – perhaps keeping that potentially perfect partner by your side! But you should never try and contort yourself into an impossible psychological shape simply in order to become something else for someone. Never forget, 'To thine own self be true'!

The trouble is, that we don't always know who we are and what we're capable of; with one person we may feel like an insignificant nonentity, while with another person, who loves us, we may shine like the sun.

10

That is one of the most wonderful things about being in a perfect relationship; and I don't just mean a 'love' one. Being with someone who cares for you and respects you has an extremely powerful effect. How many times have you woken up and looked at yourself in the mirror, not really liking what you saw? The outside world seemed grey and gloomy, you felt ill at ease with yourself and everyone else; then, suddenly, you received a compliment from someone you respected or loved, and you started to see everything in a totally different light? Giving compliments is therefore equally important.

Putting out negative vibes really can create negativity in your life. If you believe that the perfect relationship will forever be elusive to you, it can easily happen that way.

There are other possible dangers to face in a love relationship: the danger of becoming too deeply involved too fast with someone who is not right, and the danger of not giving your heart to the right person and losing them because of your own indecision. It is not only Librans who suffer from being indecisive! Many people faced with having to decide whether to make a relationship permanent suffer similar pangs of 'will it work or won't it?'.

Therefore it's important to recall that it can be better to be alone than to have made the wrong decision; and usually a right and perfect partner will know that *you* are right too, making non-coercive gestures to attract you.

If you have doubts in any kind of relationship, always express them; when you feel you have something very special and unique, express that too. Always remember that words are among the most powerful keys to success in love and in life, if they are used well. And this has nothing to do with cleverness, for plenty of people know how to be clever and fast-talking, full of snappy comebacks, but are dumbfounded when it comes to sincerity and seriousness of feeling. To be serious does not mean you have to be dark and gloomy; it means only that you have to be absolutely straight with yourself and your partner – and, indeed, everyone else you relate to.

In a perfect relationship there ought not to be any necessity to prove something to your partner, like spending a great deal of money which you don't have, or dressing in a certain way, which deep down you know does not feel right to you.

It's important for people to care for each other for his or her own sake, and not just for what they can get in the way of power. Many strong and lasting relationships are built within a circuit of friends and shared interests.

In a love relationship, problems often arise because of one or both partner's attitude to sexuality. No one will think you're perverted for wanting to know more about your partner's body; but you can't always ask them questions about what he or she likes, for that can destroy the mystery and enchantment, and besides, you should like each other physically well enough to begin with, or like each other spiritually, which itself is sexuality; for sexuality can also be called the spirit expressing itself on the physical plane. If you turn sex into something dirty you are only reacting to the controls of superstition, and fear of the body, and the powerful forces of sexuality. To make fun of it is ridiculous. But to find greater pleasure in sex does not mean that you should discover this or that technique (sorry, Scorpio!). No one likes to feel they're being made love to by the rule book; and certainly complete innocence isn't always the best guide.

One question which invariably raises its ugly head when two people embark on a love relationship is that of faithfulness. The trouble about this is that if both partners have had many affairs or marriages in the past, doubts are often going to creep in. However, it really isn't fair to assume that because one person is born under a particular star sign they are more likely to play around. It's true that some signs are more sensual and hedonistic than others, but in a perfect relationship people *do* become devoted to each other exclusive of all else. You have to learn not only to trust more but to remember always that your partner did have a life before you came on the scene. If you have been truly honest with each other about the past, why do you have to be any less honest in the future?

A perfect love relationship will involve sharing thoughts, ideals, aspirations, learning to adapt to each other. It's also important not to let your code of behaviour slip. It might seem rather outmoded to talk about manners. But if you start to take your partner too much for granted, or vice-versa, the

12

relationship is going to be out of balance.

A relationship can also be out of balance when one person, for instance, thrives on action and excitement, and the other prefers a much more placid life and needs more routine. However, if you genuinely love your partner and he or she feels the same way about you, this is something which can be overcome, especially when you are prepared to learn more about the characteristics of your mate's star-sign. Besides, it's not necessary for two people to be the same in order to get on well. The attraction of opposites can never be understated.

In every star-sign there is something of its opposite, and there is always something to learn about ourselves by learning more about this opposite sign. If you're an Aries it's not difficult to realize that Libra's ability to weigh things up is usually sadly missing in the Ram's impulsive headstrong behaviour; and the passive attitude of Taurus could benefit from a little more Scorpio intensity.

When I first started writing this book, many people asked me the same question: 'What *is* a perfect relationship?' Sometimes they were teasing, sometimes genuinely curious as to how I would reply.

Of course, the perfect relationship can mean many personal things to many people. Some people go through their entire lives searching for what they believe they want or need. It can involve illusion and delusion; romantic fantasies; a quest for material security; emotional contentment; a practical working partnership; so many different things. Not all people involved in a love relationship consider that a blending of mind/body/spirit is of paramount importance; not all people place major importance on financial security; and not everyone is prepared to work at holding on to their so-called perfect relationship even when they do find it.

We're living in a consumer culture where there are thousands of merchandisers trying to help us to have 'fun'. We're encouraged to spend, spend, spend on items to make us more beautiful, more elegant, enjoy greater comforts in our homes; we're in a technological age where machines are prepared to do our thinking for us.

But do you truly believe that there is any machine which can help you to have a perfect relationship? No matter how many successful dating agencies put you in touch with the so-called 'perfect partner', compatible in every possible way, you will still have to work at it yourself.

You will also have to remember that the differences which first attracted you can, after a while, create their own conflicts. You love to be the recipient of your Cancerian partner's protective and sentimental gestures, yet sometimes so much domestic cosiness makes you feel hemmed in. It's wonderful to receive extravagant gifts from your Leo lover, until you're living together and discover that the mortgage payments have fallen way behind.

On the positive side, you will realize how much you also have to gain from these same differences. Perhaps you're a Sagittarian who has yearned to settle down; your wanderlust ways are no longer your *raison d'être*; you long for a partner who understands that feeling inwardly free doesn't mean you're going to be unfaithful. At the same time you can bring your wonderfully positive and optimistic outlook to the partner who believes in you, enabling him or her to experience the joy of being totally committed yet retaining *their* independence too.

Relationships tend to be approached in different ways at different stages of our lives. As a teenager you might have had your own romantic dreams of settling down forever with the perfect partner by your side. But your first important love relationship was probably based almost totally on physical attraction. That's fine, if you bothered to learn everything else about each other's personality too.

When you're very young you think that love will conquer everything. Of course there are people who married very young and who will always stay together. But in these days of instant gratification and quickie divorces, where 'triangle' situations arise all too frequently, it's almost too easy to go from relationship to relationship, discarding one because you feel it has outlived its purpose, feeling that there is no longer that excitement and thrill which dominated your life in the beginning.

In any relationship it is important to be able to communicate.

For some people this is the easiest thing in the world; for others it is a long and painful process before they can trust anyone deeply enough to reveal all.

Work relationships and family relationships are not usually affected by age differences; and even in love relationships the age barrier is becoming less and less of an issue. There was a time when it was considered fine for a man to have a relationship with a much younger woman but it was looked down upon when a woman became involved with a younger man. Today there are many references to 'toy boys' but there are also many blissfully happy relationships between women and their much younger mates.

When you find that perfect blend of mind/body/spirit with your chosen partner, it transcends age differences. You may even feel there is a karmic bond between you: that you have met before. Or there may be a feeling of *déjà vu* between each other.

But it's not simply a question of deciding which star-sign you're best suited to, and resolving that no one else will do. In *The Seductive Art of Astrology* I made the point that you can get on with every sign by learning more about yourself – and about them too.

In the same way, I want you to realize that by becoming more knowledgeable about your partner's needs and desires, strengths and weaknesses, positive and negative characteristics – you can build and maintain the perfect relationship, regardless of your sign and theirs.

Of course there will be changes along the way; children will bring many people even closer together; some of you will be affected by changes in professional status, or through material influences; or some of you will sadly realize that an initial passion has cooled over the years. For some, divorce may become an inevitability.

But one thing to remember, which must always remain constant, is that if you truly learn to love yourself you will always attract loving people to your side and all your relationships will grow from strength to strength.

Always remember too that it's not what 'other people' have done that matters now. It's what *you* can do to make *your* relationships more contented and more fun too.

Part 1
You in a Relationship

Building and maintaining relationships are not part of a school curriculum, although they are definitely an important part of growing up. For once you have realized the value of an in-depth look at your personal characteristics and your needs, you can gain even more enjoyment and fulfilment out of life.

The brief guides to 'How you see them' and 'How they see you' and 'How to make things even better' at the end of each star-sign are preludes to what you will discover when you read the chapter on your partner in the Zodiac. You will then find out why they behave as they do and understand them that much better.

You have to realize that relationships of every kind are a bit like balancing acts, and this doesn't just apply to love but to every other relationship too; from all of them you hope to receive the sort of moral support that you're prepared to offer, and when you have begun to know yourself better you will soon see how much happier you can be.

However, in any astrology book one has to generalize to some degree, so if while reading the 'You in a Relationship' chapter for your star-sign you do not recognize certain facets of your character, remember that this can be due to your Ascendant or Moon sign, or various other influences in your particular chart. Nonetheless, I'm sure there will be a great deal which you *do* relate to, and which can help you to enjoy better relationships with the people in your life.

Aries

Ruled by Mars, that fiery God of War, your birthsign coincides with the very first day of Spring, and your attitude to life invariably tends to be 'me first' or 'I want it yesterday'. You might think that this attitude is perfectly acceptable, and that it's managed to get you where you are now, but are you really convinced that it's always been for the best?

You're a real go-getter; one of the most enthusiastic and enterprising signs in the entire Zodiac. A born survivor, you're someone who thrives on challenges, loves life, and possesses a natural exuberance which makes you one of the friendliest souls around. Full of energy, you throw yourself headlong into everything you undertake — headlong into relationships too.

Impatient, impulsive Aries. There is something wonderfully innocent and vulnerable about you. Somehow you manage to remain eternally youthful. At heart you'll always be the child who never wanted to grow up. But, unless children learn that they can't always have things all their own way early on, life can be tricky as the years go by.

Sometimes you can appear aggressive and even arrogant when people meet you for the very first time. Astrologically, Aries rules the head, so I suppose you could be forgiven for perhaps being slightly too concerned with your ego. However, why should anyone else be aware of that, unless they're a keen student of astrology and have instantly realized that you're far more timid than you appear?

Just because Aries is the first sign of the Zodiac, and because you are endowed with natural qualities of leadership, that doesn't mean you can always take the lead. Even if your friends let you boss them around when you were all seven or eight years old, it didn't mean that once you reached adolescence and adulthood your experiences would be the same.

But you have to be very honest with yourself when reading this chapter, for it might be far too easy to sit back and tell yourself that you've never been bossy or aggressive in your life. You may say you've simply been enterprising and assertive, and that you have only initiated things because nobody else was prepared to make the first move, and that deep down you've always waited for someone else to take control. And subconsciously that might well be true. The trouble is that there isn't always the time to scratch below the surface and find out what makes someone tick. And if you want to achieve the perfect relationships in your life, then you need to clock up more obviously positive characteristics than negative ones.

One of the most important things to work on in your personality is inevitably the need to exercise a little more patience. You invariably try to do everything too quickly. To maintain perfect relationships in your life you do need to take things a touch slower.

Besides, you know how much you thrive on challenges. If something doesn't run as smoothly as you would like, think how proud you will feel when it starts to improve because of your positive attitude and determined efforts.

When it comes to love, you must surely accept that you're up against something you can't control. As romantically idealistic as Pisces, and often as self-critical as Virgo, even the toughest Arien will usually admit that while you enjoy being independent and renowned for your qualities of leadership, deep down you do thrive in a blissfully happy emotional relationship, with someone who understands the real you.

But what do you do so often? Your headstrong, impulsive ways send you falling head-over-heels in love with the most impossible partner, and not only when you could perhaps excuse yourself for being too young to know any better. Your knees turn to jelly, you dream of living happily ever after, and you're determined to prove that you're irresistible. You don't necessarily wait to ascertain whether this dream partner is interested in you or not, let alone whether he or she has the strength of character you need. You're quite prepared to make the first move and take it from there.

The snag is that sometimes you rush so quickly into something that before very long you realize you've made a mistake. To have and to hold the perfect relationship in your life, you have to learn to take things a touch slower. But as a typical challenge-loving Aries, your heart bursts into flames when you fall in love.

You're passionately emotional, and a lover who doesn't satisfy your sexual desires will not be your perfect partner for very long. But equally a physically gratifying relationship which doesn't give you very much satisfaction outside the bedroom will be just as short-lived. A totally fulfilling involvement must combine romance, good sex, and mutual interests.

Your Mars-ruled personality gives the impression that you want to control situations from the word go. But it's not that you're totally selfish, and expect the rest of the world to revolve around you. Although you possess a large ego, you're also one of the most loving and generous signs of the entire Zodiac. You're amazingly adept at attracting admirers to your side, and it's simply a matter of allowing them to take things at their pace instead of yours.

Anyone who has ever been emotionally involved with an Aries of either sex will also soon realize that you can be as jealous and possessive as any Scorpio. You tend to have blind faith in anyone you love, so it always comes as a great shock if you realize it has been misplaced. And while you thrive on challenges, your fiery passion will burn itself out in bitterness and frustration if you feel you're being two-timed; so coping with a 'triangle' situation is never your forte.

It's not just in emotional relationships that your impatience and urge to control can create problems for you. You're quite capable of behaving like a spoilt child if you don't get your own way with your family or friends. And heaven help a boss or colleague you don't respect who is responsible for telling you what to do. It's always difficult for a headstrong Arien to be given orders by anyone they can't relate to.

But don't get me wrong: you're never usually a snob. You can happily relate to anyone you're involved with in any way, just as long as you do respect them, and age differences never bother you.

However, while everyone invariably mellows as the years go by, a typical Aries does find it hard to slow down, to be more patient, to accept that there really is a time and a place for eveything, and therefore you sometimes give yourself unnecessarily difficult moments.

Why not try to stop wanting things yesterday, to give other people a chance to be leaders and enjoy the freedom which you like to have yourself? You have so much energy and vitality to give to the world, so don't burn yourself out by missing it.

This is also a good moment to tell you that inside every starsign is a part of their opposite sign trying to get out! And that is absolutely perfect for you, since your opposite sign in the Zodiac is Libra – the sign of balance, peace and harmony. Think about those Libran scales when you feel yourself doing your leadership act a little too much. Visualize them in your mind – the power of your mind is incredibly strong, so use it. Next time you feel the urge to tell someone what to do, count silently to ten and think it over again. Were you about to order them around unnecessarily? Were you being selfish, putting your own needs before anyone else's? Were you creating an unnecessary challenge for yourself?

You don't have to turn overnight from a fiery Ram into a meek little sheep. But equally you don't have to make quite such a noise and wear everyone else out with your amazing energy. You can learn to walk instead of run, perhaps even try not wearing a watch when it isn't absolutely necessary. You can learn to be a little less extravagant financially. Many Ariens never seem to have enough money to cope with all their needs, even though they're quite capable of earning it. And it's no use making the excuse that it's part of your astrological make-up to be both extravagant and generous when you know that you also have to overcome any of your negative characteristics – and over-extravagance can be very, very negative.

Because you're a Fire sign you're not always sufficiently practical with your feet on the ground. But you're perfectly capable of modifying this. You're also perfectly capable of becoming less impatient and less involved with your own needs. Of course you enjoy being put on a pedestal and having lots of action and excitement in your life, of having innumerable goals and challenges, of having earth-shatteringly good sex in your love life and of tirelessly proving that being the first sign of the Zodiac is a privileged position.

But since you also value relationships which can become more fulfilling and contented as the days and months go by, and since you're invariably aware that you're far more vulnerable than you appear, why not stop putting on quite such an act. Your refreshing mixture of adventurous enthusiasm tempered with courage and faith, your passion combined with that childlike innocence will mean you will never be alone for long.

It is up to you to control your impatience, to explore your feelings step by step, to learn to take advice as much as you like to delegate responsibility, and to discover as much as you can about your partner's needs and desires so that your relationship can always remain as perfect as the first moment it began.

★

How you see Aries Think of this relationship rather like looking in a mirror. You'll recognize and understand almost every facet of your partner's personality. Challenging in every sense — you can be perfect soulmates or two strong egos battling for control!

How Aries sees you It's that mirror image once again. Your Aries partner will know that this is the challenge to end all challenges, and one which they are determined to win — for who could know each other better than you two?

To make things even better Pretend you're a Libran: practise a little indecisiveness and just for once be happy to let someone else make the very first moves — it could be a lot of fun.

★

24

How you see Taurus   You're both equally romantic, but even if you're just wild about Taurus, remember the sign of the Bull hates to be pushed. You want instant gratification — they live by slow, deliberate consideration and love to watch things growing — try to learn some vital lessons from this!

How Taurus sees you   Taurus will be captivated by your fiery personality — but Taureans put up a barrier against being swept off their feet. They want to get to know you better — at their pace, not yours.

To make things even better   No one is asking you to be an immovable object, but start to take life slightly slower and enjoy the bliss of seeing this relationship grow from strength to strength.

★

How you see Gemini   You can have a wonderful relationship with Gemini once you admit that you enjoy flirting almost as much as they do, and that you're quite prepared to be faithful for ever more — just as long as they are!

How Gemini sees you   Gemini enjoys a challenge as much as you, but in their case the challenge is whether your active mind can keep up with theirs, more than who can win hands down on the passion stakes.

To make things even better   Never let your attention slip when Gemini has something to discuss. Learning to be a good listener will enhance this relationship in the best of all possible ways.

★

How you see Cancer   You relish the idea of moonlit walks along the beach, and cosy domesticated evenings in front of a log fire. You know that your moods can sometimes swing almost as much as theirs — but that you are both equally sentimental when it comes to love.

How Cancer sees you   Cancer can be just as forceful as you, so it might be pleasant to let someone else take charge for a change. Cancerians will soon make it very plain that a happy domesticated life is what the perfect relationship is all about.

To make things even better If your Cancer partner wants to crawl into that shell from time to time, don't make quite so much fuss – everyone needs some private moments alone with their thoughts.

★

How you see Leo The two of you can make beautiful music together if you remember that Leo is determined to be boss. You learn that being the leader of the pack is no longer quite so important when your Leo is around.

How Leo sees you Leo understands your fiery nature but sometimes finds it hard to cope with your impatient attitude to everything in life. This sign's passionate desires blend beautifully with yours.

To make things even better If being in command is what makes Leo so happy, continue to go along with that from time to time – at least till you have recognized each other as equals! Then you can take turns.

★

How you see Virgo You sometimes resent the way Virgo picks holes in what you say or do. But a little self analysis will lead you to admit that constructive criticism helps you to know yourself better.

How Virgo sees you This sign needs someone as positive and outgoing as you to believe in them and stop them being *quite* so self-critical, but a little reflection might lead you to admit that Virgo is often right and could help you to know yourself better.

To make things even better This relationship will work best if you each make resolutions to understand your personalities a little more and don't constantly harp on each other's faults!

★

How you see Libra You've met your true match. Libra can be

26

your perfect soulmate if you stand still long enough to listen to what is being said. You need balance in your life – Libra can provide it.

How Libra sees you Libra wants peace while you thrive on excitement; Libra is indecisive – but your impulsiveness can often lead you astray. Opposites attract and Libra will invariably be fascinated by you.

To make things even better Take a leaf out of Libra's book. Visualize those Libran scales and practise doing a little balancing act on your personality so that this relationship can go from strength to strength.

★

How you see Scorpio You may feel slightly intimidated by Scorpio's passion in the early days, and wonder if life will really stay this good. You're intrigued to know everything about your Scorpio partner's life.

How Scorpio sees you Scorpio is equally intrigued and charmed by your idealistic childlike faith in life, and that Scorpio intuition lets this sign see that you're nowhere near as independent as you seem.

To make things even better Both of you will have to work harder at being less jealous and possessive if this relationship is to last on a permanent level.

★

How you see Sagittarius You're captivated by Sagittarius' happy-go-lucky approach to everything. You imagine a life where the two of you together can conquer the world.

How Sagittarius sees you Sagittarius is delighted to find someone almost as free-spirited as they are – but isn't quite so happy if you're always the one who gives the orders.

To make things even better Both of you need to retain a certain amount of independence in your lives for this relationship to get better and better. Always remember to make each other laugh — a sense of humour is so important.

★

How you see Capricorn   You'll really have to persevere to make Capricorn believe that you're looking for a permanent relationship and not just interested in having a good time while the fun lasts.

How Capricorn sees you   This sign could easily worry that you'd get bored once any kind of routine sets in. Your exuberance is sometimes hard for them to accept when they often seem to have the worries of the world upon their shoulders.

To make things even better   Prove that you can be just as serious about life as they tend to be, and don't be afraid to admit that a secure relationship is what you've been dreaming of.

★

How you see Aquarius   You envisage a relationship where your flights of fantasy become reality with someone who is even more idealistic than you. But emotionally you worry that Aquarius is sometimes too cool and detached.

How Aquarius sees you   Aquarius has such unpredictable moods that one day you're the flavour of the month, the next they might almost wonder what they ever saw in you to like — let alone love!

To make things even better   Practise a little unpredictability yourself if you want to keep this relationship as intriguing to Aquarius as it is to you. You have a very special soulmate here.

★

How you see Pisces   You dream of romantic bliss for ever more with a Pisces partner — but all that Aries aggressiveness and passion can sometimes make your Pisces swim away to calmer waters.

How Pisces sees you   Pisces needs a partner who sets as much store by tender sentimental love as passionately physical declarations of your emotions. Anniversaries must definitely be remembered in any relationship with this sign.

To make things even better Resolve that you'll never be too brash and forceful in this relationship. Let Pisces see you're as incurably romantic as they are — and always remember that Water *can* put out Fire.

Taurus

Ruled by Venus, Goddess of Love, your idea of the perfect relationship is one which brings you security in every possible sense of the word. You're not looking for a flash-in-the-pan affair, the kind that may start off with overpowering intensity but which may fizzle out a short while later.

When you meet someone you really like you're quite prepared for things to take their time, building gradually from friendship into a deeper bond. While Aries wants it 'yesterday', you're prepared to wait for tomorrow or even next month. You don't believe in rushing into anything before you know for certain that it's truly what you want. But are you always so convinced of all the answers? For instance do you not hold back sometimes for so long that you lose out on opportunities? And I'm not just talking about love.

The trouble with being a Taurus is that while you're wonderfully dependable and down-to-earth, you can also be amazingly stubborn and obstinate in your attitude to life. Just because you're a Fixed sign do you have to be quite so set in your ways? It might do you a lot of good to relax and accept that life can take you unawares sometimes, bringing unexpectedly joyous moments your way. Try and let this happen and don't always negate surprises simply because *you* don't think the timing is right.

It can take a lifetime to really know one's self. But whatever your age you have probably realized that there is often a conflict within you between your materialistic needs and your more spiritual ones. Your Taurus feet are set firmly on the ground, but your feelings are controlled by your senses. Sight, smell, touch, sound – you have to admit that these are what matter in your life, and negating your own sensuality would never work.

But sometimes you give yourself an especially hard time by somehow feeling that Earth signs are supposed to be so practical and realistic that they can't let themselves go. No one is asking you to become a romantic dreamer who lives way up in the clouds. But if you're really honest with yourself you have to admit that you have just as many idealistic yearnings as any Piscean, so why do you have to lock them away?

To enjoy more romance in your life it doesn't mean that you have to be irresponsible. But it does mean that perhaps you will have to let a few of your defences down and admit that you're not always quite so tough as you seem.

To achieve the perfect relationship you need to show there is a vulnerable side to you too. Sometimes you deliberate for so long over every action that its meaning almost becomes lost. Self-restraint and self-control are admirable qualities but letting yourself go a little more doesn't have to mean losing your strength!

You have such highly attuned senses that you usually know when there is someone you want to see more of. It is true that your sensual nature sometimes means you're physically attracted to someone who doesn't blend with you in other ways. But that's when you can use that self-control in a more positive way.

Honest, patient, gentle Taurus, building and maintaining a relationship is no great challenge for you. You love to see things growing in the ground, and watching a relationship bloom into something permanent can bring you so much pleasure no matter what the differences of age or station. You don't mind how long you work at it, when you know deep down that it's right.

But first of all you have to recognize that you are sometimes too slow to admit to yourself – let alone the other person – that you've fallen in love. And for someone who is normally as honest as you, that is definitely a personal danger zone. Be aware of what you're feeling and don't hold back your thoughts. Bottling things up inside is no way to allow a relationship to grow. A relationship needs the air and sun of communication. Caution is one thing, but refusing to accept what is happening to you is simply being stubborn yet again.

You also need to recognize that you have an inner fear about your financial security. But emotional security is as important as the material kind. Never sell yourself short on this, for money in the bank will never make up for a lack of romance in your life as the years go by. And, for you, maturity can only deepen love.

Do you really believe that with the Goddess of Love as your planetary ruler you can dismiss romance, friendships and attachments to family as feelings which are not terribly important in your life? Never fool yourself about that! You can't do without them or you really will begin to feel like a plant which hasn't been watered.

Sometimes you're so busy looking for what you consider to be the 'right path' in the practical sense that you forget about your inner needs. You're fully aware that physical satisfaction is highly important but you forget about the soul level too.

Once you have opened up completely to a lover you also open up to life and become incredibly passionate; love-making is definitely something at which you are highly skilled. Touch is everything to you and your sexuality can never be understated. You need a partner who is as pleasure-loving as you are − for the pleasures of the flesh are high on your agenda too!

Determined yet stubborn, pleasure-loving yet highly sensitive − you expect a great deal out of life but at least you don't expect it all to happen overnight! You are extremely loving and affectionate, loyal and generous. It's easy for you to have admirers flocking towards you − never so easy for you to make the first move.

Just like your opposite sign of Scorpio you can be extremely jealous and possessive. But then you often tend to be possessive about everything in your life, whether its your home, your friends, everything you own. You work hard to realize your desires, and although no one could accuse you of being selfish, you have a fear of losing possession of things. It all comes back to your need for security.

Deep down you dread being let down in any way. You're not the sort of person who would behave irresponsibly towards people you care for, and you expect the same behaviour from them.

It would be hard for you to cope in a 'triangle' situation, although if you were really determined that it was meant to be in the long term, you would not suddenly walk away from the person you loved. However, hurting anyone, even a stranger, is not something you are able to do very easily, and breaking up someone else's home and family is invariably against your morals and belief in the sanctity of marriage.

In a work situation you're not always the most ruthless of people, and often not even that ambitious. As long as you're doing something you enjoy, where the financial rewards are adequate, you don't have a burning desire to be at the very top. You're quite happy to take second place to someone you respect. But sometimes you undervalue your own talents and abilities too much, and need to be pushed into taking a more assertive attitude.

Astrologically, Taurus is the second sign of the Zodiac, and if you feel you have been taking second place in too many areas of your life for too long, then you should take steps to do something about it.

You have such great strength of purpose when there is an objective you intensely desire, but because you basically dislike the idea of change, any kind of change, you sometimes go along in the same old rut year after year. You also don't like to make mistakes — but we all have to make mistakes at times, and as long as we can admit them and learn from them they can transform into very positive steps towards making our lives and our relationships better than ever.

Sometimes things can go awry for you because of your fear of change — so remember life is never ever static, and since, deep down, you possess such boundless common sense, you're unlikely to go off on a wild tangent that will land you in disaster. Nonetheless don't be so serious and insecure about life: you have an innate sense of humour — so use it!

You're one of the most courageous and dependable star-signs around. Everyone can lean on your shoulder, but it's about time you employed these qualities a little more for your own benefit. If anything *is* wrong in your life, don't plod on in the same old way, simply accepting 'the way it has to be'. If a relationship goes through a difficult patch, resolve to talk things over calmly and rationally with your partner. You probably worked so hard at building it in the first place that it would be frivolous to allow problems to take over to any major extent, without taking positive moves to overcome them.

All in all − you need someone who understands that although you are a tower of strength to all outward appearances, you're actually a highly sensitive and loving person who needs to lean on someone *else*'s shoulder once in a while.

Planning for the future is something which comes naturally to you, and it is as if you've been doing it from your very first breath. You don't have any lessons to learn on that score. But make sure you engage yourself with friends, and a partner, who also understand your great need for beauty, peace and harmony so that your fulfilment never fades. And vow that you won't be quite so stubborn about taking more of a chance on life. Learn to appreciate the joy of doing things spontaneously, and forget about planning for tomorrow just once in a while.

Allow more rein to your emotions; don't always hide them so deeply below the surface. It's not that you have to try and switch your personality and become someone totally new, but you *can* let your defences down just a little without the whole world going off its axis.

The best relationships are those which are allowed to grow stronger day by day, and year by year − and discovering more about your partner's needs and insecurities will bring you as much benefit as facing up to and admitting your own.

The influence of Venus makes you a warm and loving person; vow you'll love yourself a little too. You don't have to be quite so rigid in your beliefs and principles when it comes to your earthbound view of life!

★

How you see Aries You're not quite sure you're prepared for this firebrand in your life. You believe the best relationships start slowly and take time to build up. Aries wants to get something rolling right away.

How Aries sees you Aries is attracted by your sensuality, feels that there could be a passionately exciting time ahead, and doesn't even want to start thinking about tomorrow.

To make things even better *Both* of you will benefit by learning more about each other's star-sign personalities − but if Aries really attracts you then don't be *too slow*.

★

How you see Taurus Is this what it feels like when two immovable objects meet each other? 'Do I really take so much time letting someone know I care?' 'Am I quite that stubborn?'

How Taurus sees you Your Taurus partner recognizes a kindred spirit, backs away, hesitates, thinks again, and decides it's all too much to think about in one day. They want things to grow slowly, remember!

To make things even better Remember that Venus is your ruling planet and don't be shy about admitting it when you *know* you're in love.

★

How you see Gemini It doesn't take you long to realize the importance of mental stimulation to this Air sign. But you wonder if this social butterfly of the Zodiac can give you the security you cherish.

How Gemini sees you Gemini wonders if all that down-to-earth practicality could be a little too much to cope with. This sign needs to have lots of fun and variety in their life.

To make things even better Try to make Gemini sit still long enough to listen to all your wonderful plans for the future. And make sure you keep up-to-date with what is going on in the world so that Gemini never gets bored.

★

How you see Cancer   You envision a lifetime of domestic bliss but are slightly concerned that Cancer's up-and-down moods could sometimes be too much to take.

How Cancer sees you   Cancer is delighted to be with someone who has similar feelings about enjoying a secure domestic set-up, but feels that sometimes you're much too stubborn and resistant to change.

To make things even better   Resolve that you'll keep out of the way if Cancer *is* in a mood, and promise that you won't be quite so obstinate in the future.

★

How you see Leo   You're slightly concerned that Leo will try to boss you around too much, but you're willing to worship and adore them − within reason!

How Leo sees you   Leo recognizes someone who can be a tower of strength when needed but is happy to take second place without making a fuss.

To make things even better   Recognize that you're both pretty determined people in your own way, and remember to have plenty of give-and-take in your relationship.

★

How you see Virgo   You're delighted to have such a hard-working partner alongside you, but you wonder if you'll be able to put up with all that criticism!

How Virgo sees you   Virgo sometimes wonders if you're just too slow getting your act together in your everyday life; but can't find too many faults to criticize!

To make things even better   Remember, you're both Earth signs and things that grow in the earth don't shoot up overnight. Let your relationship take its own pace.

★

How you see Libra You're delighted that Libra is ruled by Venus, just like you, and look forward to a relationship which is full of tender, loving care.

How Libra sees you Libra is charmed by your warm and caring personality, but has heard that you can be a bit like a bull in a china shop when you don't get your own way!

To make things even better Use your powers of persuasion to make Libra more decisive, and promise that you'll never throw your weight around too much.

★

How you see Scorpio You recognize that you've met a powerful partner here. Your opposite sign of the Zodiac is someone who frightens but fascinates you and you want to get to know them better.

How Scorpio sees you Scorpio feels a strong sensual attraction to you but wonders if you're going to be too set in your ways to envision an exciting life together.

To make things even better Let yourself go more and don't be quite such a stick-in-the-mud. Ensure that jealousy never becomes a bone of contention between you – you're both very possessive!

★

How you see Sagittarius You wonder if the Archer's free and easy approach to life is too much for you to take. You fear they may never want to settle down for long.

How Sagittarius sees you Sagittarius enjoys having someone around who is so dependable but doesn't want to feel tied down by too much routine.

To make things even better Let Sagittarius feel inwardly free and they won't want to roam once you've shown what a lovable partner you can be.

★

How you see Capricorn Two Earth signs striving for a common cause — security is the name of the game for both of you. You're delighted to come across someone with such serious intentions.

How Capricorn sees you Capricorn recognises the same things in you as you discover in them, and wants to get to know you better.

To make things even better Don't be quite so serious about life. It's up to you to draw Capricorn out more and get them to relax and feel less inhibited about enjoying themselves.

★

How you see Aquarius You're not sure if all that unpredictable behaviour is not too much for you to cope with. You worry that Aquarius is too unemotional for someone as physical as you.

How Aquarius sees you Aquarius might feel you are so resistant to change that life could become boring after a while. And all that sensuality could even frighten them away!

To make things even better Take a leaf out of the Aquarius book and be a little more unconventional once in a while — it will give you a whole new vista on life! Remember that Aquarius finds it hard to reveal their deepest feelings and don't push them too hard.

★

How you see Pisces You love the fact that Pisces is so romantic, but you're a bit concerned that this sign's impractical ways could create financial problems in any relationship with them.

How Pisces sees you Pisces loves the idea of romantic bliss with someone as devoted as you, and relishes having a tower of strength to lean on.

To make things even better Try to be the one in charge of the finances without ever making Pisces feel that they have let you down in any way at all.

Gemini

Ruled by Mercury, planet of communication, you tend to rush through life, apparently as free as Air — the element you were born under. You are often described as 'the social butterfly of the Zodiac' and you're rather proud of that. You enjoy flitting from place to place, and it is unlikely that you will ever feel lonely since you are so brilliant at attracting friends, lovers, and companions to your side.

You're one of the most perceptive and mentally alert signs of the Zodiac. But sometimes you don't have enough patience to *work* at making a relationship grow.

When you're very young, the idea of settling down with one person for ever more probably sounds like a dismal fate. You enjoy your freedom to the utmost, creating a rich social calendar, meeting different people from all stages of life, having lots of varied interests which fill your days. You can't bear the thought of being tied down to anyone or anything for very long. Often you are the life and soul of a party, capable of chattering away about a myriad of subjects while your eyes continuously notice every interesting newcomer who enters the room. It's certainly not unusual for you to stop abruptly in a conversation and move away to talk to someone else. You seem to get bored very easily, but it's not necessarily boredom that rankles you, it's more that you hate to feel you could be missing out. 'The grass is always greener ...' could be your motto.

Sometimes, you get a reputation for being very fickle, too

much of a flirt, a philanderer, someone who strings an admirer along for a while and then drops them at a moment's notice. When the astrological cognoscenti want to be really nasty about you, they point out that you were born under the sign of The Twins, making you dualistic: therefore you're 'a two-faced Janus' or worse, 'schizophrenic'.

But just because there is this dualism in your personality it's a bit unfair to turn you into a two-headed monster. Every sign has its dark and light sides, its positive and negative characteristics, and to imply that Gemini is necessarily worse than anyone else is unfair.

However, if you're totally honest with yourself then surely you will have to admit that your Mercurial mind leads you off into so many different directions that sometimes you don't stop still long enough to consider and reflect what you really want out of life. Just because you are brilliantly adept at making friends and keeping up with the latest trends and the 'world information updates' doesn't mean that you are quite as successful at attaining the perfect one-to-one relationship.

Of course, there are plenty of Gemini people who are happily married, or who have cohabited with the same 'co-vivant' for years. I'm certainly not trying to intimate that it's impossible for you to settle down and be happy with one person. But it is often difficult for you to reconcile yourself with the fact that you're going to want to settle down and renounce doing things as and when you want to, without having to take into account the needs and desires of another person, i.e. a partner and children in a wider family setting.

It sounds as though you could be very selfish, but thoughtless is more like it. The difficulty with you is your active mind — it switches tracks so fast that it takes a great effort for you to concentrate on any one thing for a long time before you're riding away on a totally different subject. You often convince yourself that true love is a state so elusive that it's not worth searching for: that it would only turn out to be a mirage if it came into view, and that you're quite happy as a colourful 'butterfly' anyway.

All this means that you must be attentive to putting enough

energy into a promising relationship when it does come along. You place so much value on being mentally stimulated by your partner but don't necessarily give enough of yourself in return.

It isn't just Aquarians who find it difficult to reveal their secret selves; you're pretty much the same on that score. You're fine when it comes to making a particular point in a conversation, but you sometimes find it irksome making those little sentimental and affectionate gestures which are all part of a loving relationship. A little more body language and a touch more sensuality will not go amiss. How on earth do you expect the person that you care for to understand your feelings when you refuse to give away even the slightest indication in your words and actions? It's almost as though you're nervous to show too much of yourself in case it reveals a weakness you'd prefer to hide. But being clever and intellectual is one thing – it doesn't mean that you can't be warm and loving too!

Because you're such a restless person, it can be incredibly frustrating for those involved in any kind of relationship with you, whether it's a family tie, a friendship or a work situation. It is hard to pin you down to anything, to get you to commit yourself to meetings, even for you to phone at a certain time – there is always something going on in your life, and your mind never seems to stay still long enough to enable you to organize yourself a little better.

If you had ever taken a course in 'How to build and maintain a relationship', you would have learnt how to examine your personality a little closer, evaluate your needs, and discover what you might have been doing wrong. It's never too late, however, to learn new ways to get on even better with people – and recognizing that you often allow too little time to get to know them really well is perhaps one of the best lessons you could learn. It would help you not only in personal relationships but also financially and in business as well.

When it comes to love, you are often as idealistic as any other sign, but you're frightened to trust what you feel. Of course, deep down you're probably searching for a partner who needs to feel as inwardly free as you do, and it could come as a shock to find that you've fallen hook-line-and-sinker for a lover who is far more possessive and jealous than you could ever be, yet what are you going to do? Negate the chance of being blissfully happy just because you resent this? Are they really so jealous, or is it simply that you consider anyone who cramps your style in any way is a real drag? And have you ever considered that if you were deeply in love with another Gemini you might also feel a few stirrings of jealousy while you watched their behaviour?

You often give the impression of being someone who will play around, but the truth can be very different. Mental flirtation is one thing, but you're perfectly capable of being a loyal and devoted partner when you're committed to the person you love. Although reaching the point when you know you want a total commitment is hard for you, to have and to hold the perfect relationship you definitely have to take the risk and be prepared to give more of yourself. Astrologically, you are well aware that mental compatibility is highly essential to you, so it's not likely that someone could sweep you off your feet by sexual chemistry alone. If, therefore, you are immersed in someone who can satisfy you mentally *and* physically, and you're prepared to accept that love isn't an elusive dream which has passed you by, just be more giving of yourself and enjoy the pleasure that this love will bring.

There are two sides to your personality — it's not that you're Dr Jekyll and Mr Hyde — nonetheless your mood swings sometimes make you difficult to live with: for instance you change your thoughts and ideas at a moment's notice. A little more organization could work wonders in your life, and that goes for organizing your thoughts a little better too. Don't be quite so scattered in your approach to family, friends, and business associates. Plan a little more carefully — write yourself little lists so that you know what's on your schedule for the day.

You're a natural communicator, but sometimes you use this too much on a surface level and forget about the soul level below. In any important relationship you must learn to be more open, more trusting of your own intuition as well as other people's.

Try not to be quite so impatient; don't always expect your partner to fit in with all your ideals. Relationships have to be worked at in order to grow stronger, and you need to be more prepared to try a little harder at understanding someone else's deepest needs and desires. You're so clever at living by your wits but sometimes you can be sarcastic without even realizing it, and create needless hurt at the same time. You can be almost as tactless as your opposite sign of Sagittarius.

Changeable, unpredictable, easily bored (i.e. you always think you're going to miss out on something) — perhaps this is why you have a desire to have at least half a dozen things going on all at the same time. But don't risk spoiling a potentially perfect relationship by refusing to pull your weight in making it endure.

Don't be one of those Gemini people who search for the quickest escape route when they feel bored. Ask yourself *why* you feel bored. Is it because you're too concerned with yourself to be really interested in what is going on around you? Resolve that you'll be a better listener, more prepared to fit in with other people rather than to go on helter-skelter. Being footloose and fancy-free is often wonderful, but when you're in a promising relationship it is much better to remember the benefits of practising a little more give-and-take.

A Gemini needs a partner who recognizes and understands your fear of being tied down too much, and who will let you be secure without trying to possess you totally; someone who will be a companion in every possible sense, and who will help to balance your life so that you realize the happiness of being in a perfect mind-body-and-soul relationship without feeling the need to search for something more.

So, it's up to you to channel your restless mind and concentrate on what is really important in life — making relationships and any kinds of personal associations better than they've ever been before. You also need to organize yourself a little more realistically on the financial level so that you don't create unnecessary problems for yourself.

★

How you see Aries As someone who can communicate with you on all levels, but whose patience level seems to be even lower than your own. You're not sure whether all that Fire is safe to be around!

How Aries sees you   As someone who is fun to be with but might be exhausting on a long-term basis because you always seem to be on the go from morning to night – even more than they are.

To make things even better   Both of you will have to fit in with each other's needs a little more. Fiery passion becomes even more exhilarating when mental stimulation works the bellows.

★

How you see Taurus   As someone who will always be there come rain and come shine, but you're slightly scared that so much security could bore you after a while.

How Taurus sees you   As an exciting whirlwind who breezed into their life, but your restless ways could make them wonder if you'd be off again far too soon, searching for something new.

To make things even better   Prove that you can be just as dependable as Taurus once you've recognized that you're in a relationship which fulfils your innermost needs and desires.

★

How you see Gemini   As Dr Jekyll or Dr Hyde – who else could make you realize you have two sides to your personality? Fascinating, stimulating, and a great deal of fun!

How Gemini sees you   Unless their personal horoscope shows evidence to the contrary they're bound to see you in the same way too.

To make things even better   Stop being so concerned with talking about yourself and listen to what your alter ego has to say for once!

★

How you see Cancer   All that sentimentality makes you realize that you're not too good at putting your own feelings into words, and you're not sure you're ready for someone as protective as Cancer in your life.

How Cancer sees you   As too much of a wanderer to ever want to settle down into a steady relationship. They might hide away in their shells when you pass by!

To make things even better   Learn to appreciate the bliss of having a marvellously domesticated set-up, and resolve to take more time in getting to know this homey sign.

★

How you see Leo   As someone who might try to cramp your style and give you too many orders, but you're perfectly willing to give praise and adulation when you consider it's due.

How Leo sees you   As a witty and fun-loving playmate, but would like you to be a bit sexier and more passionate too. Leo also fears you could be too much of a flirt!

To make things even better   Always let your Leo partner feel secure in your love so that they don't go on worrying about your flirtatious ways, and let yourself go more, physically, without feeling inhibited.

★

How you see Virgo   As someone whose intellectual powers match yours, but who worries far too much about things which never even occur to you − and you don't like being criticized!

How Virgo sees you   As a restless free spirit who stimulates them mentally but makes them worry that you're impossible to pin down for very long.

To make things even better   You'll have to do everything in your power to prove that even an elusive Gemini can be constant when they're in a good relationship. Vow that your Virgo will start to worry less and enjoy life more.

★

How you see Libra   As the perfect sort of partner who only exists in books. but you're always changing your thoughts and

45

ideas, and could be off and away before you've had sufficient time to know them better.

How Libra sees you   As someone to balance their scales on the mental wavelength, but whose changeability could lead to problems on a permanent basis. Also Libra doesn't like arguments . . . but wants to win debates.

To make things even better   Remember that you're both Air signs and try to stand still long enough to appreciate the pleasure of having such a perfect partner in your life.

★

How you see Scorpio   All that burning intensity overpowers you instantly, but you're not sure whether you can cope with someone who can read your mind as easily as this sign can.

How Scorpio sees you   As someone who stimulates them on an intellectual level but might not show quite enough passion for sexy Scorpio.

To make things even better   Try to loosen up a little sexually and don't be quite so reticent about letting your partner know what you feel deep down. Emotional satisfaction with mental compatibility can be a mind-blowing experience.

★

How you see Sagittarius   As someone who needs to feel free just as much as you. Your opposite sign of the Zodiac is the one person to help you balance your life.

How Sagittarius sees you   As someone to talk to and travel with on a voyage of discovery around the world — but on a permanent basis wonders if you each have enough patience to keep a relationship running smoothly.

How to make things even better   Admit to yourself that you've found a kindred spirit, and vow that you'll do everything possible to ensure that any roaming you'll do will be with your Sagittarian partner by your side.

★

How you see Capricorn As someone who will give you material security and bring into your life a feeling of belonging to someone that you've maybe never really known before.

How Capricorn sees you As someone who might be too flighty ever to want to really settle down with someone who has such traditional values. Capricorn is fascinated by your ability to charm the birds down from the trees.

To make things even better The inner strength of Capricorn is a marvellous balance for your free-spirited ways – so it's well worthwhile working hard at this one.

★

How you see Aquarius As someone whose unpredictability makes you feel you've discovered a true soulmate. You're convinced that life will always be exciting with this partner by your side.

How Aquarius sees you In almost the same way, knowing that you can be very compatible. But Aquarius can be just as reticent about revealing their true feelings as you!

To make things even better Don't spend so much time talking about inconsequential things when the important factor is to get to know each other better on every other level too.

★

How you see Pisces As sometimes too much of a romantic dreamer to cope with the realities of life. Your need for mental stimulation sometimes puts too much pressure on this partner.

How Pisces sees you As a wonderful person to talk to long into the night, but Pisces needs more sentimental affection than you are always able to give.

To make things even better Let Pisces see that in your own way you're just as much an idealist as they are; and enjoy the magic that their dreams can bring into your life. Don't be afraid to be more sentimental too.

Cancer

Ruled by the Moon, you are emotional, sensitive, sentimental and imaginative, and you're also accused of being moody – particularly at Full Moon time!

Your home and close family-ties are tremendously important to you: they're probably the most important factors in your life. For this reason you are keenly aware of the need for a strong, steady income. You usually know from an early age that what you want more than anything else is the cosy domestic environment with the 'simpatico' partner by your side. You love looking after people, have a wonderfully protective quality to your nature, and emotional fulfilment is your greatest desire. The danger is that you tend to be overly protective, sometimes to the extent that the people you care for feel they're being smothered. When you have children who are ready to leave home, you may try to weave a pattern of reasons why they shouldn't go.

You come across as being very shy, sometimes you seem to doubt yourself, which is strange when there is a side of your character which is exceedingly strong and determined. Why not remember, a little more often, that inside you there is also something of your opposite sign of Capricorn, and instead of creeping into your Cancerian shell, think about the Capricorn mountain goat climbing up to the top of the mountain, overcoming obstacles along the way?

I'm not asking you to negate your own personality, to try and be something you're not. But, thinking about the characteristics of one's opposite sign and recognizing and making use of the positive attributes they can bring will be tremendously useful in personal relationships, as indeed in business contacts.

In any event, as you get to know yourself, you will understand that you're a whole lot tougher than the image you sometimes project. Never forget that you were born under a Cardinal sign, and you're supposed to be a leader.

You're an interesting mixture, a blend of leadership and dreamy sensitivity, this inner needing to control combined with the urge to be protected yourself. There are definitely moments in your life when you need to stand still and take stock of what you want and what you need.

Some of you who gave in to that urge for emotional fulfilment and emotional security when still quite young may have entered relationships convinced that they were all you ever wanted to guide you in life. It's as though you've been conditioned from the very beginning almost to subjugate your own personality and live your life through the people who share it with you, and it is they who 'justify' your existence.

You are also pretty determined when you want to settle down with your chosen partner. But there is a side of your personality which makes you unable to admit when you've made a mistake. It's wonderful if you have worked together carefully with your partner to make your relationship grow better and better over the years. But if things ever reach the point of no return, for one reason or another, don't be quite so outwardly tenacious, clinging on when you've tried every avenue to improve impossible situations. I'm certainly not advocating that you scream 'divorce, divorce' every time you have a row — you don't have to go to extremes!

If you want to achieve perfect relationships in your life, you have to understand that sometimes your moods really do upset people, especially if they don't know you terribly well. When you feel one of those downers creeping up on you, why don't you somehow let your partner know that it's much better for you to go into your own private reverie, or inner 'crab stew', letting the moods boil and be done with than to get involved in convoluted discussions which end up in argument? But also resolve to let your partner deal with *their* own ups and downs in their chosen way too. It isn't only Cancerians who have bad moods!

You often possess a wonderful sense of humour, but this has to be the moment to say to you that you're not very good at laughing at yourself. It's important to be not quite so uptight. You seem to have an inner fear of people making fun of you. Is it because you're so ultra-sensitive? Is it because you know you can be close to tears so easily when you feel upset? Being able to laugh at yourself is crucial; it's also important for everyone around you, and it will help you to snap out of your down moods much faster too. This type of release can improve your workaday style and smooth the way in a competitive situation.

You're invariably a very physical person. In a love relationship you have strong sexual feelings. You want to give and receive in equal amounts. When you tell someone you love them, you aren't playing around in any way. You mean it, and you want it to be for keeps. You have very high ideals, and your feelings run incredibly deep.

In business you expect impeccable behaviour from others, but you must remember that other people cannot always be as outwardly perfect as you. Learn to forgive mistakes. No one will take you to be a fool for that.

One of the most important things for you in your personal relationship is that after making love with your partner you should be able to snuggle up close to each other and feel totally at peace with the world. For this reason, 'triangle' situations are not very easy for you. Especially if you're left alone with your thoughts for too long, because then the negative aspects of the situation take on a much gloomier outlook. However, because of the tenacious side of your personality, you often find it possible to hang on to this kind of relationship for longer than many other signs, even if it seems that your perfect partner may never be free to start a life with you. And it's necessary for you to make a firm decision as to whether this is what you truly want or whether you're simply scared to let go.

Letting go is all part of growing up. It applies to love in the same way as it applies to many other aspects of our lives, but no one ever said that it was going to be easy. You feel so deeply that it's not surprising it *is* so hard for you to contemplate letting go of someone or something you believe in. If you're a typical Cancerian you will have to admit that hanging on to people and to possessions is something you've done all your life. Because you're so sentimental, it's difficult for you to imagine being any other way — but everyone has to do it sometimes, so why not you! Your leadership qualities make you want to dominate, but the Moon which rules your emotions heightens your innermost yearnings and your insecurities too.

Just like a little child you want everyone to love you. How melancholy you become if you ever feel rebuffed — how quickly your protective shell becomes a barrier against supposed hurts or slights. Because you are so sensitive you always need the right surroundings: if you try to live in a place in which you really don't feel happy, it is extremely difficult for you to function at your best. But you don't insist on something extremely grand. It just has to have the homely atmosphere which you thrive on.

Material security *is* important to you, and you are not often a spendthrift. You want to save for the future, and no one could accuse either male or female Cancerians of not being good providers. You'll happily work alongside your partner to make your domestic haven secure.

In your working relationships you're equally loyal, and equally sensitive! It's important to make sure your moods never create insurmountable problems. You can't avoid responsibility just because you feel down or under-the-weather.

Sometimes you dwell so much in the past, remembering all the good times (and the bad times too) that you forget all about the present. Sure, hanging on to your memories is a wonderful thing to do, and you certainly don't have to stop doing it, but watch out that you don't ever spoil your chances of having a perfect relationship by being too scared to trust because of hurts in the past. At the same time, remember about that tendency to hang on. Vow that you'll never be so clinging to anyone that you lose your own identity. You know how much you hate to have your feelings hurt so resolve that you will try hard not to hurt anyone else by being too possessive or demanding if they feel they need more freedom.

Don't be quite so determined to look after other people in the way *you* feel they need to be looked after. Learn to accept that there are occasions in your life when it will be wonderful to have someone who can look after you.

You feel everything so very deeply that your imagination sends you to the very heights of happiness. Don't miss out on even more enjoyment from life by sometimes hiding away in your shell.

You will always need security in your life, especially if your own childhood left something lacking in that direction. And you will always have your Cancerian moods, fluctuating like the tides of the sea. No one expects you to change your personality, but with a little more positive effort you will be able to control those negative aspects a little more.

One wonderful part of being born under your star-sign, is that you don't mind how much effort it takes to work through conflicts to make a success of a relationship. You know that it's what you need more than anything else to make you feel one hundred per cent secure. So stop all the dwelling in the past and think about the marvellous future you have in store.

Still waters run very deep – and your deep feelings can bring so much joy to your partner when you've learnt to understand each other even more.

★

How you see Aries As a fiery passionate bombshell who bursts into your life and expects you to forget about yesterday, and not think about tomorrow. Madness or Moon magic?

How Aries sees you As someone to bring domestic bliss into their lives – but fears your melancholy moods.

To make things even better Enjoy the passion, seduce Aries with your cooking, and don't ever be too possessive with this impatient Fire sign.

★

How you see Taurus As someone who will understand your yearning for security, and who is wonderfully sensual too. You picture this relationship growing stronger day by day.

How Taurus sees you   As the warm and loving partner they've dreamed of all their life, and is delighted to discover someone equally practical and dependable.

To make things even better   Vow that neither of you will be quite so stubborn if arguments arise. And watch out that this domesticated heaven never turns into some boring routine.

★

How you see Gemini   As someone whose flighty ways could make you feel much too insecure. You realize you'd have to become a lot more independent to make this work.

How Gemini sees you   As a tender loving partner but one who could try to cramp their style just a little too much. Gemini always needs to feel inwardly free.

To make things even better   Learn to have more faith in the people you care for. They're not going to abandon you just because they need their own space, too.

★

How you see Cancer   It's like looking at your own reflection in the moonlit water − so you have to be truly happy with what you see! But who could know you better?

How Cancer sees you   Unless their personal horoscope gives them totally different characteristics, your Cancer partner will see and feel the same way as you, and know all about those high and low tides too!

To make things even better   Don't give each other a hard time when the Full Moon comes along. But remember to remove those protective shells more often and enjoy being in perfect harmony.

★

How you see Leo   As a strong supportive partner who will make you feel totally secure. But you're not so keen on being bossed around.

How Leo sees you   As someone to give them all the love they crave for, but their love has to be strong enough to enable them to enjoy your moody side too.

To make things even better   Accomplish something for yourself rather than depending too much on your partner all the time.

★

How you see Virgo   You see Virgo as a supportive perfectionist and admire them tremendously, but fear Virgo's critical capacity because you know how soft and sensitive you are behind your shell.

How Virgo sees you   As someone who will work as hard as you at creating a wonderful domestic set-up, but Virgo is not prepared for your vulnerability.

To make things even better   Be patient, loving and generous and vow not to be quite so ultra-sensitive if Virgo does have a few critical remarks to make from time to time.

★

How you see Libra   As someone to bring more peace and harmony into your life, but you wonder how to make them decide that you're the perfect partner for them.

How Libra sees you   As a wonderfully romantic soulmate, who can make living together the best thing in the world, but they can't cope with too much moodyness around them.

To make things even better   Try to balance your moods a little more, and help Libra to balance their scales. Mutual love and understanding can work wonders here.

★

How you see Scorpio   As a sensitive emotional partner who will make you feel more desirable than ever. But so much passion sometimes sends you scurrying back into your shell.

How Scorpio sees you   As someone with whom to share all those sentimental dreams; but doesn't want to feel you're prying into their past too much.

To make things even better Learn to understand each other's need for quiet moments alone from time to time. Be generous with your love but never too possessive.

★

How you see Sagittarius You love the way Sagittarius always sees the brighter side of life. And you appreciate having someone around to help you do the same.

How Sagittarius sees you As a marvellous helpmate who will create the most secure home base you've known; but they worry slightly that this could tie them down too much!

To make things even better Show your gratitude for having this optimistic partner in your life by allowing them to feel inwardly free. Start to be more secure about yourself.

★

How you see Capricorn As the partner who compliments you in the best possible way, but you wonder how you're going to bring those deep-rooted Capricorn emotions to the surface.

How Capricorn sees you As someone who feels the same way about traditional values and the joy of having a settled secure home as they do. But they do realize they're not as sentimental as you.

To make things even better Resolve to gain a little more insight into the Capricorn personality, and remember that the attraction of opposites can be very very strong.

★

How you see Aquarius As someone who is fascinating but not as sentimental as you'd like. All that cool detachment is a little hard for you to bear.

How Aquarius sees you As deliciously romantic and as idealistic as they are. But they are worried that all that sentiment would be hard for them to live up to. And it's often hard for them to admit they care.

To make things even better   Don't try to put words into your Aquarian's mouth. There's a time and place for everything, so let your understanding of each other move along at its own steady pace.

★

How you see Pisces   As a true romantic just like you. But, remembering how impractical Pisces can be over material issues, you're bound to worry that this could be a problem.

How Pisces sees you   With just the same romantic connotation, recognizing a kindred spirit. They realize that domestic bliss doesn't have to simply be a dream any longer.

To make things even better   Relax. You can be practical enough for both of you. Isn't it wonderful to feel in total harmony emotionally? You can give so much to each other and learn so much too.

Leo

Ruled by the Sun, your bright and breezy personality makes you a joy to be with. It is never difficult for you to attract admirers to your side, and being in love is something which comes more naturally to you than almost any other sign.

The Lion is the lord of the jungle, and you're the regal ruler of the Zodiac. You're a true leader, a Fire sign just like Aries and Sagittarius, seemingly without a vestige of insecurity beneath your surface. You are also one of the most loving and generous signs around; financial extravagance comes far too easily to you. It's not just that you yearn for luxury at all costs, surrounding yourself with status-symbol items whenever you can; but you're equally fond of giving to the people you care for, showering them with gifts to show just how much you care.

But being a leader is one thing; knowing how to harness your powers of leadership is something else. Sometimes you create your own problems in a relationship by wanting to control, taking charge from the very first moment, and refusing to relinquish the reins. You're so forceful and charismatic that it's hard to tame you once you get going. But humility is something which everyone needs to learn from time to time, and is something to remember the next time you are told that you're being too bossy. This will apply to your work relationships too.

You are often as aggressive as Aries, as convinced that you know all the answers as Sagittarius, but, because you can be so idealistically romantic about having the perfect partner, isn't it worthwhile harnessing all your positive energy into toning down some of your ultra-domineering ways?

What Leo wants, Leo is *determined* to have, but learning how to make a relationship an equal one will benefit you immensely. Don't be quite so fixed on yourself, try to be more yielding and diplomatic; let someone else take centre stage once in a while.

It's often so hard for you to be out of the limelight for long. You thrive on praise and adulation, and being placed on a pedestal by someone you love is a wonderful feeling for Leos of both sexes. But have you ever been completely honest with yourself? Have you ever thought carefully about what you really want from a relationship? Are you completely happy when you're the one in charge, or do you secretly yearn for someone to look up to and who might even dominate you? Although you're supposed to be such a very strong sign, deep down you have your vulnerable side too. And deep down you thrive when you're able to lower your defences and allow yourself to be looked after for a change. You're not looking for someone to boss you around, although I've often felt that this could do some Leos a world of good! But secretly you're enchanted to know just how it feels to be told what to do for a change. And provided you're in accordance with what you're asked, you're quite willing to comply. Besides, it does you good to be on the receiving end of orders; it shows you what it feels like, and might encourage you to tone down your dictatorial ways.

Sometimes it's difficult for you to admit to any faults. You have immense self-esteem, more than any other star-sign. You find it hard to imagine that you could make any mistakes. You're a bit like Sagittarius, optimistically convinced that you're always right. Besides, you certainly don't mean to upset anyone by your manner. You'd be mortified if you discovered how many people were fearful of your lion's roar and preferred to do your bidding rather than risk a row.

And you're such a giving person that it would really upset you to know you had unwittingly made anyone else unhappy. That's why it is even more important to create the right balance in your relationships.

Learning to make submissive gestures and take second place,

allowing loved ones and friends to have the right to have their say, to make certain decisions, and to live their own lives alongside you, is certainly not a sign of weakness, but a sign of accepting the wisdom of letting other people grow too, which in turn will help your relationships to become even stronger.

In love you sometimes rush in as quickly as Aries. You may think you have patience, but more often than not you're racing ahead of yourself, planning the future without taking anyone else into account! You expect a great deal from a love relationship, which can be very positive. It's when you start to 'demand' love that trouble begins! But since Leo rules the heart, is it any wonder that you do need love to make you feel complete in every way? Accepting that need and enjoying it will make your life even more enjoyable.

And just because you're also passionately emotional and are fully aware of the power of a sexually compatible relationship, it is still possible to allow your partner to take command. In this area of your life, as in so many others, you are often far too accustomed to being the dominant one. Perhaps you have a partner who is totally happy this way, but if not, it is definitely worthwhile changing your act a little! Giving pleasure is something which is second nature to you − so, you're not usually a selfish lover even though you can be a demanding one.

You are extremely loyal when you're involved with the perfect partner; there's not much chance of your wanting to roam and search for someone new. Although, if you feel you're not being appreciated enough, and flattery comes from a different direction, you might be tempted to indulge in a little flirtation just to teach your partner a lesson. But you're not usually very good in a *ménage à trois* situation. You'd find it very difficult to sit back and fit in with someone else's life, without being able to do anything at all about it. That's when it *would* be hard to take second place. You'd have to be convinced that the love you felt would overcome every possible problem. And since you also hate the idea of hurting people it would cause you all sorts of inner doubts and feelings of guilt.

You want everyone to be happy. You cannot bear to think of the sadness and misery in the world, without being able to do anything about it. On the other hand you also thrive on an audience to applaud your performance in life; that's also why achieving the perfect relationship with someone can be a real challenge for you. It's never as simple as meeting, falling in love, and settling down to live happily together ever after in a rose-covered Lion's Den. You know that you can be possessive, jealous, sometimes even aggressively selfish when you're caught up in a relationship. But you're also prepared to build your life around making that person really happy too. It's all a question of Leonine meditation, taking more time to nurture the good life that you have and watch it grow stronger day by day.

Please, Leo, don't change your personality, and become so meek and mild that you couldn't take charge of anything at all. But just don't be quite so dramatic in your approach to your everyday life in general, and your relationships in particular. You're always concerned with how people see you, how they will react to what you say. Leo is the sign which relates strongly to showbusiness – so many of you are actors and actresses at heart. But since you've already been told you can't be on centre stage all the time, why not have a go at being in the audience once in a while? Step back, look at what is going on around you! You've spent so much time controlling people and situations that you've only seen it all from one perspective. Enjoy seeing how different it can be from a different vantage point.

You'll *always* need someone who appreciates your strength, your generosity, your sense of humour; someone who knows how to show love and affection in the same aggressively positive way as you. You would find it very difficult to love someone you couldn't respect, and if you're totally honest you'll have to admit you need a partner who can give you material security as well. But, because you *are* often such a spendthrift and couldn't imagine having to cut down on your generous gestures, love could fly out of the window all too fast if money worries entered into your relationship.

But you'll work like a Lion alongside your partner to ensure that financial problems don't become insurmountable. You are not someone who likes merely to spend money without thinking about where it comes from. You are well aware it doesn't grow on trees and you're certainly aware of the benefits it can bring.

You have a very strong ego, and this does not diminish with age. But you're perfectly able to tone down your dictatorial ways and be the lovable, playful cub instead of the roaring King of the Jungle.

There *will* be times when you have every right to feel superior, and that's when you must remember the benefits of a little more humility too.

You have such incredible warmth and vivacity, it's no wonder that people are drawn to you. As host or hostess, your skills are phenomenal, but you know you can't spend your life simply having fun and giving parties. You must resolve that you'll start to develop a little more insight into your partner's needs, hopes and desires. You know how much you thrive on attention, so give your beloved a little extra too. Don't always make your own needs the unconscious priority in your life. It's not that you do it on purpose, but when push comes to shove you are usually willing to admit it's second nature to you. Learn to control your dictatorial ways, and don't be afraid to show you can be vulnerable too; put your heart and soul into showing your appreciation of your perfect partner. It isn't only Leos who thrive on being appreciated – it's a marvellous way to boost someone's confidence and make then feel even happier with you.

The perfect relationship isn't often something which bursts into flame overnight, reaching its highest potential straight away. It's something which needs to be carefully nurtured with love and affection. And it takes two to do that. So always try to give as much as you like to receive, and remember to sit on the other side of those footlights too.

★

How you see Aries   You recognize you've come up against a real challenge here. You're attracted by all that fiery passion, but wonder if Aries will ever do anything that you ask.

How Aries sees you   As someone with immense strength but may not be ready for such total domination. But in the game of love they recognize an equally passionate playmate.

To make things even better   Both of you need to slow down a little and let things take their own pace. And both of you need to resolve you'll take turns in playing 'leader'.

★

How you see Taurus   As someone wonderfully sensual who is relieved to play second lead to your principal role. You envisage a good long-term relationship developing here.

How Taurus sees you   As someone to look up to and admire, but they're not quite sure they want to be bossed around quite so much. They recognize a sexually fulfilling relationship when they've got one though!

To make things even better   Since you are both such powerful personalities, neither one of you needs to be ashamed of taking second place to the other if the necessity arises.

★

How you see Gemini   As a wonderfully stimulating partner on the mental plane, but fear that Gemini's flirtatious ways could make you feel somewhat insecure unless you've learnt to totally trust.

How Gemini sees you   As a powerful and charismatic partner – who might just try to control them a little too much unless you're prepared to understand their personality in greater depth.

To make things even better   Go easy on the strong stuff – there's a great deal of sensitivity here which will benefit the quality of your life in the long run. Again, trust is the key.

★

How you see Cancer   You love all that sentimental affection, and it's great to be worshipped this way. But you fear that too much domesticity could make you feel too hemmed in.

How Cancer sees you   As the strong support they've yearned for all their life. But they're also pretty determined to do a spot of bossing around themselves from time to time.

To make things even better   Realize you both have lots to give and to learn from each other. Accept the fact that both of you expect a great deal from your home life, and enjoy it!

★

How you see Leo   One minute as the other half of a perfect duo – the next as someone who might take too much limelight away from you! You're fascinated, but fearful too.

How Leo sees you   In almost exactly the same way, unless they're not prepared to admit they thrive on adulation! They may need more time to think about it all.

To make things even better   Use your sense of humour to the utmost in any tough moments. Always be loyal to each other, and take it in turns to share the limelight!

★

How you see Virgo   You're not sure you're ready for someone to criticize you the way this sign does. But you like the idea of showing Virgo how to unwind and relax a little more.

How Virgo sees you   As a bright ray of sunshine bursting into their life. But as for changing all their ways to fit in with you – that's something to contemplate cautiously at first!

To make things even better   Allow yourself to be criticized once in a while – especially if you feel deep down that Virgo is right. Don't frighten Virgo away by being too dominant until you know each other better.

★

How you see Libra   As a charming, easy-going partner and a perfect foil for you. But you'll need to exercise more patience when you want any decisions from this sign.

How Libra sees you   Libra wants an easy-going life and won't put up with being bossed around too much. But recognizes that you both believe that love makes the world go round – which makes everything okay.

To make things even better   Forget about your own pride and vanity and remember to give Libra plenty of compliments too. You both expect lots of happiness out of life so always be lovable to each other.

★

How you see Scorpio   As someone who can be even more powerful than you. You know you'll never try bossing this sign around too much, and you're excited by all that passionate intensity.

How Scorpio sees you   Scorpio admires your strength but wonders if they'll have the patience to give you the adulation you crave. No Scorpio likes to take second place for long.

To make things even better   Recognize you've met your match in the power game, and never give Scorpio reason to doubt your loyalty. Flirting with other people is not advisable. Scorpios don't forgive or forget easily!

★

How you see Sagittarius   You admire the Archer's independent attitude to life, and feel their optimistic views will make life more fun, and more exciting too.

How Sagittarius sees you   As a bright and sparkling personality who could sweep them off their feet. But they won't want to feel you're going to tie them down too much.

To make things even better   Read up all you can about each other. Two strong Fire signs together should definitely be on the right track. All it needs is a little more work.

★

How you see Capricorn   As someone who will bring you material security in abundance, but wonders if they will share your love of life in quite the same way.

How Capricorn sees you   As someone who might be too much of a party-lover ever to settle down and take life really seriously.

They also fear your spendthrift ways could land you both in trouble.

To make things even better Promise you won't be quite so extravagant, and let them believe that your greatest luxury in life could be having them by your side. Let Capricorn see you're even prepared to forego being boss! This could turn out to be fun!

★

How you see Aquarius As someone whose unpredictability could drive you wild. But you realize that opposites can and do attract. It depends on whether or not you're ready for the challenge of meeting someone who won't be tamed.

How Aquarius sees you As someone who tends to show off and demand attention a little too much. They don't want to be dominated but their opinions can change from day to day!

To make things even better Accept that you've met your opposite and try to forget about taking the lead all the time − Aquarius won't follow unless they're good and ready anyway.

★

How you see Pisces As someone who will be easy to dominate and who can fulfil your romantic dreams without ever demanding too much in return. You feel it could be true love.

How Pisces sees you As someone to prevent them from swimming downstream and getting lost. They adore your protective quality and are happy to pay you all those compliments you think you deserve.

To make things even better Enjoy what you have, and don't spoil things by being too extravagant with money. You will both benefit by this. Always remember that Pisces sets great store by sentiment.

Virgo

Ruled by Mercury, planet of communication, your birthsign is known as 'the sign of service', and since you are always so good about doing things for other people it's surely worthwhile to consider yourself a little more too.

The trouble is that because you're such a perfectionist in almost every possible way, you never seem to appreciate yourself enough. We all know just how picky you can be at finding faults in other people's characters, although no one can go on at you *too* much for this, since you're equally critical about yourself.

You're one of the most hard-working people around; you're often brilliantly organized, totally dependable, and can be very witty when you allow yourself to relax and enjoy having fun a little more readily. But being such a perfectionist means that you often give yourself an unnecessarily hard time. Everyone has faults. Think how boring life would be if we were all perfect in every way. Why do you persist in seeing the flaws of life, instead of the beauty which lies there too?

Sometimes you can dampen people's spirits much too fast by taking a pessimistic, over-critical view of life. Perhaps you need a few Sagittarians around you to show you the benefits of being positive and optimistic.

Being called 'the sign of service' ought to be taken as a compliment; but it's not meant to be the hard and fast rule by which your life needs to be run every minute of every day. Surely you're not intent on being such a masochist that you consider taking time off to have fun to be a crime?

Your planetary symbol is the Virgin, and it's true that you do have a purity which is unmistakably your very own. It shines through like an unflawed diamond and you'd hate to think of its becoming blemished in any way.

You should learn to value yourself a little more instead of running yourself down so much. Haven't you ever realized that until you learn to love yourself it is going to be much harder to have a really good relationship? How do you expect your partner to appreciate you, if you don't appreciate yourself? So many people born under your sign seem to have an incredibly low self-esteem, and from an early age too. It's as though it were drilled into you at school that you must write down all your faults a hundred times a day and memorize them for ever more. But do you really enjoy this, and finding faults in others? Or is it just a *habit* you'd be wiling to throw aside?

No one is asking you to switch personalities overnight, and suddenly decide that you're living in a perfect world for that would be equally wrong, and certainly untrue! But at least you could make a resolution to try to be a little less analytical at those times when analysis is unnecessary.

Learn to exercise a little more self-restraint the next time you're compelled to tell someone just what you think if you feel it's an unnecessary criticism. If they ask you for some constructive advice that's a very different thing, and there is no reason for you to hold back. But since you don't normally wait for them to do this, it can be very off-putting to the person concerned. This can apply to all your relationships with family, friends or business but it's sure to apply especially when you're in love. Sometimes it's almost as though you're afraid to let anyone know just how much you care about them. You feel you're letting too much of your inner self be discovered, and that you've given yourself another fault to criticize!

Although you're an Earth sign and your feet are supposed to be firmly on the ground, you can be as shy, vulnerable and sensitive as any Water sign.

Stop worrying quite so much about what might happen if you

do this, or they do that ... or what could happen next week, or next month. Start to enjoy life more, and please live one day at a time. I've never met a Virgo yet who doesn't have something to worry about. Of course you might say that everyone has worries, but I'm sure others don't all give them quite as much priority as you do.

You're one of the kindest, most generous people around, when you *are* doing things for other people, which is all the more reason to love yourself more and give to yourself too.

At work you can create problems for yourself by never quite believing that anyone else can do any tasks quite as well as you. This can mean you're hesitant to delegate, which not only means extra work and longer hours for yourself, but can unnecessarily alienate your colleagues. With your family, your excuse will be that everyone knows you by now, and therefore knows exactly what you're like. But that is the lazy way out of admitting that you're often just too fussy for your own good.

Things can go wrong in even the most perfect relationship if neither partner will admit their own faults, and work harder at overcoming them. Stop considering that you have more than anyone else, and make a resolution from now on to be a lot more positive about yourself. You might be amazed just how beneficial this can be.

Moreover when it comes back to your analytical prowess, have you ever taken a step back and analysed what *you* need in a relationship? Do you really know what is essential to make you feel happy and secure? It's clear that you need someone you can look up to and respect. And since you do have your Virgo feet so very firmly on terra firma it's unlikely that you could be happy for long with someone who was for instance, an irrepressible spendthrift. You have very strong feelings about money and material security. You can't bear to think of being horribly extravagant and having to worry about your security in the years to come.

You know what is worthwhile in life and you don't want to sacrifice precious moments on things which are a waste of time. You're quite prepared to work alongside your chosen partner to make a better home; there doesn't have to be a busy social life to make you feel happy.

Because you're also normally so neat and tidy it would be hard for a totally disorganized partner to keep to your high standards, and hard, too, for you to cope with someone who wasn't practical and had their own feet on the ground.

You're almost as much of a workaholic as Capricorn, and you're a stickler for detail in everything that you do.

You have strong ideas on diet, and sometimes fuss so much about health that you're accused of being a hypochondriac − all things which may need to be modified a little if you're involved with someone who finds it hard to understand your stomach.

You may appear to be so busy worrying, that you don't even allow yourself sufficient time to enjoy a mutually satisfying sex-life with your partner. But while it might almost seem as though you could sometimes veer towards the frigid, or prefer to have more of a platonic relationship than a passionately physical one, it's usually just that you need the right partner to encourage you to let yourself go and open up completely to what you are feeling. Your sex drive isn't necessarily any weaker than any other sign. But in your heart of hearts you know that you need a total mind, body and soul communication if you're going to enjoy sex to the full.

You're always so determined to do everything right − it's as though, because your symbol is the Virgin, you feel that having a virtuous life is the only way to live. Any kind of 'triangle' situation would be difficult for you to accept, although you can also be pretty determined to have what you want, and if something became very serious, you're likely to wait to see if a satisfactory outcome could be worked out without anyone suffering too much hurt. You definitely don't like hurting people if you can possibly avoid it.

You need someone who is prepared to work at understanding you, at getting you to come to terms with being *you*, as you are, and to break you away from this feeling that you fall short of what you think you need to be to live up to everyone's expectations, or your own idealized expectations of what you would like to be.

You also need someone who has a well-developed sense of humour, and will help to make you laugh at yourself a little more. Don't be quite so busy doing good deeds and being so industrious that you end up exhausted at the end of the day.

To have the perfect relationship with the star-sign of your choice you must constantly remember to give yourself a little more tender loving care as well as fulfilling the needs and desires of your partner. Try to erase those niggling negative thoughts that creep up into your mind and those unnecessary worries that wake you in the night. Remember that your opposite sign in the Zodiac is that romantic dreamer of all time − Pisces − and, since every sign has a little of its opposite one in its own personality, resolve that you'll be more romantic from now on too. You don't have to take your feet too far from the ground, but once you start to indulge in a few idealistic daydreams and discover just what a wonderful sensation that can be, you might find it even easier to show the love you feel inside of you.

Even the most perfect relationship can have its pitfalls from time to time. So why not vow to use your critical ability in a more positive way? If problems arise in any relationship, your keen insight can help you come up with the best way to overcome them. Sort them out in the best possible way and resolve that you'll do all in your power to ensure that they never happen again.

Spend time learning all you can about your partner's needs and desires. Understanding each other better will ensure that your relationship really can achieve that perfect state when you know you have a soulmate by your side.

Love yourself more − and you'll discover you'll be even more lovable in everyone else's eyes too!

★

How you see Aries   You think this sign is almost too much to take at first; but you soon realize there's a childlike innocence beneath that aggressive exterior, so you stop being quite so critical.

How Aries sees you   As someone who has a lot going on below the surface, but they wonder if they can cope with being on the receiving end of your analytical probing for very long.

To make things even better Stop worrying about each other's faults and start to learn more about the positive characteristics you both possess in abundance. Aries can bring excitement and fun into your life.

★

How you see Taurus As someone who is on the same wavelength as you in many ways, but is perhaps a little too stubborn for your taste. You're a bit shy about all that sensuality.

How Taurus sees you As someone who appreciates security as much as they do. But they wonder if you sometimes lack a little warmth when it comes to the physical side of love.

To make things even better Remember that you're both Earth signs and should have a great deal in common. Try to unwind a little more and enjoy the pleasures of life for Taurus won't let you down.

★

How you see Gemini As someone who is even more restless than you. Although you're attracted by this sign's personality, and have plenty to talk about with each other you may find Gemini too flirtatious.

How Gemini sees you As a perfect partner on the intellectual level, but they don't want to have their lifestyle cramped in any way, nor have to take constant criticism.

To make things even better Recognize that Gemini needs to feel inwardly free, and always make sure there is plenty of mental stimulation in your relationship. It's the perfect way to keep them by your side.

★

How you see Cancer As someone to share a wonderfully domestic life together. You're even prepared to put up with some of Cancer's bad moods if there isn't too much else to criticize.

How Cancer sees you As someone who worries too much about the future, and they want to show you just how pleasant domestic harmony can be with the right partner by your side.

To make things even better Accept that, just as you've always been picky, Cancer has always had those up-and-down moods, and learn to adapt to each other's personalities a little better.

★

How you see Leo As someone whose bright and sparkling personality is almost too much to take at first. But you realize that they can bring a great deal of happiness into your life if you stop fussing quite so much.

How Leo sees you As someone who is far too self-critical and insecure. They feel you have a great deal to give, and want to draw you out more without frightening you away.

To make things even better Relax and stop worrying about life quite so much. Leo has a great deal of strength and isn't going to let you down, as long as they know they're important in your eyes.

★

How you see Virgo As that mirror image you've been criticizing all your life. But why don't you start to look at all the positive factors too. Stop being quite so sensitive and admit you like each other!

How Virgo sees you In the same way no doubt! And deep down they know that no one could understand them better.

To make things even better Stop analyzing each other quite so much and get on with enjoying life together. Remember all those ideals and ideas you have in common.

★

How you see Libra As someone who might be too indecisive and too self-indulgent for a long-term relationship. But you also recognize that you need a little more balance in your life.

How Libra sees you As someone who might pick too many faults in their personality, but they're prepared to be patient and work at getting to know you better.

To make things even better Always remember that Libra can be just as logical as you in the long run, and don't waste precious time criticizing their faults when they bring so much harmony to your life.

★

How you see Scorpio You fear that Scorpio's famed sexual prowess could be too much for you, but you're certainly intrigued to find out what else they have to offer!

How Scorpio sees you As someone who might be too cold and unemotional for a perfect love match but they're prepared to see if you might thaw out. But deep down they also hate to be criticized!

To make things even better Relax, and take things step by step. Don't underestimate this invincible sign.

★

How you see Sagittarius You worry that all that positive optimism is heading for a fall. You think that Sagittarius could be just too free and easy for you.

How Sagitarrius sees you As someone who might be interesting to get to know better but they fear that their Archer wanderlust tendencies would irritate you after a while.

To make things even better Stop questioning whether this can work or not. A free-and-easy approach to this relationship could work wonders for both of you, and bring more fun into your life.

★

How you see Capricorn As someone who could be on a perfect wavelength in almost any relationship. At last you've found someone who is prepared to work as hard as you.

How Capricorn sees you   Capricorn recognizes that they have found a kindred spirit, someone whose goals and aspirations match their own.

To make things even better   Start to be much more positive about life and enjoy learning everything there is to know about each other.

★

How you see Aquarius   As an unpredictable visionary whose ideas nonetheless fascinate you. But you realize that Aquarius is very fixed in their beliefs, and hates to be criticized!

How Aquarius sees you   As someone who might be too concerned with living an orderly life, with a great deal of routine. And that is definitely not their scene at all.

To make things even better   Recognize that you have completely different personalities, and if the attraction is strong enough you'll want to try to understand each other more.

★

How you see Pisces   As your opposite in almost every way, except that deep down you feel you could be almost as romantic as Pisces if you ever let yourself go.

How Pisces sees you   As quite a challenge if it means trying to make you relax and become more sentimental; and they won't like being criticized about their impractical ways.

To make things even better   Don't try to switch personalities overnight, you couldn't do it anyway. But resolve to allow a little more time for romance in your life. You'll start to blossom in quite an unexpected way!

Libra

Ruled by Venus, Goddess of Love, you're the sign of the Scales, the sign of peace and harmony, and your charm and diplomacy are renowned.

You're marvellous at helping to create the right balance in everyone else's lives. You genuinely enjoy being around people and making them happy. You're quite prepared to do everything in your power to help their relationships grow from strength to strength; you're willing to listen to their hopes, fears and insecurities, and give constructive advice when you can.

But what about you? Do you always know what *you* need in a relationship to balance your own Libran scales? And if you do know, are you sometimes too indecisive to do something positive about it?

Astrology books always tell you that you *are* indecisive, but your own personal horoscope will modify this characteristic, and many of you can probably make up your minds even faster than an impatient Aries when you want. However, the vast majority of Librans must surely admit that having to make up your mind can present you with an insurmountable problem if you really don't know what it is you're aiming for.

Knowing yourself is something which can take a lifetime to achieve; that absolute sense of being totally in tune with yourself, which is actually so important, for you are then able to relate so much better to the other people in your life.

You invariably know that you enjoy and understand life more

75

with a partner than completely on your own. But perhaps you never even realized that this is also because Libra is the seventh house of the Zodiac, and the seventh house relates in turn to marriages and longstanding relationships.

Of course, you can function perfectly well on your own, but you are far more fulfilled when you have someone to share your hopes and dreams, your plans for the future. And once your Libran mind *is* made up on something as important as the perfect partner, that's good enough for you. You don't want to then spend hours agonizing as to whether you've made the right choice.

Sometimes you're accused of not only being indecisive but of being lazy too. This is really just another example of your Libran scales not being properly balanced; you can go to extremes far too easily, and it's important for you to maintain your equilibrium both physically and mentally.

You will also have realized early on that you do enjoy being in love. It's the most wonderful experience you have ever known, and you can't imagine ever being without this one person who is your ideal partner in every way. You genuinely want to settle down and live happily ever after. You don't want to flit from lover to lover. You're an idealistic romantic who believes that love is the be-all and end-all.

You believe that age differences don't matter to you, and as long as you always look younger than your partner it's true! But then if you're a typical Libran you always do manage to look younger than your true age.

One of the nicest things about a Libran in a love relationship is that you don't let it take over your life to the exclusion of everything else. Your family and your friendships don't suffer. You want everyone to get on well with each other, but if they don't, it doesn't mean that anyone is going to see any less of you because of it.

Since you have such a natural aptitude for diplomacy and tact, you're unlikely to create problems in any of your relationships by ever arguing too much. You'd much rather talk things over calmly and rationally. There is a great deal of logic in the Libran mind, and you know that fighting over something unreasonably can only lead to further difficulties. The good thing about this is that you're always prepared to see both sides of a situation. You're never unfair, even if it means having to criticize yourself as well. You see the pros and cons of everything, weigh them up and then come up with your balanced view of what needs to be done.

You're often much stronger than you seem. Anyone who thinks they can dominate you is in for a rude awakening. You know what you want, and what you want is perfection, even in this imperfect world of ours! You need to see beauty around you, and you're prepared to work hard to create beauty in the lives of the people you care for.

But if this sounds as though your perfect partner has to match up to the stereotyped idea of good looks, that isn't it at all. It's the beauty inside you care about, and a harmonious blending of mind, body and soul.

However, because of your Libran scales you sometimes swing up and down too much. You can miss out on really great potential relationships because you do waver over what you want. It's all back to being indecisive yet again. But doing that when you're very young is one thing − just remember that part of becoming more mature is to recognize your needs and be more resolute in admitting that making a decision is often not only important but also imperative.

Whatever your age, you've surely also recognized that you function so much better as a team. In work relationships you can achieve much greater success and earning capacity when you have the right 'in tune' colleagues around you, sharing the ups as well as the downs. You're an incredibly loyal colleague, and anyone who has you as a boss couldn't want for anyone more fair-minded than you.

But have you sometimes thought it would be easier to discover a needle in a haystack than to find the perfect soulmate? Have you ever fallen head-over-heels in love with someone before you realized that they were actually more indecisive than you?

Have your ever wondered whether, because you love beauty and perfection so much, you might sometimes expect just too much?

One of your greatest requirements from any relationship is day-to-day companionship, which is why it's so important for you to be with people who are on the same wavelength. You need a partner you can look up to, and who respects you too. It's hard for you to function if that respect ever begins to slip, so, invariably, you want to ensure it never does. But you certainly don't want to dominate *or* be dominated.

The perfect partner definitely has to satisfy your physical desires too. You don't necessarily consider yourself as sexually demanding as Scorpio or Aries, but a love relationship which tended to border on the platonic could soon leave you feeling very dissatisfied, and almost convinced there had to be something wrong with *you*, rather than with the relationship as a whole.

You also need a partner who won't be quite such a spendthrift as you. Blame it on your eye for beauty if you like, a sort of aesthetic 'sweet tooth', but you're not usually brilliant with money; not unless your own particular horoscope is strongly influenced by Taurus, Virgo or Capricorn. It's just not easy for a typical Libran to be highly practical where money is concerned. But always remember that a great many problems arise when material issues are at stake, and resolve to try to remain realistic even if you're in a really extravagant mood.

There is also a part of your character which is often quite stubborn. And that has nothing to do with being indecisive! It's simply that when there is something you're totally against you're likely to dig in your heels and refuse to budge. You can become more bull-headed than Taurus and more sulky and sensitive than Cancer!

Dare I say it, but could you also be so used to charming your way through life that you've become used to getting what you want? And that sometimes you don't want to give as much as you want to take?

Sometimes you enjoy being the centre of attention almost as much as Leo. Flirting with members of the opposite sex is something which comes naturally to you, but you can become surprisingly jealous if your partner behaves the same way. However, there is such a deep-rooted sense of fair play in your make-up that you would never wittingly hurt the people you care for. And you value 'togetherness' far too much to risk ruining a special relationship by going off and finding a new lover just for an idle fling.

Building and maintaining a perfect relationship is not something which can be hurried along too much. That's one reason why being indecisive can often have positive connotations too. It gives you time to let something grow at it's own pace. It allows you to examine your feelings and to understand your partner's needs and desires a little more too.

Your balancing act can be a perfect foil if someone ever tries to sweep you off your feet. You much prefer to step back from the situation and weigh things up carefully. Although you're an Air sign and a true romantic too, your feet can be very much on the ground.

But one of your greatest danger zones is if, or when, complacency sets in. Sometimes you like to coast through life without experiencing any major alterations in your routine. You don't want to have great highs and lows − it's back to those scales all over again. Depression is almost a dirty word to a Libran, and you tend to behave more like a Cancerian if it does creep up on you, preferring to go into your shell and forget about your usually sociable ways. Don't allow inertia to creep into your everyday friendships and family ties. When you're ensconced in the perfect relationship you may not be inclined to bother to pick up the phone and see what is going on with your closest friends.

Sometimes you may also hate to face up to the fact that any problems might exist in a relationship. Is it a fear of finding yourself alone that sometimes makes you put up with the kind of behaviour from a partner which would horrify you if it was described by a friend? Don't simply sit back and accept the things which aren't so good, burying your head in the sand. Bring them out in the open − it's much better that way. And since relationships always are a bit like balancing acts, think of the experience that you have to gain by learning to keep your own personality in balance too.

As the years go by, your need for peace, harmony and companionship grows stronger, so continue to work hard at making all your relationships with friends, lovers and companions grow stronger too.

★

How you see Aries   You recognize and admit that Aries is your opposite. You're indecisive − they're impulsive; you're the peace-loving sort − while fiery Aries thrives on excitement.

How Aries sees you   They realize they've met their match at last. Your calm, soothing approach to the things which have them tearing out their hair makes them realize they should listen to you!

To make things even better   Think of your relationship rather like those Libran scales − enjoy learning to balance them and keeping them that way!

★

How you see Taurus   As someone who will always be as romantic as you and who is wonderfully dependable when you need a shoulder to lean on.

How Taurus sees you   As a charming diplomatic soulmate and is willing to be the decision-maker to make your life easier.

To make things even better   Make up your mind that you really do have a lot going for you, and be thankful that Venus, Goddess of Love, rules both your signs.

★

How you see Gemini   As a wonderfully intellectual partner who keeps you on your toes. But you fear that their flighty ways might bring out a jealous streak in you.

How Gemini sees you   As someone who is sweetness and light but sometimes just a little bit too laid back and seemingly lazy when it comes to getting your act together.

To make things even better   Never ever let inertia come over you when you're happily ensconced in a relationship with this sign. Two Air signs together can make heavenly music.

★

How you see Cancer   As someone to bring you masses of emotional fulfilment, and you envisage wonderfully lazy evenings at home. But you're concerned about those crabby moods!

How Cancer sees you   As a kind and tolerant partner they can definitely grow to love more and more − but they wonder if they'll be able to convince you to feel the same way.

To make things even better   Resolve you'll spend more time alone with your Cancerian partner to understand their up-and-down moods a little better. Never let Cancer feel insecure.

★

How you see Leo   As a bright beautiful ray of sunshine, one of the most loving and generous partners you've ever known. You don't mind giving a little gentle adulation when you know it's due.

How Leo sees you   As someone to be proud of when you're by their side. They're bowled over by your lazy indolent charm and desire to please.

To make things even better   Don't ever lose out by being indecisive when Leo is around. This sign wants quick answers, especially when true love is involved.

★

How you see Virgo   As someone who searches for perfection just as much as you do. But you fear that Virgo is too intent on finding the flaws to enjoy life to the full with you.

How Virgo sees you   As someone who would be easy to love if you weren't quite so hesitant about deciding what your next moves should be. But your ability to weigh things up secretly impresses them.

To make things even better   Resolve to use Virgo's criticism in a positive way. And don't be afraid to criticize *them* if you feel they're ever being unfair.

★

How you see Libra   As the perfect soulmate with whom to relax and enjoy an easy-going life — but how are you going to convince them to reach that decision too!

How Libra sees you   If they're a true Libra they'll no doubt see you in exactly the same way too.

To make things even better   Both of you will have to learn to make up your minds a little quicker so you don't miss out on a perfect balancing act.

★

How you see Scorpio   As someone whose fiery intensity will always sweep you off your feet. But are you slightly scared that all that passion could overpower you just too much?

How Scorpio sees you   As the beautifully romantic sensitive partner they've yearned for. Their instinct tells them this could be a very loving relationship as time goes by.

To make things even better   Don't be frightened away by Scorpio's magnetic charisma. Get to know them better and you'll discover a sensitive and highly sentimental side to them too.

★

How you see Sagittarius   As a wonderful friend who can enhance your life in so many positive ways. But you worry that Sagittarius might have too much of a wanderlust for a permanent relationship.

How Sagittarius sees you   They're fascinated by your ability to be so tactful and diplomatic, and could easily fall for your lovable personality.

To make things even better   Never try to tie Sagittarius down too much — and don't waste precious moments being indecisive if they're obviously keen to see you more and more.

★

How you see Capricorn   As someone who could bring total security into your life. But you realize you'll have to work at drawing them out when it comes down to love and romance.

How Capricorn sees you   As someone who might just be too relaxed and fond of having a good time to contemplate having a serious relationship . . . with a serious person.

To make things even better   Work at proving you can be not only a perfect soulmate but a perfect helpmate too. Don't let Capricorn think all the hard work has to come from them.

★

How you see Aquarius   You feel a strong attraction between you. Mentally you're on a perfect wavelength; but emotionally Aquarius might be rather too detached for you.

How Aquarius sees you   As a perfect blend of mind/body/ soul. They're captivated by your lazy, indolent charm and friendly manner. *And* you're both Air signs too.

To make things even better   Don't worry so much if Aquarius can't always reveal their deepest feelings. Enjoy thinking up new ways to show them just how perfect you can be in every way.

★

How you see Pisces   As someone to fulfil every romantic dream you've ever had. But you wonder if their impractical ways and your indecisive ones could lead to disharmony.

How Pisces sees you   As perfect in almost every way. Pisces isn't always the most realistic of signs and can easily be swept off their feet by your beauty and charm!

To make things even better   Resolve that neither of you will be too lazy or unrealistic to work at building up your relationship on every level − not spend all the time gazing into each other's eyes.

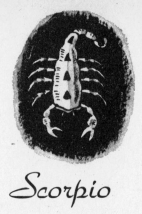

Scorpio

With two planets ruling your sign – Mars, God of War; and Pluto, Lord of the Underworld – it's no wonder that you consider yourself invincible. Or perhaps it's simply astrologers who consider you this way and deep down you're just as insecure and confused about love as the rest of us.

One thing is certainly true – you're not afraid to rush in where angels fear to tread when it comes to romance. You thrive on challenges just like Aries, that other Mars-ruled sign, but you're not quite as impulsive and headstrong as the Ram; you have a slower, more burning intensity when seeking out that perfect person with whom to share your life.

Passionate, smouldering Scorpio! Can't you understand why you sometimes hear a note of trepidation in people's voices when they learn your star-sign? At a party is it sometimes 'Oh, "Scorpio"'! as they move briskly away? Do you wish you'd never been given the Scorpion as your planetary symbol, so that you would never again have to hear about the 'sting in your tail'?

Just as a leopard can't change its spots, you can't change being a Scorpio. It's far too late for that! Now, what you have to do is to learn a little more about *you*, in order to achieve the perfect relationship in your life without being worried that your Scorpio personality will send your potentially ideal partner scurrying away far too soon, before they have a chance to find out how wonderful you really are.

You're intense and powerful and you're bent on searching out the mysteries of life and love. It's really difficult for you to accept that sometimes you give yourself problems by having a very strong ego. It's not necessarily inflated, but you know that what you want out of life simply cannot be second-best.

Sometimes you're unfairly accused of being cruel and unfeeling when it comes to relationships. That's a sad thing to say when you're actually one of the most loyal signs in the Zodiac, and it's about time people stopped maligning you before they get to know you well.

One aspect of your personality which does often create difficulties in your life is that you find it so hard to forgive anyone, let alone forget anything which you feel to be unfair. It would be great if you could learn to be a little like Libra, the sign which precedes yours, and try harder to see both sides of a situation instead of taking an instant stand.

Scorpio, you have such intensity of purpose, learn to harness it in a positive way. Since you're always so intent on finding out what makes everyone else tick, don't be quite so sensitive next time someone tries to find out a little more about you.

Anyone who has anything at all to do with a Scorpio will soon learn that there is an essential part of your personality which is private to you, and you alone. You need your inner space, and your outer one as well. But, paradoxically, you can be jealous, possessive and suspicious if you feel that anyone you care for has secrets they are holding back from you. This is something which has been with you from your early childhood on; it's not something which will necessarily mellow with age. In fact, some Scorpios tend to become very bitter and frustrated later in life because of it. So try to be a little more understanding of other people; they may need their own private spaces too, even if they are born under different signs. This is especially applicable in a love relationship, for real love must never turn into possession – the possessed would only start to feel trapped and most likely resent the situation, creating problems.

Interestingly enough, while you are invincible in so many ways, there is a rather beautiful form of sensitivity which shows when you do fall deeply in love. There is a fear of rejection, an insecurity which transforms all that passionate intensity into something more delicate. You would hate to think you were showing your vulnerability, but it's about time you began to realize that being vulnerable is all part of building the perfect relationship too. Or are you so determined to be in control that you hate to think of your partner seeing any weaknesses you might possess? It's true, Scorpio — you spend your life protecting your deepest feelings, as though you don't trust anyone enough for you to reveal the real you.

You're also not very good at coping with weaknesses you discover in others. And while you are perfectly prepared to be a strong shoulder to lean on, there comes a time when you feel that the person needing your help and support should learn to stand on their own two feet, as you invariably do yourself.

But things can go wrong in any kind of relationship if you're only prepared to delight in the strong characteristics of those people you are involved with, and don't have enough patience to understand their insecurities. For when you're building and maintaining a relationship, it really is important to empathize with your partner. Find out why they may be feeling bad. Start to become more patient, and talk things through calmly. Don't lose your temper and start to become coldly sarcastic — it's far too easy to do that.

There is a part of your personality which can be very self-destructive. Sometimes you may need to project more of a sense of humour. No one can deny that you're often brilliantly witty, but are you able to laugh at yourself too?

In a working relationship your invincible quality is seen all over again. You are determined to achieve success, and don't mind how hard you work to attain it. You're an extremely loyal colleague, and a strong and forthright boss. In professional relationships you definitely don't tolerate any weaknesses, and you can be quite ruthless if you're involved in a power struggle, invariably knowing that you have the ability to come out on top. Sometimes you can make enemies in your working life, but you're not out to hurt people willingly if it can be helped.

With family ties you can be as devoted as any other sign, and it's often easier for a Scorpio to accept and put up with a rift between family members if serious problems have arisen. It all comes back to your attitude towards forgiving and forgetting. But you're happy to do everything in your power to prove your love and affection to the people who are closest to you in your life.

Friendships are very important to you. It may be difficult for people to get close to you in the beginning, but once they've proved their own particular brand of loyalty, they are assured of yours as well.

Most men and women born under your sign are well aware of your description as the 'sex symbol' of the Zodiac. Astrologically, every star-sign rules a different part of the body, and Scorpio happens to rule the sexual organs. But it would be ridiculous to assume that every single Scorpio has but this one thought on their mind. It would be equally ridiculous to pretend that good sex in a love relationship was not a very important issue. You have a great deal of passion simmering away inside you and it needs to be expressed. When you're in love you need to have a sexually fulfilling relationship with your partner. Anything veering towards the platonic would be very hard for you to take. When you have total empathy with your perfect partner it's a mind-blowing experience in the best possible sense of the phrase. It has to be mind, body and soul. Your opposite sign of the Zodiac, Taurus, is one of the most sensual signs around – and you have a great deal of this Taurean sensuality within you. Being with a partner who failed to understand this almost visceral need would be impossible for both of you to take.

It's interesting that you can be so compassionate and yet so ruthless when you're thinking about your own situation in life. Sometimes you're so set on your own course, so fixed in your own ideas and opinions that you give yourself an unnecessarily hard time. You blow hot and cold with the greatest of ease: why don't you sometimes exercise a little more tolerance and be more prepared to forgive and even forget? Never forget that you're also one of the most psychic signs of the entire Zodiac, so use your intuition a little more when you are relating to others.

Financially, you also blow hot and cold. When you have plenty of money you are sometimes inclined to spend it as a form of emotional release. At other times you can be accused of downright stinginess.

You're an 'all or nothing' person. You can survive with very little, and like the phoenix rising from the ashes you'll overcome the greatest problems and soar to the heights. Even coping with a 'triangle' situation would not be insurmountable if you were deeply in love. Perhaps it's yet another example of your ruthlessness. But having a marvellous relationship with the perfect partner will bring you so much happiness and help you to release those pent-up emotions you spend so much time building up.

Never forget that you're a Water sign, romantic, idealistic and dreaming your own special dreams. You're so keen to unravel the riddles of both life and death: why not work a little harder at unravelling the mystery of what makes your own personality the way it is?

Scorpio is said to be ruled not only by the Scorpion, but by the Eagle too. Learn to be more like that eagle, towering high in the sky. No one should ever underestimate you – particularly yourself. Building and maintaining the perfect relationship is something you can do so easily, provided that you forget all about that sting.

★

How you see Aries As almost as power crazy as you, but not quite so focused and patient. You recognize that this can be a passionately goal-orientated relationship.

How Aries sees you As a sexually stimulating lover, but is slightly scared about those possessive ways of yours.

To make things even better Both of you will have to be more cool, calm and collected, and talk things over before making any rash decisions.

★

How you see Taurus As your opposite in many ways but you find this sign infinitely sensual and wonderfully dependable.

How Taurus sees you As passion personified but they fear that

88

your jealousy might be just too much to cope with. And depending how stubborn they are they might just back off.

To make things even better   Be prepared to give a little more of yourself — and try not to be quite so overpowering in your attitude to life and love.

★

How you see Gemini   As much too flirtatious and fickle for you to cope with. But think what a challenge it will be to keep them by your side.

How Gemini sees you   As the most passionate lover of all time, but isn't so keen on taking the mental telepathy that goes along with it.

To make things even better   Learn more about the power of self-expression and the value of bringing things out into the open.

★

How you see Cancer   As a wonderfully sentimental dreamer but you're worried that you'd be tied too close to home. Domestic bliss is one thing but you don't want to be protected too much.

How Cancer sees you   As a dramatic fiery partner but recognizes that underneath there's a great deal of sentimentality and sensitivity too.

To make things even better   Try to understand that Cancer *is* one of the most protective of all the signs, and explain gently that you hate to feel smothered.

★

How you see Leo   You admire Leo's bright and golden personality and are drawn like a moth to a flame — but then you remember you hate taking second place to anyone!

How Leo sees you   In practically the same way, but is even more fearful of the secret sting of Scorpio. However, Leo is enticed by your sexuality.

To make things even better   Leo can be one of the most affectionate signs of the Zodiac and Scorpio one of the most passionate. If you give up your power games and learn to co-operate you can conquer the world.

★

How you see Virgo   You see Virgo as calm, cool and critical, but it doesn't take you long to realize that this sign can be undeniably passionate too.

How Virgo sees you   As overwhelming in the sexual department but the Virgo curiosity is intrigued to find out what else you have to offer.

To make things even better   Wait a minute! Be prepared to take a little criticism for it could do you the world of good. Don't be so intent on taking the world by storm.

★

How you see Libra   As the angelic partner you have always dreamed of. Intuitively you sense that this could be the most romantic relationship of all time.

How Libra sees you   Somewhat warily. Your sexual hunger shakes Libra to the knees but Libra would love to have the abandonment to fulfil your intense desires.

To make things even better   Be sensitive of Libra's aesthetic sense of balance. Take time to use your Scorpio intelligence to its best advantage and you'll discover a lifelong friendship and sentimental romance rolled up into one.

★

How you see Scorpio   At first as the ideal mate. The at-oneness is almost startling but after a while you begin to wonder if you should have just been friends instead of lovers.

How Scorpio sees you   In just the same way – how else could it be?

To make things even better   Respect each other's power and learn to live and let live.

★

How you see Sagittarius   You're torn between following Sagittarius to the opposite end of the earth, but then you wonder if they will ever care quite so deeply about life as you do.

How Sagittarius sees you   As someone with amazing charisma but the responsibility of having to live up the Scorpio extremism might be almost too much to bear.

To make things even better   Relax and start to enjoy life more without taking everything quite so seriously if you want to stick around with Sagittarius.

★

How you see Capricorn   As powerful in a different way from you – but you fear you could be bogged down by their need for so much security.

How Capricorn sees you   As an extremist whose passionately sexual desires could interfere too much with their workaholic mode of life.

To make things even better   Try to realize that Capricorn works so hard to make a better life for both of you.

★

How you see Aquarius   As someone who fascinates you because you never know quite how they're going to behave from one day to the next. An interesting challenge.

How Aquarius sees you   As a powerful mental combatant in the game of life, but refuses to be overpowered by your need for sexual domination.

To make things even better   Always remember that coming on too strong is never a turn-on to Aquarius. And that they have an intensely private side too.

★

91

How you see Pisces You can't wait to swim upstream with this romantic dreamer by your side, but you fear that Pisces is just too impractical for you.

How Pisces sees you As someone who can be unbelievably sensitive beneath the surface, but is almost too intense in their approach to love and romance.

To make things even better Never forget you do have that sensitive side to your nature – Pisces needs lots of love and support. You can both use your psychic powers to understand each other more.

Sagittarius

Ruled by Jupiter, planet of good fortune, you're the eternal optimist, the truth-seeker of the Zodiac born with an irrepressible wanderlust which doesn't diminish with the passing years.

Sometimes, you come across as the sort of person who functions much better on the friendship level than when it comes right down to a close relationship. Moreover you are one of the most gregarious signs around: there is nothing you like better than to be in the midst of congenial company. You enjoy talking for hours about every subject under the sun, and you love hearing what other people have to say, but since you're also known as the Sage or, Counsellor of the Zodiac, you also love to give advice.

But this might be the moment to point out that sometimes you're a little too fond of giving advice when it's not called for − or even wanted. And the trouble is that many of you have the habit of thinking you are always right. Of course sometimes you are − but there is a side of your personality which can be so brutally frank that it comes over as lack of tact. Take a leaf out of Libra's book. Weigh things up a little more before you upset someone with what they consider to be a scathing viewpoint even if you do feel it's simply an honest appraisal of the situation.

Lovable, happy-go-lucky, free-spirited Sagittarius. You can be the most wonderfully positive and optimistic star-sign in the entire Zodiac − and usually are. It's so refreshing to meet someone with so much energy and vitality, so much *joie-de-*

vivre! Your enthusiasm and adventurous view of life is refreshing, especially at a time when so many people are becoming jaded by what they read about and see in the world. You're such an independent character, so convinced that you can succeed at whatever you want to achieve, and you have a wonderful ability to get on with almost anybody you meet.

But there is also something in your personality which often makes it hard for you to contemplate settling down with one person for ever more. Of course there are many many Sagittarians who have been happily married to or with the same 'co-vivant' for years. That's probably because they have been wise enough to know exactly the sort of partner they needed from the start.

The going isn't always so easy. Knowing yourself and knowing what you want and need out of life can take a lifetime. The wanderlust part of the Sagittarian personality isn't something which is always easy to harness. You need a partner who not only understands but also accepts your restlessness, your inner need to feel free. It's not as though you want to play around with other people once you're immersed in an important love relationship. It's just that there is a part of you which rebels if you do feel you are tied down too much. You're almost the sort of person who would thrive best in a close relationship or marriage if you and your partner were (perhaps due to your respective careers) forced to spend periods apart from each other. It isn't even a case of absence making the heart grow fonder but simply that you do need your own space at times.

However, needing your own space almost makes it sound as though you're as secretive and private as Scorpio. In fact, quite the opposite is true of you, for you are totally honest about everything you feel and think. You're not someone who could be involved in a 'triangle' type situation without going through an incredible amount of soul-searching. You hate to hurt people, and it's so hard for you to keep anything under wraps. Life isn't meant to be a subterfuge for you: everything has to be open and above-board for you to function at your maximum potential.

But sometimes in a one-to-one relationship you lose out because of your fear of giving up your freedom. You're so hesitant about making a commitment, that even when someone comes along who fulfils your vision of a perfect partner, you can be almost as indecisive as Libra. You want them as your friend — that much you're sure of — but can you cope with something deeper?

There is an innocent and childlike quality about you. Refreshingly naïve, you can be as impulsive as any Aries, leaping into a love affair with reckless abandon. You want to love and be loved — but it has to be on your terms and you're certainly not going to lie about it. It would probably take another Sagittarian or a Gemini or Aquarian to understand you totally. You need lots of mental stimulation, that's for sure, and you need your partner to be your best friend too.

Because you are such a friendly and outgoing person, your relationship with your family and friends is invariably an easy-going and harmonious one. You're not necessarily prepared to be around all the time — but you somehow manage to stay in touch no matter where you are. You love bringing people together, having parties where you can be a marvellous host or hostess.

You're not the sort of person who bears grudges when arguments arise. You're usually quite prepared to forgive and forget. You hate to think of becoming bad friends with anyone — it really hurts you.

Your spirit of adventure means that you are invariably great fun to be with. But you can be irresponsible too.

Financial security is never quite as important to you as it is to many other signs. But perhaps that is also because deep down you know things will always be all right for you. I hate to use the word 'luck' in astrology, but it truly seems that with Jupiter as your ruling planet you are often blessed with a really high percentage of good fortune. It is maybe why so many of you have that gambling instinct, the ability to take risks where the rest of us would shy away. When you have money, you're one of the most generous people around, and you can be unselfishly extravagant. When you don't, your optimistic streak shines through and, somehow, something always comes along to restore your belief that you always will be sufficiently supplied for your needs.

You're marvellously adaptable to your surroundings, and you don't demand the trappings which can go with material security: the big house, the wardrobes full of expensive clothes. You could be happy living in a tent if you were with the right person. Besides, you don't usually like to think of living in the same place all your life.

For someone who often finds it hard to contemplate settling down you're extraordinarily idealistic about love. Perhaps it's because of the philosophical, questing side of your nature. Symbolized by the Archer aiming his arrow far into the sky, you, in turn, are questing for your ideal soulmate, someone who can fulfil your mind, body and soul and never leave you feeling bored or restless. But just because you are so fond of challenges, it doesn't always mean that your friends or lovers feel the same way about life. Make sure you're never too wrapped up in your ideas of what you want for yourself that you forget about the needs of the people you care for most: sometimes there can be something almost selfish in your insistence on being free to roam.

You don't always come across as being highly passionate and emotional, although your sexual desires are no less strong than anyone else's. However, it's highly important that your lover *is* a true friend as well. Sex alone is rarely sufficient to fulfil you. There has to be mutual compatibility on every other level too. You need to communicate totally with your partner, to have an understanding of each other's everyday feelings. You hate to have strings attached, but if you're totally honest you will also admit that it's your deep-rooted fear of losing your independence which often makes it hard for you to give of yourself completely.

You need a partner to accept you as an equal, and not to try to dominate you. By the same token you would find it very hard to be with someone weaker or less intelligent than you are. Not that you're a snob – social backgrounds, different races or nationalities don't worry you – but your aims and objectives in life need to have a common ground.

In a work relationship you're usually easy to get along with. But if you're tied down to too much uncreative routine, your freedom-loving Sagittarian spirit begins to rebel. Also, you're not good at taking orders from anyone you don't respect.

Building and maintaining any kind of relationship is not necessarily the easiest thing in the world. But think what a great benefit it is to have your innate optimism about life. You know very well that when you're determined to work at something and achieve the very best you can invariably do just that.

Sagittarians are very hard to pin down, but at least when you recognize that you have met the perfect partner, you are not afraid to admit it.

You are someone who would never be comfortable alone for very long. If the ideal relationship seems to have eluded you, it might just be that you are not ready for it. And, since you are naturally very sociable, all you have to do is get out and about in the right places; be in the swing of things, and you're sure to attract interesting people to your side.

Just because you're also known as the 'long-distance traveller' of the Zodiac, it doesn't mean that you're always searching for new pastures to roam. If you're in a relationship with someone who prefers to stay put more than you, why not learn to adapt your personality a little? Don't insist on having things the way *you* want them every time − be even more giving of yourself, be more sensitive to the needs of your partner, and always keep your wonderful optimism. Things will work out for the best. When you channel your energies in this direction all your relationships will grow stronger and more fulfilling.

★

How you see Aries   As someone who enjoys freedom as much as you. You enjoy the warmth of being with another Fire sign who shares your enthusiasm and *joie de vivre*.

How Aries sees you   As an ideal soulmate in a myriad of different ways. But they are slightly worried that you might be torn between *your* sense of freedom and your possessiveness.

To make things even better   Admire each other's colourful individuality and never try to fence each other in. Be totally

honest, but remember that Aries is sensitive under that aggressive exterior.

★

How you see Taurus   As someone who will always be a wonderfully dependable support. But you recognize that they have your
feet far more on the ground that you ever will.

How Taurus sees you   As a bright, adventurous free spirit. But
they fear their jealous streak could start to show after they've
been around you for very long – and your wanderlust ways are
not for them.

To make things even better   Both of you will have to adapt your
personalities a little more; Taurus has to be less stubborn – and
you have to be less of a know-all.

★

How you see Gemini   Gemini could be your perfect travelling
companion. You both have your need for freedom and you're
both great communicators.

How Gemini sees you   In the same way, but they wonder if you
have enough patience to put up with their flirtatious ways.
Meanwhile there's plenty of mental stimulation here.

To make things even better   Learn even more about your opposite sign of the Zodiac's personality – you'll find new ways to
make this relationship grow stronger.

★

How you see Cancer   There are times when you love to feel so
protected and needed, but with your optimistic approach to life
you fear you'd run a mile from too much smothering.

How Cancer sees you   Wistfully, recognizing that they will
never be as independent and freedom-loving as you, but they will
do their best to feel as positive about life as you.

To make things even better   Think yourself lucky to have
such a deeply rooted domestic partner to give you an anchor to

your tendency to wander. Resolve you'll try to understand Cancer's fluctuating moods.

★

How you see Leo   You're happy that Leo enjoys being the life and soul of parties just as much as you. But you don't relish being bossed around too much — even by another Fire sign.

How Leo sees you   They would love to follow you off into the horizon but they are much too used to being the leader. They also realize they have a greater need for admiration than you do.

To make things even better   Accept that you both have a great deal going for you. Accept each other's ways and get on and enjoy life to the full.

★

How you see Virgo   As an interesting companion on the intellectual level, but all that constant criticism could have you packing your suitcase much too fast.

How Virgo sees you   At first in a critical light but they appreciate your ability to see life in such a creative way. They secretly wish they could be a little more like you.

To make things even better   Let Virgo do some nit-picking from time to time. Remember that your bright and bubbly personality can put more colour into your Virgo's life.

★

How you see Libra   As someone who could benefit from your exuberant personality to inject a little more go into their life to balance their Libran scales.

How Libra sees you   As a true soulmate but they go through agonies of indecision as to whether this could really last. They need to believe that you will stick around.

To make things even better   Even though Libra's indecision can sometimes make you wild, you realize that you both love to be loved and that you must be decisive enough for both of you.

★

How you see Scorpio   As someone who might sometimes be too secretive for you, which makes you unjustifiably suspicious that they may have too much to hide from you.

How Scorpio sees you   As someone so adventurous and free-spirited that they're almost convinced it's *you* who must have some skeletons in your cupboard.

To make things even better   Stop going back into the past and learn to enjoy each other in a much more positive way.

★

How you see Sagittarius   You love the way that your Sagittarian partner knows how important it is always to be good friends.

How Sagittarius sees you   They totally agree with you that friendship really is the basis for all true love.

To make things even better   Recognize that each of you will always think they know best but never waste time arguing when you have so much going for you.

★

How you see Capricorn   As someone who sometimes lacks sufficient sense of relaxation and ability to enjoy life, but you value the sense of belonging they bring you.

How Capricorn sees you   As someone who gambles too much with life to provide you with the stability you need. But they're fascinated all the same.

To make things even better   If you can keep your feet on the ground a little more and stop Capricorn being quite so pessimistic, the two of you could be really good for each other.

★

How you see Aquarius   As someone who is as adventurous and excited about life as you are. You love the way they need their freedom but wonder if emotionally they're demonstrative enough for you.

How Aquarius sees you   As an easy-going, happy-go-lucky personality they want to know more about. They like your air of independence — it makes them feel freer too.

To make things even better   Let things take their own pace. Don't frighten Aquarius away by expecting them to tell you exactly what they feel about you — it's easy for them to do that!

★

How you see Pisces   As an appealing romantic, but you're not sure whether you have the sentimentality it takes to convince them to put up with your independent air.

How Pisces sees you   They're envious of your free-and-easy personality, but dream beautiful dreams of travelling the world with you by their side.

To make things even better   You can be more sentimental if you really try. Start to appreciate how beautiful it can be when your deepest romantic dreams can be fulfilled.

Capricorn

Ruled by Saturn, taskmaster of the Zodiac, you have a wealth of powers to offer the perfect partner in a serious relationship.

Cautious, practical and realistic, you approach life in a most determined manner. Where others are off dreaming and gazing at the sky you are hard at work. The danger inherent in your approach to life, though, is that too much seriousness can alienate the people you inwardly care for most.

So, Capricorn, it might be good advice for you to try and let off steam now and then, and occasionally adopt a more unconventional outlook ... you might even find that the unconventional approach may solve problems even faster than a traditional way, and since you're also a person of high ideals and pride yourself on the ability to solve problems it might even tempt you to loosen up once in a while.

Self-discipline, for which you're so well-known, is great in a work situation, or in a crisis, when everyone around you is losing his head, but in the ups and downs of relationships and in the subtlety of love and affection an entirely different approach is needed which you may have to learn to cultivate.

Dare I accuse you of being almost too materialistic, of setting so much store in the right background of people you associate with that you can miss out on the one thing that you need? The spark of love cannot be fired in a vacuum!

You're an Earth sign, so it's quite natural for you to have both feet firmly on the ground, but when those first stirrings of romance begin to cast their golden light in your heart and mind, why do you negate them and brush them aside as mere futile fantasies which have little importance in your so carefully constructed lifestyle? Don't you realize that 'love makes the world go round'? Having both feet on the ground doesn't mean that you're not also meant to enjoy the fruits of the Earth to full measure!

No one is asking you to alter your personality, but if this challenge seems reasonable to you, why not risk being more open, positive and optimistic? If you really don't know how to do this why not invite a Sagittarian around and listen to the way he or she talks?

Deep within your personality, there is a very sentimental side, and it's often that you need just that right person around you to express it. So, when you find that perfect person, please don't project yourself as being so self-sufficient that you won't allow them to get close to you, until you've satisfied those high idealistic standards about people you've set yourself.

Stop being quite so rigid in your approach, just because Saturn *is* your ruling planet, you don't have to be quite so hard on yourself: you're entitled to have some fun! Start to look at yourself in a more optimistic way. You know that when you're determined to achieve something you're a worker of miracles!

Relationships may always be a serious business for you, and there is certainly nothing wrong with that. It's marvellous for your chosen partner to know that you're such a calm and practical person, and so dependable too − a veritable tower of strength.

You're not the sort of person who wants to embark on a string of different affairs. It's not only because you have such deep-rooted moral views on life, but because you're a traditionalist too. You believe in the sanctity of love and marriage. You don't want to spend your life changing partners, not when you've found someone whose personality can blend with yours. And you often set such high store by financial issues that living with a spendthrift would be almost impossible for you to contemplate.

You're sense of responsibility is wonderful: you will never let anyone down. You're thoroughly dedicated to doing the best that you can in every situation; but are you really as self-sufficient as you make out? Or, is it an act you've perfected until it has become second-nature to you now? You're not really a loner: you know how satisfying it is to have the perfect partner by your side.

You have so much to give if you'll just allow yourself to unwind and relax a bit more. Try to stop thinking quite so much about sticking to what is tried and true − be a little more adventurous and not quite so mistrusting about what life has to offer. Is excitement something you're frightened of? Do you feel you'd lose ground by experiencing the adventures and ecstasies which other star-signs enjoy?

Very often the first thirty years of your life are the hardest − after that you start to bloom in a new and self-confident way. It's as though you have had to come to terms with who you are and what you want to be. You finally release all the deadwood and move on with greater confidence and awareness too.

Whereas age differences in a love relationship don't necessarily have much bearing on many relationships, with you it could be difficult to contemplate a serious relationship with someone a great deal younger than you, unless in many ways they seemed older than their years. This is usually because even as a child you seemed to relate better to adults than to children of your own age. Life always *has* been a serious business to you, and you're fully aware of the importance of the right mental communication in any important relationships. Once again the practical side of your nature comes to the foreground, and although obviously your own personal horoscope will modify certain of your characteristics, you are unlikely to veer far away from your conservative and rational approach to life.

But don't let your search for the right partner allow you to become too serious about life all the time! Sometimes you're far too preoccupied with thinking you know exactly what you need, without bothering to realize that the art of building and maintaining a relationship means learning and understanding your partner's needs too − so that the two of you can grow together.

It's a fantastically positive attitude to have such a determined sense of purpose, to know what you're aiming for in life. And to have the right person by your side sharing in all this is a wonderful experience.

In a physical relationship you sometimes give yourself an unnecessarily hard time. It's as though you're holding back, afraid to let yourself go in case it means losing a little of your strength. You're often very vulnerable under your cool and controlled exterior. But you have incredibly strong feelings once you allow yourself to let them go. Perhaps it's also because of your almost old-fashioned views that you could find it extremely difficult to indulge in light-hearted flirtations or affairs without a real commitment in view. But strangely enough there can also be an almost ruthless side to your personality which enables you to be the third party in a 'triangle' situation – as long as you feel you and your partner are totally committed to each other.

There's probably no way you're suddenly going to turn into a laugh-a-minute comedian, but you'll be able to improve *all* your relationships if you do allow yourself to become a little more light-hearted. Why not try it and see?

You are immensely loyal to your family and friends. Anyone in a relationship with you must remember never to run them down and criticize them in any way. Hopefully your partner will get on with everyone who *is* important to you: if not this could place a strain on your relationship.

In a work situation, your capability and determination to achieve success is phenomenal. Just like that mountain goat circumnavigating the craggy mountain side in order to reach the top, you will put in incredibly long hours to reach your own chosen pinnacle. But remember that this, too, can place other relationships under strain. Having a workaholic around is not always easy. Never let your partner feel that they are taking second place. Always let them realize that your desire to achieve greater material security is to benefit them as well.

Always remember too that although you do come over as such a self-sufficient and well-organized person, you also thrive when you know that you have someone who cares immensely about you.

Even though your feet *are* so firmly on terra firma, you want to love and be loved just as much as everyone else.

Money and social advantages will never be enough for you if you're truly honest about your deepest desires, so open yourself up more to the possibilities which life has to offer.

Stop being so frightened about what might happen *if* . . . A marvellous facet of being born under Capricorn is that life invariably does get better as the years toll by. Resolve to relax a little more and become more aware of yourself as someone who can achieve anything they want.

Don't have such preconceived ideas of what the ideal relationship must be. Life can often surprise you in the most unexpected way. Enjoy it to the full without questioning it quite so much.

There's something of your opposite sign of Cancer inside your own star-sign. Its not only domestic security which makes your life more fulfilling, but allowing yourself to open up and be more sentimental and romantic too.

★

How you see Aries   As bright, breezy and exciting to be with . . . but what about when the routine starts to set in and Aries feels the urge to roam?

How Aries sees you   As someone who'll bring stability and security into their life, but they fear you could sometimes be too practical and materialistic for their idealistic ways.

To make things even better   Show that you have a wonderful sense of humour when you're prepared to stop worrying about what might happen tomorrow. Let your hair down once in a while.

★

How you see Taurus   As a perfect blend of soulmate and helpmate. You recognize that Taurus will put as much effort as you into making this relationship work on every level.

How Taurus sees you   In virtually the same way, although Taurus is slightly concerned that their sensuality could sometimes distract you from your workaholic ways.

To make things even better Relax and enjoy the bliss of building a relationship with someone who has their feet almost as firmly on the ground as you do.

★

How you see Gemini As a fascinating and delightful companion who would never bore you. But you're scared you'd never be able to keep up with their pace, and you fear they might get tired of you.

How Gemini sees you As the tower of strength they know would be good for them; but they're not quite sure if they want to feel tied down in any way.

To make things even better Enjoy what you have between you and don't spend quite so much time thinking about the future. Always try to keep Gemini mentally stimulated.

★

How you see Cancer As someone to share the perfect domestic set-up with you. One part of you loves to feel so protected, the other feels that so much sentimentality could distract you from your work.

How Cancer sees you As someone to watch over them when they eventually get home from work! They're delighted to meet someone as security conscious as they are.

To make things even better Accept the fact that deep down you have a greal deal in common with your opposite sign of the Zodiac and don't fight it!

★

How you see Leo You're worried that Leo is too much of a party-goer ever to settle down to a permanent relationship with someone as committed as you.

How Leo sees you As the Rock of Gibraltar but they wonder if you have the exuberance for life that they have.

To make things even better Enjoy the prospect of forgetting all about work once in a while, and never forget to give Leo plenty of praise and compliments when they're due.

★

How you see Virgo   As the perfect partner in so many ways that you're determined they will find nothing to criticize in you.

How Virgo sees you   As someone to share life's ups and downs – two kindred spirits working towards a common goal.

To make things even better   Start to become more optimistic and be happy that Virgo cares as much about total security as you do.

★

How you see Libra   As being a little too laid-back sometimes but all that charm and diplomacy goes a long way towards alleviating your doubts.

How Libra sees you   As someone who will always be dependable, but they wonder if you could be too staid and rigid in your outlook on a long-term basis.

To make things even better   Don't assume that you will have to do all the work. Libra might have bouts of laziness and an easy going disposition but don't underestimate them.

★

How you see Scorpio   As a powerful and intriguing partner whose magnetic charisma makes you see there is something else in life besides your work.

How Scorpio sees you   They recognize that they've met an equal in the power stakes but wonder if you realize just how important it is to be sexually compatible too.

To make things even better   Admit to yourself that you have physical needs the same as everybody else and that passion can enhance your life in a truly positive way.

★

How you see Sagittarius As a free spirit whom you yearn to tame, recognizing that their particular brand of optimism is just what you need to add extra brightness to your life.

How Sagittarius sees you As a strong supportive focal point, but they are mindful that you don't always know how to wind down as easily as they do.

To make things even better Tolerate and start to appreciate each other's differences, and be grateful for the wealth of optimism that Sagittarius can bring to you.

★

How you see Capricorn Two workaholics together. You initially think that this is total bliss but wonder if you'll ever have sufficient time to get to know each other better.

How Capricorn sees you They could be really attracted to you for reinforcement of their own ideals − or run away from such a vivid mirror image.

To make things even better Accept that you can work *and* play together if you choose − and enjoy it all.

★

How you see Aquarius As someone whose unpredictability is like a breath of fresh air in your more staid conventional life − but you're not sure you're quite ready for it!

How Aquarius sees you As someone with whom to settle down and be really serious with − but your need for total stability frightens them a little too.

To make things even better Respect each other's individuality − and don't try to tie down Aquarius too much.

★

How you see Pisces As a wonderfully sentimental romantic dreamer − but you're not sure if you have enough time for romantic dreams.

How Pisces sees you   As the tower of strength they've hoped for all their life — they long to help you open up and be more sentimental too.

To make things even better   Show that even a self-disciplined Capricorn can put away their workload with a sensitive soulmate at their side.

Aquarius

Your vision of the world as a whole is one in which there are no wars, no enemies, no frontiers. You genuinely want everyone to get along with each other. You are the greatest humanitarian of all time. Yet you're also the most unpredictable and unconventional of all the signs in the Zodiac, even though you can be almost as stubborn as Taurus when it comes to admitting any of your faults.

You were born under a Fixed sign — you refuse to follow anyone else's doctrines. Contrastingly, you also need to feel as free as your element of air. But in a love relationship you sometimes create unnecessary problems because of your inability to say what you really feel. You love no less intensely and deeply than anyone else, but when someone becomes very close to you are you frightened that it will leave you much too vulnerable? Or are you scared to admit that you need anyone else?

It often seems that you would make a much better friend than lover, but even as a friend you have a few things to learn, like fitting in with other people's quirks and foibles. It is also often impossible to know just how you're going to react to anything at a given time, and this too can be part of your endearing characteristic of unpredictability!

It is not easy to tell what you are like in a relationship, nor what you need from one; you can sometimes hurt the people closest to you by not levelling with them and letting them know just how important they are to you. They might get the impression that they are 'here today and gone tomorrow' in your mind.

Since every star-sign has something of its opposite in its own make-up, it is interesting to realize that Leo is your own opposite sign, and that you're often just as bossy and domineering as the Lion. You can also be just as bright, sunny and sparkling as the King of the Jungle, but you certainly seem to switch your moods a whole lot more than the Lion!

Ruled by Uranus, planet of change, invention and also disruption, you're never prepared to fit in with anyone else's preconceived notion of what they'd like you to be. You are unique – and that's the way you want to remain. The demanding planet Saturn is also associated with your sign, and you can be just as serious and determined as any Saturn-ruled Capricorn when it comes to achieving your aims and ambitions in life. But unlike Capricorn you're more inventive, more inclined to go off on your own various tangents. You don't want to conform, to be too conservative in your outlook, or rigid in your approach to life.

In some ways, you're a mass of contradictions. Deep down, your idealistic yearnings for a true soulmate to understand you and share your life cannot be understated. But on the surface you fear the idea of being trapped in something which might become boring and unexciting as the years go by.

Learn to trust your instinct a little more: let yourself go – and admit to yourself *and* your partner when you know that you're in a good relationship.

Anyone who has ever been emotionally involved with an Aquarian of either sex will discover that you can be everything and nothing! A strong statement perhaps, but sometimes it's as though you switch personalities faster than any Gemini. You can analyse as deeply as a Virgo, and yet your romantic idealism can also be greater than any dreamy-eyed Pisces.

The detached side of your personality enables you to be a party to a 'triangle' situation without perhaps being too deeply involved, but the unselfish side of your nature finds it hard to think of hurting someone you might not even know. It's this conflict within you which can make building and maintaining the perfect relationship a hard lesson to learn if you're not also prepared to adapt to your chosen partner a little more resolutely. Sometimes you're so practical and resourceful – at other times your idealism has you building rainbows in the sky. You need to balance yourself a little more.

One thing is certainly true of almost every Aquarian (depending of course on your personal horoscope too) – your need to feel inwardly free cannot be understated. But while a Gemini or Sagittarian would understand this very well, it's often hard for other people to realize that it's far more of a mental feeling than a physical one; and a possessive and over-protective partner could find it difficult to appreciate this. Jealousy has little place in your life; you consider it far too much of a negative emotion to allow it to take control of you.

From an early age you have probably enjoyed having lots of people around you; friends have always been an integral part of your life. But whereas many people enjoy having really close friendships, it's almost as though there is a part of you which has always preferred keeping your friends at a certain distance. Perhaps you considered it a 'safe' distance, never giving away too much of yourself in order to avoid becoming in any way vulnerable.

But anyone who really does take the time and trouble to break through the barrier which you've built up to protect yourself will discover a wonderfully amusing, off-beat, creative and unique individual. So what if you do need your own space from time to time, or are sometimes so changeable in your thoughts and actions that you're impossible to keep up with? Isn't life more exciting that way? That's the way *you* see it anyway, and since you're a true visionary you recognize that that's the way it can be with the right person by your side.

You'll fight through hell and high water for anyone and anything you believe in. You'll be totally loyal and devoted – but you have to do what you believe in. And you have to experiment with life too.

Often it's easier for you to maintain friendships than love relationships. It's interesting to realize that someone who is probably a believer in greater sexual freedom can be extremely shy when it comes down to your own personal sexual desires. Communicating on a mental wavelength holds no barriers, but letting down your defences and admitting to your physical needs is a whole different thing. For you love has to be an equal blending of mind, body and spirit. Satisfying the flesh alone is invariably never quite enough, not for very long anyway.

You need a partner who understands this; someone who is neither too dominant nor too passive. Someone who understands that you're afraid to experiment but that you're also likely to turn off almost at a moment's notice without this signifying some deep and dark secret! Inwardly you yearn for intimacy − yet when you have it you can almost run away.

You're invariably honest, and you expect anyone with whom you're in any kind of relationship to be equally so.

Material issues don't usually create great problems. You're neither a spendthrift nor someone who puts immense value on financial security. You're willing to share what you have, to work together with a partner you respect to create a good life together.

When you're living with your partner, you don't neglect your family ties or relationships with friends. But here again you don't like to be tied down, although you will always be around if you're needed.

You have a unique ability to see far into the future, far more than the rest of us. But it will help you achieve more balance in your life if you're prepared to pay more attention to what you need today. Sometimes you *are* still too concerned with what is happening for mankind as a whole to notice what is happening right next to you. Don't ever allow problems to arise in your relationships by failing to recognize danger signals, and even worse, failing to find out why they arose.

Your intuition and inspiration are such highly positive traits when they're used in a truly positive way. In a working relationship you can be an absolute genius − as long as you're not tied down to too much routine. You hate anything which is too repetitive, anything which takes away your freedom and ties you down to set times and tasks. But since not every Aquarian can have the sort of freelance occupation you might crave for, you'll sometimes have to knuckle under and fit in with other people a little more.

In any relationship you're not usually bothered by age differences. But you're well aware that you need a partner who stimulates you on the mental wavelength as well as being a good friend in every other aspect.

When you have the right person beside you, you feel you can conquer the world, so why don't you start to reveal a little more of yourself so we can get to know you a little better? Try to be a little more trusting when you fall in love and more tolerant of your partner's feelings.

It's wonderful to be a truth seeker − but don't sheer away from the truth about yourself. Use your ability to analyse in an even more positive way − enjoy discovering more about yourself and about your chosen partner too.

You have a great deal of patience when you're working towards something you totally believe in. And working towards maintaining the perfect relationship will never seem too daunting for you.

★

How you see Aries As someone whose enthusiasm and vitality has even you coming up for air at times . . . but they give you an extra challenge in your life.

How Aries sees you As a wonderfully free-thinking and idealistic soulmate but they yearn for you to be physically demonstrative too.

To make things even better Try to be a little more predictable from time to time. Give full rein to your feelings instead of hiding them away.

★

How you see Taurus As a loyal, dependable helpmate to stick by you for ever more, but you're not quite sure if you can cope with someone as obstinate as the Bull.

How Taurus sees you As someone to bring the unexpected and exciting into their life — but they realize they need a little more stability too.

To make things even better Accept that with a patient supportive Bull by your side you can conquer the world.

★

How you see Gemini As someone to brighten your life in a myriad of different ways and stimulate your intellect. But could their flirtatious ways drive you wild?

How Gemini sees you As someone with whom to share life's adventures and they will never feel too tied down with you.

To make things even better It's already good so you won't need much extra help here — just be yourself.

★

How you see Cancer As someone to curl up in front of the fire with on cold winter days — but you don't want to feel smothered by Cancer's protective ways.

How Cancer sees you As someone fascinating but too much of a will-o-the-wisp to share your dreams of domestic bliss.

To make things even better Recognize that you're both so different but enjoy what you can offer each other too.

★

How you see Leo As a wonderful party companion — but you're not always in the mood to play second fiddle to such a forceful and ebullient partner.

How Leo sees you Your unpredictability sometimes drives them wild but the challenge of trying to tame you is one they'll fight through to the end.

To make things even better Enjoy it! If Leo wants to play the leader once in a while, what have you got to lose?

★

How you see Virgo As the nit-picker of all time. But in a way you realize that a little criticism can be incredibly helpful too.

How Virgo sees you As a unique and almost irresistible partner – but they fear you could never fit in to their orderly scheme of life.

To make things even better Don't expect a Virgo partner to stop criticizing you overnight – you're sure to have a long way to go before that happens – but it's worth it!

★

How you see Libra As someone to bring more romance into your life – but you're not sure how long it will take for them to make up their mind that you're right for each other.

How Libra sees you They're instantly attracted and feel you could be the perfect partner to balance their scales.

To make things even better Remember that Libra needs some positive proof of the affection you feel – thought transference isn't enough.

★

How you see Scorpio As someone who is one of the most exciting people you've ever known, but you worry that their jealousy could tie you down too much.

How Scorpio sees you As a mystery they can't wait to unfold, but they're almost scared to let you know how strongly they feel.

To make things even better Remember that if you're too unpredictable they might decide the challenge of taming you is just not worthwhile.

★

How you see Sagittarius As a marvellously free-and-easy soulmate. You envision a voyage of discovery which will never ever end.

How Sagittarius sees you In practically the same way, and they revel in the thought of the adventures you will share together.

117

To make things even better   Always understand that you both need to keep a certain amount of independence in order to make this relationship grow from strength to strength.

★

How you see Capricorn   As someone who'd insist you toned down some of your unpredictable ways − and you're not quite sure how you're going to take that!

How Capricorn sees you   As someone to bring some frivolity into their life, but they need to be more convinced of your staying power too.

To make things even better   Accept that you both have different viewpoints on life, and be willing to understand each other a little more.

★

How you see Aquarius   As someone who can surely understand and accept what you're all about. You're delighted to contemplate an exciting future together.

How Aquarius sees you   How could they possibly see you in any different way? You mirror their thoughts and ideals.

To make things even better   Resolve you'll both try to reveal your deepest feelings a little more.

★

How you see Pisces   As someone whose romantic dreams could fit in with your visionary ideals. But would their compassion make you feel guilty for being almost too detached?

How Pisces sees you   As the most unpredictable partner they could ever meet? But they realize that building castles in the air together could be a wonderful experience.

To make things even better   Accept that you can both bring something a little different into each other's life. Don't be so reticent about showing Pisces that you truly care.

118

Pisces

The romantic dreamer of the Zodiac, you have a mystique which is often irresistible. You're sentimental, compassionate, sensitive, intuitive and definitely in love with love.

Is it any wonder that you're often described as 'seeing the world through rose-coloured spectacles'? Isn't it true that you sometimes live in a wonderfully make-believe world, where everyone lives happily ever after, and where unnecessarily material issues cast a gloomy shadow on your life?

Of course there are millions of practical, highly ambitious, Pisceans who will fight tooth-and-nail to climb the ladder to material success – but deep down you're all searching for the perfect emotional fulfilment to enhance your life in the best of all possible ways. In a relationship, especially one where love *is* the major factor, you're prepared to immerse yourself completely into doing everything you can to fulfil your companion's needs and desires. You're one of the most tender and devoted partners one could hope to meet.

But, sometimes, through your inner yearnings to attain romantic bliss, and to achieve that life-enhancing fulfilment, you allow yourself to fall hook-line-and-sinker, for someone who is completely wrong. Of course, every sign of the Zodiac can make mistakes when it comes to love, and many other aspects of life, but, ruled by Neptune, planet of inspiration and also illusion, you have to admit that sometimes you can be quite an expert at deluding yourself over what you want and what you need.

While it might be impossible ever to truly know yourself, at least it must be helpful to analyse your personality a little more. You're often too caught up with serving other people and being concerned with what they might be suffering, to evaluate your own needs.

Your symbol of the fish, swimming in two directions — upstream and down — represents the duality in your nature. Perhaps this should also be taken as the positive and negative paths to take, for you have to remember that you *do* have a choice. What you must never do is submerge yourself so completely into a relationship that you lose your own identity. However, anyone who thinks of you as weak is in for a big surprise! There is a great deal of strength beneath the surface of your personality, so that the impression you convey can be as equally deceptive as the illusions you so often create for yourself.

Things can go wrong for you when — ostrich-like — you bury your head in the sand and refuse to face problems realistically. You forget about your inner strength, you become depressed and this in turn can lead you to try to find an escape route. Unfortunately, Pisces is one sign which tends to turn too easily to alcohol or even drugs when life becomes really bad, but this will depend ultimately on your particular birthchart.

One of the most important things for you to remember is that you *do* have the ability to turn your romantic dreams into reality, by working on yourself a little more. You have so much psychic ability, intuition, instinct — call it what you will — why not learn to rely on that a little more? If, deep down, you know that someone is wrong for you, be braver about admitting it to yourself. Don't get yourself trapped into situations where you feel compassion and even pity for someone, and mistake it as love. Because you're so genuinely devoted to making the world a better place for others, it does mean you sometimes allow yourself to be too much of a shoulder to lean on, when you could do with someone for *you* to lean on once in a while.

You sometimes take other people's problems *too* much to heart, and because you're so sensitive this can make you withdraw into yourself far too much. It's important for you to retain a sense of humour too, to let the people who do share your life also share your own hopes and fears in the way they expect you to understand and share theirs.

Pisces is the twelfth sign of the Zodiac, and this is often called the house of one's own undoing, relating to the secrets one likes to keep from the world. You're certainly an expert at keeping your secrets, but it's perhaps time you became a little more outgoing, and had more belief in your own special talents and abilities. You are often one of the most creative people around, but without someone to encourage you and believe in you, there is the tendency to withdraw into your own private little world. This is another reason why you need a partner who will be supportive and constructively encouraging.

There is another side of your personality which makes you almost as impulsive as Aries when love comes along, which is why it's even more important to focus on what you know you need!

Problems can arise far too easily in your relationships when money is a serious issue. The trouble can stem from your own refusal to accept that material issues are extremely relevant to life. You are not necessarily an incredible spendthrift but you can be a soft touch for everyone who comes your way with a tale of woe. It's therefore going to be much more satisfactory if you're in a relationship with someone who *is* practical and who isn't going to squander away the money which is around.

No one is asking you to equate love and happiness with financial independence. I'm only trying to point out to you that love and happiness can unfortunately disappear all too fast between even the most loving couples if there are mountains of bills waiting to be paid, and no way of doing so. In a working relationship, you sometimes land yourself with financial worries because you are so intent on satisfying your artistic creative needs that you allow other people to take advantage of your talents. In a business partnership you need to ensure that you're not involving yourself with someone who could do this to you. All you need is to rely on your instinct a little more and it really won't hurt you to learn to be a little more materialistic at the same time. I'm not asking you to forget all about romantic dreams, simply to put a few more practical ones alongside of these.

There is definitely something of your opposite sign of Virgo in your astrological make-up; the desire to help other people, to work hard at the things you believe in. But it would sometimes help you to be a little more critical of other people too, not to give yourself wholeheartedly to someone else just because they *need* you. As a Water sign you're very receptive to outside influences – start being more receptive to your inner self as well.

Sex without love doesn't usually figure in your book. You know that lasting happiness in an emotional relationship needs to be on the mind/body/soul level to satisfy you. There is a very spiritual side to your make-up. You truly believe in the idea of the perfect soulmate, where you and your ideal partner can balance each other's life in every conceivable way. So don't waste precious time living in fantasy land when you can direct your strengths into so much more.

Building and maintaining a perfect relationship can be a marvellously positive learning experience. Channelling all your positive energy into helping yourself at the same time as helping the relationship to grow even deeper is always well worthwhile.

However, you do have to watch out that you don't involve yourself in a 'triangle' relationship with which you're not emotionally strong enough to cope. Try not to give so much of yourself, if you're not getting enough back. In this kind of situation you really do need to be more self-protective, and more analytical too. It's often much too easy for you to let yourself be carried along by your emotions, and what is happening around you.

Often problems arise in relationships because of a certain amount of apathy on the part of one or other partners. If you're typical of your star-sign, you'll surely have to admit that this can happen all too easily to you. But don't allow it to make you hang on to situations which need some radical changes to create improvements in your life.

Hiding away your feelings too much is never a good idea in any relationship. And you'll recognize that this is something you're often guiltier of than many other people. In relationships it's so important for partners to know how and why the other feels and reacts as they do. It helps to bring about even more growth and understanding. So don't be shy about saying what you think or feel if you know it can only be beneficial. You certainly don't have to start changing your personality overnight. You just need to be more resolute and more self-protective too.

Where family ties are concerned you're highly sentimental. There is also no way you will avoid any of your responsibilities to your relatives and friends just because you're ensconced in a love relationship with your perfect partner. Protecting others by giving of your compassionate nature is part and parcel of the real you; that is why it *is* so important that you have those around you who can and do the same for you.

You have such incredible faith in how wonderful life can be, so use it in the most positive way you can to ensure your relationships grow even stronger as the days go by.

Turn all those beautiful dreams into beautiful realities — you really can when you try!

★

How you see Aries It's wonderful to be with someone as romantic as you ... but you soon realize that Aries thrives on challenges to keep their interest riding high.

How Aries sees you As the romantic soulmate they've always longed to find; but they fear that their aggressiveness could make you swim away.

To make things even better Don't take Aries' fiery nature quite so personally. Enjoy those qualities which attracted you to them in the first place.

★

How you see Taurus As someone to transform your castles in the air to solidly built structures on the ground. You revel in having such a tower of strength around.

How Taurus sees you As a perfect partner on the romantic level, but they wonder if you'll ever learn to be a little more practical as time goes by.

To make things even better   It doesn't mean you have to be any less sentimental by being more realistic about life. Prove that you can be just as dependable as Taurus any day.

★

How you see Gemini   As someone who is delightfully flirtatious but you might feel you need more spontaneous gestures of affection than they can give.

How Gemini sees you   As someone to fulfil their inner yearnings for romantic bliss, but they realize that intellectually they can be very demanding too.

To make things even better   Keep up-to-date with everything that's going on in the world around you, and be interested in all that Gemini has to say.

★

How you see Cancer   As a perfect soulmate in almost every way. You love the idea of the two of you protecting each other for ever more.

How Cancer sees you   As providing them with all the emotional security they could ever need and they enjoy the idea of such contented domestic bliss.

To make things even better   Just remember to allow Cancer a breathing space when they need to creep off into their shell.

★

How you see Leo   As someone to look up to and adore; you'll even put up with being bossed around a little when you bask in the warm glow of Leo's love.

How Leo sees you   As someone who will willingly give them the praise and worship they need if they are convinced you truly love them.

To make things even better   Don't ever hold back from letting Leo know how much you care about them. Enjoy having your own ego boosted by such a forceful fiery sign.

★

How you see Virgo   As your opposite in so many ways and yet you realize just how caring they can be. You're determined that they will find no faults in you.

How Virgo sees you   They love the idea of allowing romance to sweep them off their feet, so hopefully they won't be too self-critical when it happens.

To make things even better   Let your Virgo partner know you can learn a lot from them. Point out that the attraction between two opposite signs can be one of the best there is.

★

How you see Libra   As one of the most charming and lovable partners you could ever meet. You're in your element when you learn that Venus, Goddess of Love is the ruler of their sign.

How Libra sees you   As someone to consider very seriously as an ideal soulmate. They realize you have so many ideals in common that this could be total bliss.

To make things even better   Learn as much as you can about each other's strengths and weaknesses and take as much time as is necessary to get to know each other better.

★

How you see Scorpio   As a highly emotional and sensitive partner, but you're somewhat scared that Scorpio's burning intensity could be almost too much to take.

How Scorpio sees you   In the same way emotionally, and they certainly appreciate and understand your sensitivity. But they realize they can be fairly overpowering to someone as shy as you!

To make things even better   Don't be quite so timid about letting yourself go. And never ever let your Scorpio partner feel jealous in any way at all.

★

How you see Sagittarius   You wish you could be as free-and-easy as them, and you love their positive and optimistic approach to life. You definitely want to get to know them even better.

How Sagittarius sees you As marvellously sentimental and romantic, but they wonder if they have too much of a wanderlust for you to put up with for very long.

To make things even better Accept each other's ups and downs. You both have a lot of good things to learn from each other, so don't run away from this.

★

How you see Capricorn Capricorn can give you the security you yearn for, and you're quite right in thinking that you can bring some much-needed romance into their life too!

How Capricorn sees you As someone to fulfil their romantic dreams when they give themselves sufficient time to think about it!

To make things even better A little gentle persuasion can help even the most workaholic Capricorn to realize what a joy it is to have you by their side.

★

How you see Aquarius As someone you'd love to communicate with better, but you're not sure if you can cope with their unconventional ways.

How Aquarius sees you As the sort of idealistic partner they need by their side. But they realize that they'll have to be a bit more sentimental too.

To make things even better Recognize that working side-by-side to achieve the same ideals can be one of the most enhancing experiences you've ever known, and don't spoil things by being ultra-sensitive.

★

How you see Pisces As true romance for ever more, and then you start to wonder if two of you together could be almost too much to take!

How Pisces sees you   In the same way of course — what else did you expect?

To make things even better   Come down from cloud nine and make realistic plans to get to know each other even better. Both of you must learn to become more practical too!

Part 2
Your Perfect Partner

Always remember that you have the ability within you to make *all* your relationships good ones. Be it a love affair, a marriage, family, a friendship or a professional partnership, you can create the perfect situation if you are prepared to put enough thought and effort into doing so.

Learning more about your partner's star-sign personality will enable you to overcome many difficulties. You will understand why one particular partner finds it easy to bring everything out into the open, while another tends to bottle up feelings and prefers to creep into his or her shell. And you should always be wary of putting your partner on too high a pedestal; it is sometimes hard for them to live up to that image! This section of the book takes a close look at all the star-signs and at what will be good and what may be more difficult in a relationship.

All in all, to have and to hold the perfect relationship takes a great deal of time and effort on the part of the two people in that relationship. It may seem idealistic to expect that initial mutual glow of attraction to be retained in exactly the same way as when it first began, but that spark is a powerful sustaining force in a permanent relationship. It is perfectly possible to fall in love at first sight, but love is not usually that simple. In order to keep the perfect partner by your side − or to keep any type of relationship properly balanced − it is necessary to nurture it. It will be well worthwhile!

The Aries Partner

★ The Aries Man ★

This partner may seem like a dream come true − at first. I'm not suggesting that he suddenly changes his personality at the drop of a hat once he's settled into a relationship, although his attitude to you might sometimes appear that way. It's just that while you were a challenge that he had to win, he practised every conceivable tactic and manoeuvre he'd ever heard of to ensure that you saw enough to be convinced he was the most wonderful man you'd ever met in your entire life.

Any faults possessed by an Aries partner are unlikely to be apparent at first. At the onset of a relationship with this man he will probably chase you so much you'll be overwhelmed by the attention, especially if you'd never known a Mars-ruled man before. You'll adore every minute of it: the phone calls, flowers and dinners in wonderful restaurants. And you have to realize that if he has decided you're the perfect partner for him, he definitely won't take no for an answer. Whether he's seventeen or seventy he has to win, and his ardour increases as he goes roaring into battle. However long it takes to cajole you into deciding he's the only man for you is fine by him, although of course he's going to find it painfully difficult if you're playing hard to get, for his lack of patience will become obvious almost right away. But what Aries wants, Aries is determined to have, and in his opinion the sooner you realize that, the better for both of you.

Even so it's best to warn you from the onset that this man is often renowned as a womanizer; depending on his age he's sure to have found that perfect relationship not once but several times before he met you. Or at least he rushed into it convinced that it was pure heaven. But when his heart was wounded, you can almost bet that more than half the problems had stemmed from him.

One of the most important things to remember about this man is that he thrives on challenges throughout his life, and not only in relationships. It's the way he's made. He's the first of the Fire signs, ruled by Mars, God of War, and he has a habit of treating life like a battlefield, invariably passionately, sometimes childishly, often selfishly, and inevitably with a great deal of impatience. When you add the fact that Aries is a masculine Cardinal positive sign, indicating that he loves to lead and give orders, you surely know what you're up against.

A relationship with an Aries man can be one of the most wonderfully exhilarating and stimulating experiences you've ever known, and you'll want it to be like that for ever. But if you're set on a totally routine life with plenty of security and a partner who is always there when he's needed, who is prepared to put up with all your moods, be patient with any of your faults, and always be willing to fit in with your plans, then Aries really isn't the right sign for you.

It's not that Aries isn't willing. He is; he'd promise you the Moon and really believe that he could provide it. He was born with an idealistic, touching faith in life. He is a little boy who never completely grew up, and, although he can come across as a horribly egotistical dictator on occasions (although he'd never admit it), deep down he is desperately looking for a partner who will love him wholeheartedly and never let him down.

Of course his idea of being let down can be incredibly self-centred. The Aries ego is somewhat inflated in both sexes, but more especially in the male.

An Aries man in good form is definitely life-enhancing. You couldn't wish for a more passionately loving and exuberant man to have around. But he's not always the easiest person to live with. His needs are always of paramount importance to him −

and I don't care how many Aries males will adamantly deny this — but there are definitely rules for him and rules for you.

He wants a woman who is independent, yet he will be fiercely jealous if he thinks your career, your friends, or family — or, heaven help you, any other man — could possibly rank in importance with him. However, if you embark on a relationship with an Aries man and you harbour a jealous streak in your own heart, be warned. Like a child he'll make you pay for it, almost deliberately flaunting himself and flirting with other women just to test your reaction.

You have to understand that this man who comes across as a tough, macho, bossy leader of others, is sometimes using a vast amount of bravado to cover up the fact that he needs to be loved and would be totally lost without you.

He knows when he's not easy to live with, when he's giving other people a hard time. But had you ever thought how in a relationship he's also testing your love, to make sure you will put up with him through the bad times as well as the good ones?

You may have thought this man's character was easy to read, even if you knew nothing about astrology. He can be so brash, so exuberant, so adventurous and have such a great sense of humour. Could such a man ever be vulnerable and insecure? Once you've started to live with an Aries man, you'll realize that he is definitely not as secure as you first thought. But if you want to make your relationship work on a permanent basis, it's wise not to make your realization too apparent — not until sufficient time has passed for him to feel that you wouldn't love him any less if he admitted to his vulnerable moments and showed how much he relied on your moral support.

Learning more about how to enjoy the good parts of a relationship with an Aries man, and also how to overcome any bad moments, will be an interesting experience; sometimes infuriating, often marvellous, and certainly never ever boring. But while Aries suffers from a lack of patience, if you want to discover just how to twist your Aries man around your little finger and make this a lifetime relationship, then patience is something which, it is hoped, you possess in enormous amounts.

If you're an Aries yourself, however, this might create more than a few stormy moments.

A business relationship will be equally interesting, since Aries definitely prefers to be boss than to work out his days in a subordinate position. He needs to be among colleagues he respects and likes. It is extremely difficult for him to knuckle under and work among people with whom he shares few interests. Striving for a common goal will obviously help, and he's sure to be the man who intends reaching that goal before anyone else.

But whether it's a love relationship or a working situation, this man needs someone to believe totally in his ability to succeed. An Aries man frustrated in love or work is a miserable soul, irrational and unreasonable. Unfortunately he also possesses an irritating habit of blaming everyone else for the situation he is presently in. He can never believe that he might have made a few mistakes. Of course he does sometimes admit to some faults, but you can be sure they won't add up to the list you may have devised. And although he will at times accept the blame for something you've accused him of, don't be too surprised if he does exactly the same thing later on.

To ensure that you keep him by your side you have to understand that an Aries man thinks he is entitled to do anything he wants, at any given moment, and without anyone's approval. That's why he is so often accused of being selfish. His independent pioneering spirit, his vanity about his looks and appearance, his need for constant freedom of expression, all make him a man who will stand out in a crowd, but if you still want him near you for ever, don't ever lose your own individuality or allow him to boss you around too much. It might be difficult when he expects you to take his side on something you feel strongly against. You will have to learn how to be diplomatic while refusing to veer totally away from your own opinions, for he needs to know that you do have opinions of your own, and a life outside the one you share with him.

Problems in a relationship with Aries the Ram can arise if he is particularly extravagant. Ariens are not terribly good with money, and although he resents being told what to do, a few well-meaning words given in an unbelievably tactful way may sometimes be necessary if money becomes a serious issue between you.

On the surface it looks as though this man is intent on being the dominant partner in a relationship, and when he's very young this definitely comes over very strongly. But as the Aries man gets older, he starts to realize that he doesn't actually want a partner he can boss around. He wants someone who is actually his equal, but who has learnt to allow him his little moments of leadership, and who is as passionately involved in learning about life as he can be.

Sex will always be important to this fiery Mars-ruled man, so never ever let him feel you're bored with his advances and not in the mood to enjoy his passionate embraces. He's one of the most physical men around, and platonic relationships will not satisfy his body, let alone his ego. He is amazingly romantic and sexually very intense. A perfect blending of idyllic sex, combined with his inner psyche telling him that you're the soulmate he's searched for all his life, will ensure that he's not going to get serious about anyone else while you're around, and even those flirtations he once enjoyed so much will pale in comparison to the happiness he feels with you.

Always remember that this man, who may go through life with a reputation for playing the field, for being selfish, spoilt, and thinking he can always do everything better than anyone else, is far more vulnerable than he will ever care to admit where relationships are concerned.

If his Aries heart has been bruised more than once in the past, he desperately wants to believe that true love can last for ever more, but he would hate to admit it and will take such great pains to cover up his insecurity that very few people will ever realize it even exists. But once you begin to understand this, and you let him have his little moments of adulation when his self-esteem needs a boost, and when you show him that your loyalty is his for ever although you'll never be his slave, the happiness you enjoy together will make you glad that you chose the first sign of the Zodiac to be your lifelong mate.

Naturally there will be high spots and danger zones in your

relationship. But would you really have chosen a partner who was the same every day and night? Of course not, or you wouldn't have picked this passionate, fiery Mars-ruled man to be your ideal soulmate.

High spots with your Aries man
He will

★ Sweep you off your feet time and time again.

★ Put you on a pedestal like no man ever did.

★ Cosset you tenderly if you're ever ill.

★ Make you feel there was never any other man but him.

★ Spoil you with wonderful extravagant surprises.

★ Take you to the heights of ecstasy with his passionate love-making.

★ Make life full of fun and adventure.

★ Help you build rainbows in the sky together.

Danger zones with your Aries man
Never

★ Question his virility.

★ Flirt with anyone but him.

★ Ever nag him.

★ Accuse him of financial extravagance if he's just bought you a wonderful present – wait a while.

★ Side with his friends against him.

★ Ever hold back sexually even if you do feel exhausted, for he'll think you don't love him any more.

★ Ever destroy his positive attitude to life by being negative.

★ Tell him about past affairs – or ask him about his.

★ Accuse him of being like a spoilt, selfish child twice in the same day.

★ The Aries Woman ★

The first thing you must understand about the Aries woman is that Aries is a masculine sign. All the signs of the Zodiac are either masculine or feminine, but perhaps it is because the Aries woman is also ruled by Mars, God of War, and possesses Cardinal qualities of leadership, that this woman entered the world as though it were hers alone to conquer.

She's not necessarily less feminine than other women, even if at times you do feel she's determined to control your life, but she was born with an incredibly strong sense of survival, the desire to be better than best; to prove that she's a woman of substance and importance, with the urge to fight to the end for her beliefs.

At first you may wonder what has hit you when you first become involved with an Aries partner. She may have seemed to take the initiative, leading you headlong into your relationship. But did you allow her to do something you didn't actually want? Or were you flattered and perhaps even overwhelmed that this desirable and independent woman obviously wanted to get to know you better.

You will eventually realize that this Aries woman who gives the impression of being able to take care of herself better than any other Zodiac sign is not quite as self-assured and independent as she appears. Deep down she possesses the same vulnerability and insecurity as her male counterpart; and just as you might never have believed they existed in him unless you got to know him well – the same applies to the female of the species. But you won't discover this for quite a while.

Tough, aggressive, fiery, impulsive and headstrong Aries – at first it may seem you've given yourself quite a handful to cope with in choosing a partner born under this sign.

If you want that 'little woman' who will never argue, will be at your beck and call, who ensures that you always have a clean shirt and remembers to pick up your favourite suit from the cleaners, reminds you to call your mother to wish her happy birthday, and is always a brilliant housekeeper – it's wiser to warn you now that you might have found it easier to settle down with a partner born under a different sign. She may not necessarily be a feminist but she will hate to feel like your slave.

Yet every star-sign has its positive and negative characteristics and it would be totally unjustified for you to think that Aries has more of the negative ones. It's just that Ariens tend to make more noise than some of the other signs. They're born with so much energy, fighting their way into the world, making themselves known from their very first breaths.

Although it may appear that she is trying to control you and everyone else around, deep down she is desperately hoping that she has met the one person in her life who is able to control *her*. This doesn't mean that she wants to be bossed around unreasonably, for that is sure to make her rebellious. But don't forget that the apparent ease with which she seems to sail through life, blasting her way through situations which would leave many another woman weak at the knees, may be achieved at quite a cost. She is fortunate in being able to put on a brave face in adversity, but don't you think she'd sometimes like to let her bravado slip and allow you to be a shoulder to lean on? Unfortunately she's spent so much time fighting her way through life that she's built a wall around herself and is fearful of totally letting herself go.

This fiery dynamo can be one of the most lovable partners in the Zodiac, but first of all you have to work at getting her total trust, which can actually be easier than you think. She needs to be convinced that she doesn't have to give up her independence to enjoy a lasting relationship; that you find her one of the most feminine and desirable women you've ever met (for you must always remember her complex about being born under such a masculine sign), and that you're the one man who will let her believe that her childhood fantasies of a knight on a white horse carrying her off to live happily ever after will turn from dream to reality if she'll only learn to trust a little more.

Like her male counterpart, the Aries woman thrives on challenges, and she too can be jealous, demanding and selfish. But once she realizes that you have begun to care so much for her that you're willing to try harder than anyone else to discover her true potential, your relationship will go from strength to strength.

One thing always to remember is that she does tend to jump into a relationship, passionately convinced that it is the be all and end all of her life. But what she cannot cope with is boredom in any shape or form. When she gives her heart, she truly wants it to be for ever, but she can also be very demanding with her need for attention.

The sexual side of your relationship will be incredibly important, she can be as dynamic in this area as in every other part of her life. And she is certainly not shy about making the first seductive overtures right from the start. She needs someone who is as passionately emotional as she is, and the man who can skilfully dominate her in bed, yet allow her to be the feminine sensitive creature she is, will understand just how much she needs a partner to whom she can give her entire physical and mental self with total trust. Sex alone will never keep an Aries woman by your side.

Living with an Aries partner can be fantastic fun. Basically she has such a positive and enthusiastic approach to life that once you've got over the hurdles of understanding her personality a little more, you will realize you have someone who would do anything in the world for the people she loves. Of course you have discovered how impatient she is, how she's always convinced she knows what's best for you, how she would rather have someone else do the housework than do it herself, and how she's often wildly extravagant with money.

But she'll always be a wonderful hostess, a mother with the ability to stay as young as her children, a lover who makes you feel that no one else could ever satisfy you so much, and she'll always keep you on your toes. You know that if you fail to pay her compliments, don't share ideas or ask her advice, and neglect to defend her if she's had a fight with her family or one of her friends, she'll start to think you're losing interest and might look around for someone new.

I'm not suggesting that Aries women are more unfaithful than any other sign. They're not actually very good at having secret affairs, at being 'the other woman', and snatching brief moments at someone else's expense. She is usually much too honest to cope with a relationship which has to be kept under cover, but she does need to know that she is admired and is not averse to harmless flirtations to make her feel great.

This is also the moment to point out that she can be unbelievably and sometimes unreasonably jealous. If you had always thought that Scorpio was the most jealous sign around, you'll have to think again. It's all down to her Martian ego. She can't bear the thought that you could find anyone more desirable than her. Those harmless little flirtations that she enjoys are ruled out in your case! However, once you're happily caught up in your relationship with your lovable, high-spirited Aries partner you'll hopefully find you won't want to risk losing her.

In a business relationship with an Aries woman, this jealousy can show up in a different way. She's determined to be a success in everything she does, and could resent it if she feels that being female could sometimes mean she is overlooked. But like her male counterpart, where mutual respect exists she will relate happily to her co-workers even if she isn't always able to be boss.

Twisting an Aries woman around your little finger so she remains by your side for ever is often much easier than it might seem. Once you've mastered the technique of making her understand you will always be there to support her without her feeling she has lost all her independence; and once she is totally convinced that she has a man who doesn't desire a slave, but a more than willing equal, your relationship with her can go from strength to strength.

Just remember to keep the excitement and passion alive always, and to admire her for what she is — a courageous idealist with a childishly innocent belief that miracles can still take place. And endeavour to make the highspots of your relationship far outweigh the low points, for they will if you really try.

Highspots with your Aries woman
She will

★ Excite you with her devil-may-care approach to life.

★ Make romance more adventurous than you've ever known.

★ Make you laugh when you feel down.

★ Always rush to your defence if anyone upsets you.

★ Build castles in the air and make them turn to reality.

★ Bring you champagne in the bath.

★ Make you wonder how you ever lived without her enthusiastic and positive personality.

★ Live up to all your expectations — if you've learnt to treat her right!

Danger zones with your Aries woman
Never

★ Make passes at her best friend, or anyone else.

★ Tell her what your mother said about her.

★ Over-criticize the way she handles the household budget.

★ Let her think she's not the most sexually desirable woman in the world.

★ Have a real slanging match — besides she'd probably win.

★ Let inertia, complacency or boredom exist in your vocabulary and in your daily life.

★ Let her boss you around too much — it could get to be a habit she's trying hard to give up.

★ Keep her waiting for anything too long — her low patience level is renowned.

The Taurus Partner

★ The Taurus Man ★

If you yearn for a partner who is solid, dependable, a veritable tower of strength, you won't have to look any further than the Taurus man for he certainly possesses those particular characteristics in bountiful supply. And yet he's not quite as simple as that. This man doesn't rush into any kind of relationship without a great deal of thought. It's not that he is Machiavellian in his techniques, but his heavy-planning strategy is definitely to be admired.

One of the first things you have to realize about a Taurus man is that he is looking for plain, old-fashioned security. Of course he's probably had his fair share of brief affairs and even one-night stands, but if questioned about them he would make the excuse that they were mistakes which he doesn't care to repeat. And if you were wise you would stop the questioning right there.

Another important factor to remember if you hope to embark on a relationship with a Taurus partner is that while *you* might be convinced from the outset that he is the perfect man for you, it is unlikely to happen that quickly for him.

And yet that isn't always true, for Venus-ruled Taurus is one of the most sensual signs of the Zodiac. He may be immensely attracted to you physically by the tone of your voice, the scent of your perfume, the touch of your skin when your hands accidentally brush, but he's not going to show it just yet. The

Taurus man has to be incredibly sure of you before he will consider you as the perfect partner. But when he comes to the conclusion that you can make heavenly music together for ever more, he will leave no stone unturned to convince you that you are part of his destiny.

Meanwhile it can be frustrating, for anyone who has had any kind of relationship with a Taurean will have swiftly learned that this is definitely one sign which cannot be pushed. Taurus is a Feminine Fixed Negative Earth sign, and Taureans have their feet so firmly on the ground that it is practically impossible to make them budge from any of the ideas which are fixed in their minds.

This man is so realistic he can make you feel you're simply a romantic dreamer even if you were always convinced you were the most practical person ever born. He's also one of the most stubborn and obstinate men you could find. It's just no use relying on feminine wiles alone to cajole a Taurus man into defining you as the partner he's searched for all his life. He would be far too inclined to see you as someone who enjoys an idle flirtation to pass away the time of day, and therefore be much more interested if you play it cool, calm and collected, showing that you have a good sense of humour and are not trying to pursue him.

From the moment he was born he realized the value of security, and more especially his own need for it. His family, his home, his toys were all sacrosanct to the Taurean child. Sometimes other people unfairly accuse Taureans of being totally materialistic, thinking only of their bank balances, their mortgages, their children's schooling. But surely it isn't a fault to consider these things important, and wouldn't you rather have a partner who understood the necessity of planning for the future rather than someone who had a totally lackadaisical approach to life? If not, then it's unlikely a Taurus man will prove to be a perfect partner for you.

It's therefore best to warn you that if you're set on having a perfect relationship with a Taurus man you have quite a lot to live up to. You won't find him as noticeably picky as Virgo, or as determined to ascertain your domestic capabilities as Cancer, although your culinary skills will certainly interest the average Taurean who has a great love of gourmet food. You will also soon realize that, if a Taurus man *has* decided you're perfect for him in every way, he is not going to give up in his pursuit. It's simply that it has to be in his own time and in the way he wants to do it. I've told you that he is stubborn and obstinate, so you have to remember that he's unlikely to take no for an answer. His courtship may sometimes seem slow and plodding; but who else would remember how you adore the scent of one particular rose, or that you love to grow your own herbs? And if you constantly remember that Taureans love to see things growing, no matter how long it takes, you will find it much easier to understand the way they like to nurture relationships so that they become more fulfilling stage by stage.

A relationship with a Taurus man can be one of the most perfect experiences you've ever encountered. Most of the time he will be so patient, understanding and easy-going you'll wonder how you ever got along without him. You'll love the way he likes to cuddle up to you, the way he doesn't care how long it takes to bring *you* to the state of sexual ecstasy that his own sensual nature craves. He is usually one of the most generous lovers you could ever meet, never selfishly thinking only of his own physical fulfilment.

He's perhaps one of the most uncomplicated men you could ever meet. His needs are apparently simple. He wants a loyal and loving partner, someone who values security as he does. Someone who truly believes that the best relationships are often those which take longer to start off but become more and more contented as the years go by.

But sometimes the Taurus man may take even longer to warm up and trust you. You might begin to feel you're wasting your time even contemplating the idea of a relationship. Try to understand that this could be simply that he wants to be even more sure of you because he hasn't got over a bad experience from the past. A Taurean who has been rebuffed, or had to cope with a particularly disastrous relationship, finds it very very hard to forget. Taurean hearts take a long while to mend if they've ever been broken and you'll need to exercise even greater patience and understanding if you've met a man who has gone through some difficult emotional experiences.

A Taurus man can bring so much happiness into your life that it's definitely worth persevering and taking the time and trouble to turn a slow-moving relationship into something more permanent, even though you might sometimes feel you're bashing your head against a brick wall. But sometimes it's hard to fathom just why he seems to take so long to realize how perfect you are together. There was such strong physical attraction between you when you met; you discovered that you had the same tastes in music; you had a similar sense of humour; you understood his feelings about possessions and security, his devotion to his family, yet still he's waiting.

Don't worry, and above all don't push it. He might be making plans for the future without your even knowing. And, besides, if he didn't really care about you he would somehow find a way to let you know, gently but firmly, so that no one's feelings would be hurt for very long.

On the emotional side of a relationship with a Taurean man always remember that he wants a woman who is definitely a *real* woman, someone who can be as sensual as he invariably is; someone who is independent but unlikely to stray for the sake of a fling with someone else; someone who is bright and intelligent and would never make scenes or belittle him, especially in front of other people.

This man neither wants nor has time for dramas in his life. He is a gentle, caring honest soul who truly believes in the sanctity of home and marriage, of permanent relationships, of living happily ever after. He knows he can be obstinate, he admits he dislikes change unless it's absolutely forced upon him. He knows all about expressions like 'a red rag to a bull' and 'a bull in a china shop'. He's very aware that he hates admitting he's made a mistake, and he doesn't need reminding about any of these factors. But never forget that he's not always as secure as he appears; that deep down he's sometimes terrified his little world could crumble all around him and he would have to pick up the pieces and start all over again. He knows he can be difficult, but then who can't at times?

Once you're involved in a relationship with a Taurus man you'll learn that mutual trust and the ability to be great friends as well as lovers will do so much to help your relationship grow even stronger. You'll learn the importance of being a good listener, of taking his constructive advice, especially on financial matters — in which he's invariably an expert. You'll appreciate his down-to-earth approach to life.

A business relationship with Taurus will invariably be a solid one. You can always rely on him to do anything he's asked, although if he does have a fault it's often that he's too content to take a subordinate position rather than be the boss. He is definitely not a risk-taker — back again to that need for security in his life. But he certainly needs to feel appreciated by his fellow workers, for himself and his creative abilities.

In his family relationships he will display the same patient, dependable characteristics with which he was born. He is aware that he sets high standards for the people closest to him, but he is quite prepared to explain his reasons for this slowly and carefully. His common-sense approach to everything makes him an ideal parent who can always be relied upon to be there when needed.

One of the most important things to remember, and another reason to ensure that your Taurus man remains by your side, is that he is one of the most genuine people you could ever meet, and that he requires a partner who is prepared to put just as much effort into making a relationship work as he does. This applies to anyone who wants to share any part of his life. He is as deeply passionate about his beliefs and needs as any other sign.

Problems will only usually arise with Taurus the Bull if you ever try to push him too far. Just because he is patient and understanding it doesn't mean he doesn't have a temper. He actually has quite a violent one when it is aroused, but happily that doesn't happen very often. And you'll learn to catch the warning signs very quickly after a while: the way he seems to dig his feet even further into the ground, the way his face and neck seem to stiffen up, his throat almost ready to emit that bull-like roar.

Never underestimate the importance of perfect sexual compatibility with this loving Venus-ruled man. His earthy passion may have taken a while to become aroused, but it won't be long before his sensually erotic love-making proves to you that anyone who unfairly accused a Taurus partner of being boring had never really known one in bed. However, although in other ways this man seems often content to take second place, he doesn't usually appreciate a woman who is more sexually dominant than himself. He likes to be master of the bedroom games and certainly won't be afraid to admit it.

Sometimes the Taurus man gets a reputation for being so concerned with the practical side of day-to-day living that he opts for security at any cost, almost refusing to fall in love with anyone he feels unsuitable in any way. But that is totally unfair – when he does meet someone he cares about he will do everything possible in order to make the relationship work. His decisions are never taken lightly, and once you're happily ensconced in a relationship with a Taurus man you'll forget to wonder why it took so long to get started.

Since he set out on your relationship determined that it would be for keeps, it's also up to you to help it remain that way. So never let him feel that his faith and loyalty have been misplaced, or that you don't love him quite as much as you first did. His place in your heart is one where he refuses to be anything but first.

Of course there will be both good times and bad times, as there would with any other sign. But isn't it wonderful to have a partner who spent sufficient time getting to know you to be totally convinced you were meant for each other? Isn't it a marvellous feeling to feel so secure in mind, body and soul? And isn't it also good to know that this man will never ever let you want for anything he can afford, and that he'll always work hard enough to make sure he *can* afford it?

High spots with your Taurus man
He will
- ★ Always be there when you need him.
- ★ Be the most tender, loving partner you've ever known.

★ Give you the domestic security you've always dreamed of.
★ Be a passionate and patient lover.
★ Show you that life really *can* get better and better.
★ And that the best things are always worth waiting for.
★ Make you feel emotionally *and* materially secure.
★ Always remember to replenish the scent you wore when you first met.

Danger zones with your Taurus man
Never

★ Nag him too much.
★ Accuse him of being a bore.
★ Argue with him in public.
★ Let him think you've gone over budget financially.
★ Let him suspect you're more sexually knowledgeable than him.
★ Attempt to push him into a relationship before he's made up *his* mind.
★ Try turning his conservative ideas into reactionary ones.
★ Ever ever be unfaithful.

★ The Taurus Woman ★

One of the first things you have to realize about the Taurus woman is that, while Taurus is a feminine sign, and while she is also ruled by Venus, Goddess of Love, endowing her with her innate desire for peace and harmony, she is definitely not anyone's idea of a submissive little 'yes' woman.

But that doesn't have to mean you've come across an ardent feminist, or someone who is going to rule you for ever more with a rod of iron. Far from it, for when this woman loves and respects you she will be more than willing to take second place. However, taking second place is something she is sometimes too prepared to do. You will have a much better relationship with a Taurus woman once you make her understand that you prefer her to be your equal, and that as such she's equally entitled to hand out a few well-meaning pieces of advice to you from time to time. She might appear perfectly content to be in the background, but the more you get to know her you'll feel it's definitely not where she should be.

When you become involved with a Taurus partner, you might wonder why it took so long for your relationship to get going. You probably remember that you knew almost from the first moment your eyes met that she excited you in a totally different way. There may have been something smoulderingly sensual about her, even though on the surface she seemed almost coldly disinterested in the fact that you were definitely giving her the eye. Depending on your own star-sign this might have spurred you on even more, making it a challenge that you wanted to investigate further. Perhaps you somehow sensed that this was not the sort of woman who would rush into any involvement before she was absolutely sure it would be something really worthwhile.

Once you have managed to know her better, you will realize that the Taurus woman is definitely not interested in short-lived relationships. Just like her male counterpart, she is searching for security in all its possible forms.

Sometimes men who have had bad relationships with a Taurus woman will sarcastically tell you that she is a gold digger, only interested in whether you can keep her in the way she expects and consequently demands. But that is unbelievably unfair, for while she will admit that security is certainly a priority in her life, she is prepared to put as much into a relationship as any other woman, and often more. She will think nothing of working long hours to help provide for her loved ones, and there is no way that the average Taurean woman will think of foregoing emotional happiness with someone she truly loves for the sake of a little extra in the bank with someone else.

That doesn't mean to say she's not concerned with money. Of course she is. She knows that you cannot have total security without it. Besides, with Venus ruling her sign she loves to have beautiful things around her, and she likes her home to reflect her artistic tastes. But with patient, kind, realistic, dependable Taurus — you've definitely met someone who is the salt of the earth and if you've been used to someone who changes moods like a will-o-the-wisp, who puts her career before anything else, who is determined to have a busy social life even if it doesn't include you, then you're in for a very different experience with the Taurus woman.

She certainly won't want simply to be in your shadow. But she enjoys the private moments you have together far more than swinging cocktail parties. Sometimes she is even quite reserved with strangers, although she is invariably a brilliant hostess, especially when it's important for you to invite your boss or some important business colleagues over for a meal. This woman is not only amazingly loyal, she is also highly practical. She will know when it is vital for you to make some extra strides ahead in your career, and she will do everything she can to help you. Her strength of purpose is indefatigable. She doesn't expect you to become the head of your firm overnight, but if it's your desire to get there some day, you couldn't wish for a better person to have by your side. It's not that she's pushy or aggressive, just that she will calmly encourage you with your objectives, use her shrewd common sense to give you advice when you need it, and be by your side to congratulate you when things go brilliantly well, and sympathize if you've had a bad day.

Of course every star-sign has its share of positive and negative characteristics, and it would be wrong to imply that every Taurus woman is a paragon of virtue. Your Taurus partner might sometimes annoy you by being much too fixed in her ideas, which is when you will have to remind yourself that Taurus is a Fixed sign, and because of this she really doesn't like making changes unless they are absolutely necessary. Of course if she has a Gemini Ascendant or Moon this will make all the difference, as will various other planetary aspects in her own particular horoscope. But sometimes her stubborn refusal to alter her viewpoint will infuriate you. Her uncomplicated patient way of taking things in their stride will also be difficult for you to understand, especially if you're not an Earth sign yourself.

What you have to understand about your Taurus partner is that she has an incredible amount of self-control. She has finely tuned senses which allow her to know just how far to go, how

151

much to take. If ever she is pushed too hard you will see a very different creature before your eyes. She doesn't like to lose her temper very often, because she knows it can create quite an explosion. She likes harmony much too much to make waves when there is no reason. She doesn't panic unnecessarily, argue with people for the sake of arguing, and she truly does value a quiet and simple life above all else.

Once you've really got to know her, you will also realize that the sensual look you first caught in her eyes was not just wishful thinking on your part. This partner might be slow to action in the beginning, but she will certainly make up for lost time once she feels she can have a secure and lasting relationship with you.

The opposite sign to Taurus in the Zodiac is Scorpio, re-nowned as one of the most passionate and sexy signs of all. Inside your Taurus woman, but perhaps locked deeply away, are the same sexual needs as her opposite sign. It's just that they aren't so apparent and they won't be revealed to just anyone at the drop of a hat. She needs to be convinced that you're in-terested in a lot more than her body before you get to reach the heights of ecstasy which are possible with sensual Taurus. She's also much too realistic ever to think that good sex alone can be the basis of a lasting relationship, even when she's young. And never forget that if she's been badly hurt in the past it might take you longer than with many other signs to convince her that you're not a philanderer.

Perhaps this is the moment to tell you that your Taurus partner can be very very jealous, although that also doesn't show at first. That's because she has learnt to control her feelings so well it's sometimes really difficult for her to let them go. She also hates to make scenes in public unless it's absolutely unavoidable. But she'll find the right moment and you'll suddenly remember all those warnings about red rags in front of bulls just too late.

Of course she's not going to pick up all her things and walk out on you instantly in a rage, unless there is something really serious. But always remember it takes a long while for Taurean hearts to mend when they are very hurt, and also that her Taurean senses are so very finely tuned. This woman will always sense when something *is* wrong between you, even though she may not necessarily want to make it apparent at first.

With her family and friends she is as loyal and dependable as she is with her partner. She is fiercely protective of them too, and would be unhappy if you didn't make the effort to get to know them well. She is basically such an affectionate person that she gets a great deal of pleasure from having everyone she cares for enjoying each other's company.

In a business relationship with a Taurus woman you're definitely the lucky one. You know you can depend on her at any time, her word is her bond. She won't mind how long she has to work if something important comes up. She will be marvellous at calming you down if there are any problems to contend with, at giving constructive advice, and dealing with difficult people. She doesn't particularly want to be in charge, unless her own horoscope shows the reasons for this, and she's happy to follow in someone else's footsteps as long as she feels they are taking the right path which has to be onwards and up. Seeing things grow is vital for her, and while she would never thoughtlessly desert a sinking ship, she always needs to see the value in what she is doing, and of course has to achieve that vital security too.

One thing you will discover early on when you have a Taurus woman for a partner is that you will always eat well and be looked after fantastically. Your emotional contentment will grow and grow, your sexual desires will always be satisfied and you'll wonder what you would have done without someone as honest and candid and devoted as she will be. But mastering that technique of keeping *her* convinced that you truly are the right partner for her for ever more isn't quite as easy as learning the alphabet.

Just because she fights against change doesn't mean she is prepared to put up with second best. She has her own romantic dreams even if her feet *are* balanced firmly on the ground. Her sexual desires may not be as blatantly obvious as your own but they are definitely there and they don't diminish as the years go by. As dependable as *she* is, always remember that she wants to be able to depend on someone too. Remember again those finely tuned senses of hers. If arguments do arise between you, her favourite music, the flowers she loves most, a romantic dinner in her choice of restaurant, will all help to show her that you really care. But don't let her down very often.

Once she feels totally secure with you in mind, body and soul, your Taurus woman will help you both create a relationship which grows from strength to strength, from year to year. So why risk changing something which makes you feel so good so often?

High spots with your Taurus woman
She will

★   Be the best friend you've ever known.

★   Combine love and romance with blissful sex.

★   Help to make you see that tomorrow *is* another day if things go wrong.

★   Be the tower of strength you've always yearned for.

★   Show you how to appreciate music and art more than you've ever done before.

★   Impress *anyone* you've ever wanted to impress.

★   Never let your bank balance go too far into the red.

★   Create the most perfect home surroundings you could want.

Danger zones with your Taurus woman
Never

★   Come on too fast when you first meet her.

★   Ever accuse her of being boring.

★   Try to change her against her will.

★   Accuse her of being a spendthrift – it's almost impossible.

★   Upset her in front of any other people.

★   Tell her you hate opera.

★   Be unreliable – it's one thing she can't forgive.

★   Forget her sexual needs are no less than yours.

The Gemini Partner

★ The Gemini Man ★

Nothing you have ever read will completely prepare you for this partner. There really isn't a stereotype for Gemini, despite the fact that so much has been written about his need for constant change and variety in his life; his perfection in flirting, his inexhaustible desire for mental stimulation, his ability to change his personality in the twinkling of an eye — and if anyone is a master at twinkling his eyes it's Mr Gemini. And so if you've been involved before with a Gemini, you might be convinced you have nothing more to learn. You survived through his flirtations, you coped with his sudden changes of mood, you pandered to his almost Leo-like desire to be the centre of attention. But weren't you still sometimes surprised and thrown completely off-stroke by a new and delightful facet of his behaviour? And unless there was a really tragic ending to your relationship can you honestly say you would run a mile from the next Gemini you met? Of course not!

The whole point is that the Gemini man is one of the most fascinatingly irresistible charmers you can ever hope to meet. Perhaps you often tried to sum up just how and why he managed to perfect such amazing verbal dexterity as he chatted up yet another interesting-looking girl at a cocktail party. For when a Gemini man first makes a play for you, his conversational skills will amaze you. He seems able to talk about everything in the world, and has such a vast array of interests. He knows how to flatter you, and to make you long for him to want to see you again. He brings out every feminine trick you've ever learnt, and makes you wish you had discovered a few more too. But somehow you sense that none of this is enough for him, and you find you've given yourself an exciting challenge.

This is definitely the right moment to warn you that this isn't just a temporary challenge that can easily be won. A Gemini partner will create a permanent challenge in your life, but what a magical experience that can be. Perhaps you can be the very first woman in his life who bothers to ask herself just why he behaves the way he does. Is it to cover up the fact that he isn't quite as secure as he seems? Could the reason for him learning so many facts and figures, so many techniques in the art of chit-chat, really be that deep down in his innermost psyche lurks the dreaded secret of his emotional vulnerability? Is he simply scared of suffering a broken heart? It could be any of these reasons, but it could equally be some others which you will never discover no matter how hard you try.

Astrologically, Gemini is ruled by Mercury, planet of communication. It is also a Masculine Mutable Positive Air sign, and the 'mutable' bit is yet another reason for all those changing ideas. Perhaps the most important factor of all is that its symbol is The Twins. How could anyone symbolized by a pair of twins be expected to have a personality which never varied? When you think about all these nasty things which can be said about Gemini people – and unfortunately often about the men in particular, such as their being two-faced, schizophrenic flirts who can't be left alone for a minute! – shouldn't that mean there are very few happily married Gemini men around? And yet of course this is not the case.

One of the most important things to remember from the very beginning of any kind of relationship with a Gemini man is that the one constant truth about his character is that he needs mental stimulation. Without it he is almost like a plant without water; its leaves shrivel and start to drop.

Referred to frequently as the 'social butterfly' of the Zodiac, he may well yearn for the perfect permanent relationship in his life, just as much as placid, patient Taurus or peace-at-all-costs Libra. Deep down he will search for a woman who appears to be as much of a free spirit as he is, but who will, in time, be perfectly happy to be a wife and mother while he perhaps goes out to play.

The Gemini male expects an awful lot out of life and he doesn't always have the necessary patience to delve beneath the surface of an initially light-hearted relationship to ascertain if something deeper could transpire. It's not even that he isn't willing to try, although the ease with which he has managed to attract women to his side from an early age will mean he may find it incredibly difficult to see the merits of settling into a permanent situation with one person. And the longer he leaves it, the harder it will become. Maybe he did have a relationship which he hoped would last, and which for whatever reasons didn't work out. Many Gemini people have been married more than once, especially if the first time was when they were very young. This can apply to any other sign, too, but Gemini is certainly up there in the front line.

By now you've probably come to the conclusion that a relationship with a Gemini man can be more complicated than most others. But it will never be dull. He will be as unpredictable as Aquarius, or as bossy as Leo, and often as romantic as Pisces. It's simply that you'll never be sure exactly what mood you will find him from one moment to the next. You'll have to accept the fact that your Gemini partner is two men at the same time – not necessarily Dr Jekyll and Mr Hyde, but definitely two different personalities. And if you're not prepared to cope with someone whose behaviour pattern doesn't fit in with your own, it's going to be hard for you to communicate on every level.

But life with a Gemini partner can be truly magical if you really do try a little harder to understand the enigma of his personality. He needs a woman who is as interested in life as he is, who has intellect, a quick repartee, is versatile and perceptive. It sounds as though he's searching for a mirror image of how he perceives himself, and perhaps he is.

The one thing to remember is that if you're the possessive, jealous sort of woman, who, whether subconsciously or not, makes her partner feel he has to account for every move, it will be very difficult to sustain a lasting relationship with the Gemini man. You must understand from the outset that, just like his opposite sign of Sagittarius, he has to feel inwardly free. It isn't that he wants to be unfaithful the moment your back is turned, but that he does enjoy exercising his ability to charm the birds off the trees. It may be nothing more than that. You might be surprised to find just how jealous he can be if you decide to pay him back with his own game and indulge in a little light-hearted flirtation yourself!

This man likes to be here, there and everywhere, both mentally and physically. But he wants to be loved as much as any other man. He just doesn't necessarily want to admit it, even to himself. He invariably knows he can be difficult to live with. Sometimes he behaves like a little boy who never grew up. He's aware of his impatience and his restlessness, his unreliability and inability to cope easily with too much routine in his life.

But the art of having a blissfully happy relationship with a Gemini man, and watching it become stronger day by day, is to remember the importance of mental harmony between you. This certainly doesn't mean that he puts more store by a platonic relationship than a physical one. Sexual compatibility is highly important to him too. But it's often the words you whisper to each other while you're making love that can stimulate this man more than your actions. It's not just your body he wants to possess, it's your mind and soul. He needs to hear you express the feelings you have for him, even if you're not quite as brilliant at doing this as he is.

He also needs to feel you trust him, no matter what you've heard about Gemini men before you met him. He can become very bitter if he is maligned for faults he knows he doesn't have. And no one can be more sarcastic and taunting if bitterness takes over. He has a clever way with words.

But the ups will certainly outweigh the downs with a Gemini partner when the right sort of mental communication exists. And when you love him you'll definitely make sure that it does, and find a million and one ways to make sure he never gets bored.

A business relationship with a Gemini man can be brilliant just as long as he isn't tied down too much by routine. He's the perfect salesman in whatever profession he follows. Nowhere does the art of communication come more naturally to him than in his working life. He needs to express himself, his ideas, his objectives, and he needs the right people around him to back him up. You will never find him staying too long in any position where he does not feel mentally stimulated, and if you're the kind of woman who wants a man who leaves regularly at the same time every morning to go to his office, returning at the same time every night, you might not fare too well with a Gemini.

Financially he can soar to the heights of success, but then suddenly things can change. He isn't basically the materialistic sort of person who thinks that money is the be all and end all of life. He is not reckless or naive where money is concerned; he simply knows that he has the ability to pick up the pieces and start all over again if problems arise.

While he is young, he invariably enjoys feeling free as the air, but as he gets older he begins to realize more and more that to have one partner who can be everything to him is worth far more than he ever thought. He has been inwardly searching for her all the time, but didn't stand still long enough to question his deepest thoughts. Yet no matter what his age there will be a little part of his personality which will always remain a mystery to any woman involved with him. It's not that he means it to be that way — it simply is. Perhaps it can be put down to the duality of his star-sign character, but it should not bother you too much for it doesn't have to affect your relationship.

You don't have to be another Gemini to learn how to twist this man around your little finger and keep him there, not if you're truly interested in learning what life is all about. Isn't it wonderful to know you have a partner who will always talk things over with you, listen to any of your problems, come up with brilliant deductions as to why this or that should work, and be a father who never neglects his children and enjoys an ideal communication with them?

Once you have understood your Gemini, you'll enjoy watching your relationship with this man of many parts go from strength to strength, and year to year. There will be both high spots and danger zones in your relationship. But so there would be with any other man. But isn't it mentally stimulating for you to know that your life can be as varied and exciting as it was when you first met and that it can continue to be just that?

High spots with your Gemini man
He will:
★ Charm you like no other man ever could.
★ Constantly challenge your mental ability.
★ Teach you to enjoy life in every possible way.
★ Constantly surprise you with a little thoughtful act.
★ Be interested in everything that you are – well almost!
★ Get on fantastically with your family and friends.
★ Make love-making a real mind-blowing experience time and time again.
★ Be everything you ever wanted – all in one man.

Danger zones with your Gemini man
Never
★ Let him get bored with you.
★ Try to stop him flirting (unless it gets out of hand!).
★ Expect hundred per cent reliability all the time.
★ Expect him to remember every single thing you tell him.
★ Be too possessive in any way.
★ Want him to grow up totally – he can't.
★ Expect to understand completely the way his mind flits from one thing to another.
★ Forget the importance of mental as well as physical turn-ons in bed.

★ The Gemini Woman ★

The Gemini woman is sure to be different from any other woman you have ever known, but then that probably includes being different from any other Gemini too. You see, she doesn't fit into any set pattern, and she would hate to think that she did.

As you know her planetary symbol is The Twins, so perhaps you're actually counting your blessings that you have two partners rolled into one. That might be one way of putting it. The truth is slightly more complicated.

The Gemini woman isn't necessarily going to be like having *two* partners, but more like a myriad of different ones depending on the way her moods change. And Gemini moods can change fast. It's not that she wants to be difficult, simply that without constant mental stimulation she becomes easily bored, and her ability to put up with boredom for any great length of time would definitely not win any awards. Ruled by Mercury, the winged messenger of the Gods, Gemini men and women have this great desire to communicate their thoughts and ideas to anyone who cares to listen. They definitely don't take kindly to the idea of having a partner who is not one hundred per cent interested in their minds as much as their bodies.

Gemini is a Masculine, Positive, Mutable Air sign, which roughly translated means that your Gemini woman is determined to get what she wants when she wants it, but that her idea of what she wants may not be exactly the same from one moment to another. Just because she is born under a Masculine sign certainly doesn't mean that she isn't feminine, but she'll be unlikely to resort to little-girl techniques to achieve her objectives.

You may wonder who you have got yourself involved with when you first start a relationship with a Gemini partner. She seemed so interested in you at the beginning, hanging on to your every word, gazing soulfully into your eyes making you convinced she found you unbelievably attractive, then suddenly she seemed totally unaware of you, her attention was miles away. Sometimes you'd lost her and couldn't get her back.

Having a Gemini woman as your partner means that to keep her interested in you will be a constant challenge in your life. She will not tolerate routine in any shape or form, but she'd be the first to admit that this isn't necessarily a characteristic she admires, it's simply one that she finds very hard to overcome.

After a while you will realize that she tends to be sceptical about hearts and flowers and true love for ever more. It's not that she doesn't want to believe in it. She does. But when she was younger she tended to like flirtations far too much to want to settle down in one steady relationship. Somehow there always seemed to be at least two people she really cared for, and she became almost as indecisive as Libra if they pushed her into making her mind about which of them she preferred.

While all her friends were settling down and getting married, the Gemini woman enjoyed her free-and-easy life, meeting lots of different people, having lots of different interests, indulging her love of change and variety. But if you think she didn't ever wonder if perhaps she was missing out on something, you'd be wrong.

Your Gemini partner probably possessed the same romantic dreams of living happily for ever more with the perfect partner as every other sign. It's only that for a Gemini it's hard to imagine being with the same person for ever, as indeed it is to foresee a life which goes on the same way day after day and year after year. Charming, teasing, perceptive, restless Gemini − are you beginning to think you've bitten off more than you can chew by selecting a partner born under this sign?

Yes, if you want someone who is totally reliable, dependable, placid, whose moods never vary, whose time-keeping is superb, and who is perfectly willing to pander to your every need without questioning anything, you should be advised that while your Gemini partner might sometimes appear to possess some of these qualities − if you're looking for them all on a permanent basis you've probably chosen the wrong sign, unless you pursue the investigation of her own particular horoscope to check whether her airy personality contains some modification such as a high percentage of planets in Earth signs.

But all this doesn't mean that the Gemini woman has more negative characteristics than positive ones; or indeed more negative points than any other sign. They just happen to be different and while other men might sometimes complain of being bored in their domestic lives, that is one complaint you will never have to make about yours, for she is engaged in an extraordinary quest: she searches for mental harmony between you as though looking for a crock of gold which lies just the other side of the rainbow.

She doesn't want someone either to boss her around or allow himself to be dominated by her. She probably doesn't give a hoot about your prowess as one of the greatest lovers of all time if you can't communicate on the right level with her mind as well as fulfilling her physical needs.

But don't start to worry that perhaps the only man ever to understand a Gemini woman would have to be another Gemini. Of course it might be a little easier for him, but then you can't have been fooling yourself all this time that life was supposed to be so easy. Anything that is worth having is definitely worth fighting for, or at least working hard for. And it's the understatement of all time to say that a Gemini partner is worthwhile – she's someone you will *never* want to be without once you've established the perfect relationship with her.

The Gemini woman will enhance your life in ways you never dreamed possible, once she has decided that you are the perfect partner for her. She'll need to be sure that you're not going to cramp her style in any way; that you won't expect her to drop all her friends, her many varied interests, her desire to learn as many foreign languages as possible all in the shortest available time. She'll expect you to trust her implicitly and not accuse her of wanting to go to bed with every man she flirts with. For you have to realize that for the Gemini woman flirting is almost as natural as brushing her teeth, and certainly more enjoyable. It doesn't mean anything more than the fact that she enjoys the attention of the opposite sex, and having the right kind of mental repartee with people who inspire her already active mind to become even more active. She loves to hear fresh ideas and gain new knowledge. And that's where it will remain.

If you do start accusing her of having affairs behind your back, she will not only be bitterly hurt, she might even decide to make you pay for your mistake by pretending to do just what you've accused her of. But it is reassuring to discover that your Gemini partner can be one of the most loyal partners in the Zodiac if that loyalty is never questioned, and unless you do something to destroy her faith and belief in you.

Like her male counterpart the Gemini woman can be impatient, unpredictable and enigmatic. And just like him she is aware that even the most compatible of soulmates will never quite discover what really makes her tick. She doesn't know that herself, even though she may have tried to fathom it out a million and more times.

When she gives her heart, she longs for it to be for a lifetime, so that her restless search for that ideal blend of mental and physical harmony can come to an end. She needs a partner who will help her realize that commitment doesn't have to mean boring routine, that being a wife and mother doesn't tie her to a life of domesticity with nothing else to offer. She needs someone who will want to share her dreams and help make them come true.

In a working relationship with the Gemini woman, she requires the same amount of mental stimulation she needs from the rest of her life. She cannot be tied down to anything which doesn't allow herself to be the creative individual she invariably is. And she always allows her family and friends the same freedom she expects to have herself.

It might seem that twisting a Gemini woman around your little finger to keep her by your side for ever will be quite a tricky task. But how wrong you'd be if you really think that. Why not vow you'll be the first man she has ever known who has really cared enough to try and understand the intricacies of her deepest feelings. See if you can learn why she sometimes becomes bored for no apparent reason; why her need for mental communication is so great. Take the time to share her interests, encourage her with her dreams and ideals.

Let her know that if there is something in your own behaviour which she finds hard to accept, she must always tell you; for even though her ability to communicate is so vast she still sometimes finds it difficult to reveal her very deepest feelings, especially in the realms of love. Always let her see that you admire her independent spirit, that you adore having a partner who never fails to surprise you, and that you will never ever allow her to be bored with you.

She might have struck you at the very outset of your relationship as a somewhat flighty woman who didn't really want to settle down. But how glad you'll be that you decided to find out more about her and managed to persuade her that you will love and cherish her for what she is — a woman of many parts — some exciting, some frustrating, all highly individual and definitely none of them boring in the slightest possible way. Let her realize that her elusive crock of gold isn't lurking behind that rainbow but is right there with the two of you in your relationship together.

You're never going to regret the hours you might have spent wondering whether your Gemini woman was really right for you. For the longer you get to know her, you will be more and more convinced you would rather have no one else than her. Work on making the highspots in your relationship even more exhilarating, and resolve that there won't be too many danger zones between you. And let your unattached friends know just what they're missing in their lives.

High spots with your Gemini woman
She will
★ Be the most fascinating yet unfathomable woman you ever met.
★ Broaden your horizons in every conceivable way.
★ Help you climb to the heights of fantasy.
★ Show you the joy of true mental compatibility.
★ Never ever bore you in any way.
★ Inspire you to learn even more about life.
★ Encourage you with your creative ideas and share in them too.
★ Be everything you ever dreamed of but never thought existed in just one woman.

Danger zones with your Gemini woman
Never
★ Let her feel bored with *you* in any way.
★ Expect her to be the perfect housewife all the time.
★ Seduce her body without seducing her mind too.
★ Accuse her of flirting just because she loves to chat.
★ Try to pin her down completely — you never will.
★ Try to beat her at Scrabble or Chess.
★ Scorn her wide variety of interests.
★ Ever ever accuse *her* of being a bore!

The Cancer Partner

★ The Cancer Man ★

At first a Cancer partner may seem to be the man you've dreamed of all your life. If you visualized a sensitive, gentle man who yearned to share his life with someone on a permanent basis, who would make you feel emotionally and materially secure, be a tender lover and a loving father to the children you would have together, you would certainly be seeing one side of the personality of this man. But you'll have to look a lot further than that.

While the Gemini partner for instance is controlled by his thoughts, the Cancer personality is totally controlled by his feelings. Perhaps you're about to say 'controlled' is a very strong word, but you have to understand that the Cancerian feelings are indeed incredibly strong, and also that Cancer is no weakling in the great wheel of the Zodiac. Just like Aries, Cancer is a Cardinal sign. And anyone born under a Cardinal sign is a leader at heart. You may have harboured a misconception that because Cancer is a Water sign and Cancerians are such compassionate and sensitive souls they are not necessarily very tough. But that would be one of your first mistakes.

Your second mistake could be to negate this man as a perfect partner because you've often heard so much about his moodyness, and not just when it's Full Moon time. But you've surely come to realize by now that someone somewhere is going to have negative things to say about every sign, and that everyone possesses their share of positive and negative characteristics in their personalities, and it therefore simply depends on how they've worked upon the negative ones as to how strongly defined they are.

If you've met a Cancer man who allows his down moods to take over his life to such an extent that he presents a sad and sorry image to the world, there is sure to be some hurt he's clinging on to and is afraid to let go.

Think about the symbol of Cancer, the Crab, first of the Water signs. This man has a protective shell around him, because he was born with it. His earliest childhood memories never leave him. If he had a happy childhood with a family which was devoted to him, especially his mother (you must have read how important the mother's influence always is upon the sign of the Crab) he will have far more faith in the outside world. But he'll then be looking for a partner who can live up to his mother, which isn't always easy. But if his childhood wasn't happy, he experienced a great loss and he felt desperately insecure, perhaps even unloved, and very vulnerable emotionally, he will search even longer for a partner who can being him security in every possible form. Because he's a Cardinal sign he doesn't equate that security with having someone who will be too dominating; he wants to remain the leader. And anyone who tries to boss him around too much will soon discover to her chagrin that Cancer claws can hurt.

One very important thing to remember about this man is that his emotions control his life. His ruling planet is the Moon, and since you know how the Moon influences the tides of the sea, it surely comes as no surprise that his emotions fluctuate in a parallel way. I've often thought that anyone involved with a Cancerian of either sex, should make a point of checking the different phases of the Moon each month, and particularly at Full Moon time. It could be an amusing exercise, seeing just how much your partner's moods were influenced by that beautiful waxing and waning ethereal silver wafer in the sky.

The Cancer man is a romantic dreamer – it won't take you long to establish that fact. But it may not be immediately apparent that he's actually a very practical dreamer at heart. If you remember to put the word 'sensible' side-by-side with 'sensitive' and 'cautious' with 'compassionate' you'll quickly learn to understand him even better.

A relationship with a Cancer man is not something you want to embark upon lightly. And that's not because it is necessarily difficult or you'd get easily bored. It's simply because this man is looking for permanence in his life. He isn't after an idle flirtation to pass away the time of day. Which of course isn't saying that there aren't any Cancerian playboys roaming the world, and good sex is certainly high on his priorities. I can only generalize, but I doubt that there will be quite as many as you'd find among some of the other signs. And when a Cancer man says, 'I love you and want to spend the rest of may life with you', you'd better believe that he means not just the first three words but the whole sentence.

The more you get to know this man you'll realize that he hates to throw anything away. His past is highly important to him; it's his, and whether it be people or possessions he will hold on to everything tenaciously. This is as good a moment as any to warn you that he can be unbelievably private about his past. It's not that he deliberately sets out to hide things from you, but until he trusts you totally there may be more than a few things he prefers to keep to himself. Even then he may feel somewhat shy about revealing some of them. The wise partner of a Cancerian man will never try to pry too hard into his past. If he's ready to talk, he will. But you have to remember that his vulnerability could mean that he encountered some tough moments while growing up, and he learnt the advantages of being born a Crab and having that tough protective outer shell to use as a shield whenever it was necessary.

The Cancer man wants a woman who is definitely all woman, someone with the capacity for love and tenderness which he possesses in abundance; someone he instinctively knows will be a perfect wife and mother. But this doesn't mean that ardent feminists instantly have to take flight, or that any of you reading this who have never been involved before with a Cancer man must immediately feel their careers are in peril and that they're about to enter a life where planning the daily menu and hoovering the carpet are going to be the highspots of their mornings.

This man respects a woman's needs and desires just as much as he realizes his urge to have his own fulfilled as much as possible. Of course if he came from a home where his mother never went to work, it might be a little harder for him — but he's not unreasonable, and his yearning for security means he will certainly appreciate the benefits of two people working together to achieve greater financial freedom for their future years together. However, you must always remember that he needs to feel he is a good provider himself, and problems could arise in a relationship where he might feel that you are contributing more than he is.

Anyone who has always believed that Taurus, Virgo and Capricorn were the most security-conscious signs of the Zodiac has obviously had very little to do with Cancer. For no one is quite so concerned with putting away for a rainy day as he is.

The Cancer man, who can display the same courageous qualities of leadership as an Aries or Leo, desperately fears rejection and criticism. Perhaps it's why he invariably strives so hard to achieve perfection, and why he sometimes needs to find solace in his private moments alone in his shell. You will also notice that he can be extremely shy and modest about his talents and capabilities. He yearns for someone to believe in him completely, yet sometimes gives himself an unnecessarily hard time by questioning it when they do.

But a marvellous thing about living with this man is that his instincts are so finely tuned, that he instantly knows when things are even the slightest bit wrong between you. He can be very argumentative and opinionated, but would never consciously hurt you by his remarks or actions, for he invariably knows what it is like to feel wounded.

His surroundings are highly important to him. Whether it's an emotional relationship, a family or work situation, the Cancer man needs to feel totally in balance. In a business and work relationship he doesn't necessarily desire to be the boss, but does need to know that he is moving up the ladder to greater financial security. He's definitely not a risk-taker, since he's far too concerned with providing for his loved ones. As a father he knows more that most about the value of love and affection, understanding and tenderness, although he can sometimes be a little too tenacious when it's time for his offspring to leave the nest!

Because his senses *are* so finely tuned, physical compatibility is essential but alone is never enough. He wants you to see the magical mysteries of love the way he sees them, to feel what you are feeling, to reach deep into your soul. He is truly searching for a real soulmate who will share his life for ever. He is also a very, very sexy man and any initial shyness will invariably disappear in a flash when he's making love to the woman of his dreams.

Problems in a relationship with your Cancer man can arise if you don't understand his deep yearning for the physical side of his life with you to be this total blending of your mind, body and spirit for ever.

You must accept that for a man who has a sense of humour almost equal to none, he is not terribly good at laughing at himself, or much worse – having anyone, and especially you, laugh at him. Perhaps it's all back to that deep fear of rejection. But it is definitely wise to remember, and save yourself unnecessary problems later on.

One of the marvellous things to know about a relationship with your Cancer man is that he is amazingly loyal. He will defend you to the end if anyone picks on you in any way. He will always be a shoulder for you to lean on if you have bad days. He will inspire you to fulfil your dreams, stir your imagination with his own flights of fancy, and make you feel protected in a totally fulfilling way which you may not have felt with any other man.

In turn you will learn how to understand how his moods might suddenly switch without the slighest warning, the way he loves to be fussed over if he's had a really bad day; the importance of showing how much you love him by the way you've learnt to cook favourite foods. It's no mere fallacy that one way to a Cancerian man's heart is through his stomach. Although if you ever mistakenly believed that this was the only way you'd be making a grave mistake. Food and financial security may be two of life's necessities for the average Cancer man, but the depth of his sensitive emotions can never be understated. You have to remember that he's a Water sign, and his feelings run deeper than the deepest ocean and then some more.

The good parts of your relationship can be so wonderful and you will feel so in tune with each other, that it will never seem too much trouble to cope with any bad times, not if you truly understand that no matter how brave a face your Cancer man puts on to the rest of the world, he cannot help those moments of doubts, when he wonders if all his tomorrows will bring him the security he has today.

If he's been hurt in the past, he'll always have his doubts, his fears and insecurities. He can't just blow them away even if you've tried in every possible way to let him see you're there for keeps. But once you've learnt to enjoy your Cancer man for the sensitive and loving partner he is; and realize that he simply wants to be cared for and protected in the way he cares for and protects the ones he loves, you will never think of any other Zodiac sign as being the right partner for you. His depth of understanding will ensure that this is one relationship you are determined will reach the heights, and remain there.

You will be wise enough to accept that there have to be both high spots and danger zones; that your own star-sign personality might sometimes conflict violently with his, even if your time together has already enabled you to enjoy so much and that perhaps you will never quite understand his constant need for possessions to make him feel completely secure. And you'll smile secretly to yourself as you imagine loving this man more and more as the years go by.

High spots with your Cancer man
He will
★ Empathize completely with your dreams of sexual bliss.
★ Protect you from life's problems in every way he can.
★ Help you believe that something wonderful can be real — and last.
★ Encourage you to trust him as no man ever did before.
★ Be tender, loving and a Rock of Gibraltar too.

★ Bring a little Moon madness into your life and make it more fun.

★ Let the depth of his emotions enhance your feminity in every way.

★ Share his life with you − for ever, if you'll let him.

Danger zones with your Cancer man
Never

★ Expect him to forget his past.

★ Criticize his family, especially his mother − even if *he* ever does.

★ Never ridicule him, especially when other people are around.

★ Waste money, even if you've worked for it yourself.

★ Let him feel neglected.

★ Think of your relationship as simply a brief interlude in your life.

★ Try to boss him around too much.

★ Ever let his down moods get *you* down − they won't last long.

★ The Cancer Woman ★

The Cancer woman is definitely not the sort of domesticated doormat she is sometimes unfairly made out to be. However, it's true that deep down, being a wife and mother is often among her earliest thoughts, and playing Happy Families was probably one of her favourite childhood games. But she is also a very independent person who will fight as hard as any other sign to achieve her aims and ambitions in life.

If you look up any astrological description of Cancer − you will read that it is a Water sign, Cardinal, Negative, Feminine ruled by the Moon, and with the Crab as its planetary symbol. In layman's terms you might loosely translate this as meaning that your Cancerian partner could be highly emotional, bossy and much too influenced by her moods.

She is certainly highly emotional, but then would you want a partner who was lacking in feelings? And anyone born under a Cardinal sign likes to think of themselves as being a leader – ask any Aries or Capricorn, plus those Librans who have managed to make up their minds about it. But that doesn't means she is necessarily bossy just because she does like to be in control of situations. When it comes to her moods, she will not deny that she is never moody. She often tries to fight against it, but then she's very aware of the strong pull of the Moon's influence on the seas, realizing that her own emotions are equally influenced by her ruling planet. So she has learnt to live with her moods, and so can you if you try.

It's not as though she is always more moody than some of the other signs can be. It's just that she's been tagged with this description for ever – and she does know how she feels at Full Moon time.

But isn't it wonderful to meet a warm and sensitive woman who truly wants to create the most perfect relationship that ever was? A person who isn't simply looking for fun and games and would opt out of anything which bore the slightest resemblance to responsibility?

At first you may have the feeling that you have met someone who could be a little too clinging, too ready to rush into settling down before she's got to know you very well. The Cancer partner is rarely looking for a brief fling, even when she's very young. She has traditional, conservative values. She was brought up to believe in the sanctity of love and marriage, of living happily ever after with one partner. Divorce is definitely a dirty word to the Cancer woman, but she is also as much of a romantic idealist as Pisces, and sadly many a Cancerian heart has been bitterly bruised since the belief that her first permanent relationship would have led her to domestic bliss for ever more.

Don't be put off if you feel that your Cancer partner is coming on too strong too soon. It doesn't necessarily mean that she is determined to have you for life, by fair means or foul! Only that if she really likes you she genuinely wants to show you just how tender and loving she is; she has a deep-rooted urge to protect the people she cares for; to bring a little magic into their worlds.

One of the most sensitive and understanding women you have ever come across, your Cancerian partner will help you to feel more emotionally secure than you would have dreamed possible, and if she's truly learned to make the most of the positive characteristics of her sign you will never feel hemmed in. She might make you wonder what on earth you would ever do without her, but that's a magical art all of its own, and she'll never divulge its strategy to anyone else!

However, this woman who can be resilient, practical and realistic is also a dreamer at heart. She always *will* believe in Happy Families, but not simply as a game. Being with the right partner, creating a happy home life, is definitely one of the things she is best at, and there would be little point in her denying it. She is far too honest for that. But don't fool yourself that she will instantly be bowled over into thinking that you fit into that mould too. She knows the importance of getting to know someone really well before committing herself totally, especially if she *has* been burnt in the past.

She knows she needs peace and harmony in her life, and while she might hate to admit it she knows she is also looking for someone who will provide for her material needs as well as her emotional ones.

Like her opposite sign of Capricorn, the Cancer partner is very security conscious. She knows the value of saving for the future; hasn't she been doing it all her life? The old-fashioned idea of having a 'bottom drawer' can only have been invented by her. But don't get into a panic, especially if you've only just begun a relationship with this woman. She's not a money-grabbing fortune hunter; she's not searching for a millionaire and won't send you packing without even a smile if she discovers you don't have umpteen different bank accounts all bringing you interest, plus a few properties here and there. No, she just wants to be sure that you have prospects, which is a very different thing to her. She's more aware than many other women that pitfalls in relationships occur far too easily when monetary problems rear their ugly heads, and that romantic dreams fall by the wayside all too fast when the mortgage repayments or school bills can't be paid.

Nor is she the sort of partner who feels it is only the man who should provide, while the little woman sits at home. She is quite prepared to work alongside you to achieve the right kind of security in your relationship.

Sensitive, impressionable, imaginative, gentle Cancer. Are you worried that her changing moods could infuriate you? Are you fearful that you can't live up to her expectations of what a good relationship should be?

You certainly won't understand your Cancer partner unless you accept from the start that she is never as strong-willed and practical as she may first appear. Never quite as convinced that she truly is the most domesticated home-maker in the entire Zodiac, whose ability to balance her housekeeping budget is admired by every other sign.

Deep down she also accepts that she needs to be protected, but only by a partner whose strength she respects and admires. Emotionally, she can be a highly sensual woman, but sexual satisfaction will never be enough if it doesn't go hand in hand with total compatibility on the mental and spiritual wavelength too. She could never envisage a lasting relationship with a man who didn't take the time and trouble to discover her innermost needs and desires. And while she may well have good old-fashioned values of what life should be all about, she needs someone who can help her spin a few dreams, search for a few rainbows, and allow life to have its fair share of fun.

To understand your Cancer partner totally you must learn to appreciate her sense of humour, but also realize that it's not easy for her to direct it against herself. Just like her male counterpart she finds it incredibly difficult to laugh at herself or her mistakes. Just like him she fears rejection or ridicule, and is often extremely shy. She also cherishes those blissful moments when she can creep away, Crablike, into her shell. She doesn't want to have fights with you, to make you suffer her intolerance if she's feeling in a really foul mood. No, she'd rather creep gently away, knowing that her little moments of solitude will make her feel better sooner than you might think.

And it's not just in an emotional relationship that she needs those respites. It never takes long for her family, friends or work partners or colleagues to understand that the Cancer woman can be as loyal and dependable as anyone else, but she does need these moments on her own to come to terms with her own thoughts and ideas. It's a sort of spiritual recharging of her batteries, so that she is then ready to face the world again.

Living with a Cancer partner can have plenty of magical moments. She is genuinely prepared to do everything in her power to make the relationship really work. It's true that you might start to feel a little neglected when children do come along − because motherhood is so strongly linked with her sign − but once she sensed this she would make up for it in a myriad of affectionate loving ways.

She will always be a lover who cares about your needs as much as her own, and she's definitely not the sort of woman who would be tempted to stray away from home for the sake of a purely physical fling.

Twisting a Cancerian woman round your little finger to keep her your very own for ever doesn't have to be difficult, not if you're prepared to show her the same loyalty, trust and under-standing she hands out in such large doses. But don't try too hard to bring out the jealous streak inside her, or let her think you were simply looking for the perfect partner to run a home and bring up children and that nothing else matters.

She knows that, important as those two things are to her, there's also a whole lot more in life as well and she's not prepared to forego it. The serenity she yearns for needs to be balanced with some excitement too.

Your Cancer partner can so easily be that perfect partner you've dreamed of having by your side. This brave, courageous woman will never let you down no matter what goes wrong. So never let *her* down by failing to appreciate her sensitivity and sentimental ways; always be there to comfort her if she ever feels lost or alone, and help her to realize that the two of you together can create a relationship which grows even more perfect as the years go by. Cherish the highspots as she will, and vow that any danger zones which come along will never seem too great.

The magic of your Moon-ruled Cancer partner is the sort of magic you will never again want to lose.

High spots with your Cancer woman
She will

★ Make you feel she's an irreplaceable soulmate.

★ Do all in her power to make you feel secure.

★ Show you the bliss that walking in the moonlight can create.

★ Fulfil your dreams of domestic harmony.

★ Always remember your birthday and every other anniversary too.

★ Be the sort of mother your own mother would be proud of.

★ Share all your dreams and come up with a few extra ones too.

★ Keep you from worrying about tomorrow.

Danger zones with your Cancer woman
Never

★ Ever betray her loyalty.

★ Tease her unmercifully if she's in a bad mood.

★ Expect her to give up a promising career before she's ready.

★ Underestimate her need for a deep and lasting relationship or the need for the right surroundings to feel happy in.

★ Make insufficient effort to get on with her relatives.

★ Accuse her of being a bad cook — that's almost impossible — or of being a bad mother — that's equally so.

The Leo Partner

★ The Leo Man ★

If you've chosen the regal ruler of the Zodiac to be your perfect partner, I hope you're prepared to bow down to him from time to time, metaphorically, of course! Your Leo partner doesn't expect a deferential curtsey from you each time he passes your way, but he does expect to be flattered and complimented and made to feel he truly is a King.

Leo is a Masculine Fixed Positive Fire sign — he's a macho man who stubbornly goes after what he wants and invariably thinks his opinions are right. Ruled by the Sun, he needs love in his life almost more than any other sign. Which is no surprise when you consider that Leo also rules the heart. But if you're beginning to think that a Leo partner could turn out to be an arrogant self-centred beast, only interested in having someone to flatter his ego, you'd be doing him a great disservice and missing out on one of the great joys of life.

The planetary symbol of Leo is the Lion, and it doesn't take a great deal to turn this man from the roaring King of the Jungle into a playful pussy cat when you've learnt the knack. However, any faults possessed by a Leo partner may not be the slightest bit apparent when you first meet him. At the beginning of your relationship he will sweep you off your feet with such intensity that you won't have a single thought other than that he's one of the most fantastic men you've ever met. And once he knows you think that way he'll show you even more devotion. The Leo partner thrives on a captive audience. He wants to be up there in the limelight, knowing that you're hanging on to his every word, and he'll be doing everything in his power to convince you that no man could ever do as much for you as he will. He's a big spender, and won't care how much it costs him to take you anywhere you'd like to go. He wants to impress you, to make you want no one but him to be in your life from now on.

Leo the Lion is certainly determined to get what he wants, and if he was spoilt as a child this can sometimes turn him into a rather arrogant despot. But invariably he is simply an enthusiastic, warm and loving man with a heart of gold, looking for someone to share his life. Or perhaps it might be more true to say he's looking for someone who will love him so much that they will be prepared to build their life around him.

It's very hard for Leo to take second place to anyone or anything. He was born to be a leader, and everything about him points that way. He's probably gone through life bossing people around, and although he was often searching for someone to love him for himself, he probably had some difficult times too by trying to control situations far too much.

A relationship with a Leo man can be wonderful if you let him see that you truly love him but that you're not prepared to be a submissive little 'yes-woman' for the rest of your life. He will respect you all the more for that, even if there could be a few raging battles at the outset when he tries to do his dominating act yet again.

If some of this sounds like a contradiction – telling you to flatter him and build your life around him, yet refuse to submit to him too, it is simply to make you aware of the need to play a rather clever little cat-and-mouse game with Leo the Lion. As long as he thinks he's in charge, he's happy. And you'll soon find it's actually very easy to have your own way too. He might fight against being ordered around but he's perfectly amenable to listening to requests – there's a subtle difference in his eyes.

A Leo partner in good form is a wonderfully sparkling and confident man with the sunniest disposition you have ever known. So what if he enjoys a little hero worship to make him feel good? And if he does sometimes have a rather inflated sense of his own male superiority? If you wanted a partner you could order around from morning to night, you wouldn't have been interested in him in the first place, for his strength of character is immediately apparent and he needs a woman who will be proud of him and appreciate him for the loving partner he's prepared to be. But he equally needs to be proud of you too. You may feel you have quite a lot to live up to, because while he's not as critical as Virgo, he has very definite ideas about the way you ought to look when you're out with him. But it's really only because he loves to pay you compliments too. He wants everyone to see you both as the perfect couple in every way. And as he's perfectly prepared to work at this, he expects you to do the same.

The Leo man isn't exactly like the beast stalking the jungle for the perfect mate, but he's definitely not a man who will settle for someone he doesn't feel will be there for keeps. He also enjoys a challenge almost as much as Aries, but will display a vast amount of patience if you're not immediately convinced that he is the right mate for you, for he's pretty certain you'll want him in the end.

You have to understand that this man who sometimes comes across as an overly self-confident and superior being is really only looking for someone to love, someone to make his life more complete. He's definitely not a loner, this fiery passionate man who exudes so much warmth and affection.

He knows he's not the easiest man in the world, he's probably been told that many times before. But his strength and courage have carried him through many difficult situations and although his sunny disposition might disappear behind a few clouds for a while it won't be gone for too long.

Once you've started to live with a Leo man, you'll soon realize he would do anything in the world for you to make you feel as comfortable and cosseted as he likes to feel himself. You'll also begin to discover more about the little boy lurking beneath the grown up man; the little boy looking for approval, wanting an audience only because he has to know he's loved.

A Leo man who has had a happy childhood and has grown up with the respect and acceptance he needs in his life, usually finds it much easier to tone down his domineering ways. He's already learnt that he doesn't have to boss people around to get them to fit in with his ideas. It's inevitably harder for him not to try to dominate you if he's really had to struggle to achieve his aims and you'll have to help him understand that his relationship with you can only grow from strength to strength if he makes more of an effort to fit in with your aims too.

The learning process in a relationship with a Leo man will coincide with so many happy moments, you'll soon manage to overcome any bad ones. It will amuse you to discover that this man who can be so energetic and forceful has such a lazy and indolent side to his character. You'll realize that he hates to have arguments or feel humiliated in any way, and that he's in no way as secure as he appears.

A business relationship with Leo isn't necessarily the easiest thing in the world unless he *is* the boss. Of course that's probably where he should be anyway. He is so much better at delegating orders than receiving them. And he is invariably good at his chosen profession for there isn't a Leo in the world who wants to be second-best. As a partner, he therefore needs to be an *equal* partner with someone he respects. If all this sounds as though he could be a real tyrant to work for, don't worry. He just thrives on success and he's perfectly happy to take you along there with him so that he can be as proud of your achievements as he expects you to be proud of his.

Sex is always going to be highly important to fiery Leo. He is invariably a passionate man, even in his laziest moments. As a lover he is wonderfully warm and tender. But Leos with excessively inflated egos will probably expect you to tell them they are the greatest lover you've ever known, and that can cause you problems on two fronts. You see, Leo doesn't like comparisons of any kind because deep down he can't believe that anyone would compare with him anyway. And a Leo with a look of injured pride on hearing that his love-making isn't up to scratch is going to be a very sorry sight. You also have to remember that he hates to think you've made love to many other men before he came along, so it's best to avoid any discussions of this sort.

He's going to be jealous – but he'll expect you to accept the fact that he definitely appreciates the admiration of other people, and especially women. He'll also expect you to believe him when he tells you that he's going to be faithful to you for the rest of his life. That part you may find hard to believe, since you've noticed how he thrives on adulation. But even a Leo man who has been the greatest Casanova of all time before he settled down into a permanent marriage can surprise you here. You'll have to understand that when Leo has found the perfect partner who will not only share his home, but also his hopes and aspirations, who will fulfil him emotionally and mentally too, he really isn't going to want to stray. For what? He's probably seen too many other relationships falter because of one or the other partner's fickle ways. He doesn't want to go through life that way.

Problems in a relationship with Leo the Lion can definitely arise if he doesn't feel he's appreciated enough. He truly does want to do everything in the world to make his chosen partner happy. However, that can also mean he can be unbelievably extravagant, showering you with gifts even if his bank balance is in the red. His magnanimous gestures are fine if the money is there – but you'll have to remember to reassure him that you don't need material things to convince you of his love. Difficulties can also arise if you do allow him to boss you around too much, because you must never let him take you for granted. A relationship which contains plenty of equality will be better for both of you, especially if you want it to last for a lifetime.

As a father your Leo partner will seem like a hero to his children, and of course he will love their adulation. He will sometimes be firm and demanding, but is usually one of the most loving parents you could ever meet, proud of their achievements, invariably generous and always someone they can lean on and turn to when they need advice.

Never forget that this man who has such a reputation for being a leader really does have a heart of gold. Even if his heart has been bruised by other women in his life, he has an innate belief in love and the joys it can bring. He will be eternally optimistic that the perfect relationship can go from strength to strength if both partners genuinely want it to be that way. He'll leave no stone unturned to discover what is going to make you happy and keep you that way. So isn't it worth letting him have that adulation he craves for; letting him see that he really is the partner you've dreamed of since you were a tiny child?

If you want a man you can always lean on, who will always have the ability to turn your gloomy moments into laughter, who will delight you with his sparkling sense of humour, and ability to shine as brightly as the sun, you'll never be sorry you picked Leo the Lion for your lifelong mate. Of course you'll have your high spots and your danger zones. But life wouldn't be realistic if you didn't go through those. And the danger zones you do encounter are sure to be outweighed by the marvellously exhilarating highspots that sunny Leo will bring into your life.

High spots with your Leo man
He will
★ Take you to the heights of happiness.
★ Make you believe that true love can exist for ever more.
★ Shower you with the luxuries you've always dreamed of.
★ Be the strong and forceful lover you've yearned for.
★ Be a wonderfully warm and loving parent too.
★ Always want the best for you.
★ Want your home to be your castle, and for you to be his Queen.
★ Be passionate, playful and unforgettable.

Danger Zones with your Leo man
Never
★ Let him feel you don't adore him.
★ Forget to think up a few playful bedtime games.
★ Criticize him for buying you an extravagant gift unless he *really* can't afford it.
★ Let him live more than a day without a few compliments.
★ Ever tell him he's a lousy lover, even as a joke!
★ Expect him to be a henpecked husband.
★ Let him lose his pride in you.
★ Flirt too much with any other man.

183

★ The Leo Woman ★

The Leo woman is like a bright shining light which can never be switched off. Ruled by the Sun, her ideal world would be one in which she could shine twenty-four hours a day. The Leo woman thrives on being the centre of attention, having a captive audience for her every word.

Leo is a Masculine sign, and the Leo woman will certainly present a forceful personality to the world. A Fixed Positive Fire sign, she knows what she wants and she is never too happy at the thought of accepting second-best. And indeed why should she? She knows her planetary symbol is the Lion, regal ruler of the Zodiac, and the Lioness knows exactly what she desires from a mate.

She is no less feminine than any other star-sign, even if she does appear to be such a dominant force when you compare her to some of the other women you have known. But look below the surface of the fiery lioness, and just as you'll find with her male counterpart, there is a playful pussy-cat who wants your love.

You must understand that the Leo woman sometimes has a hard time finding her perfect partner. Almost everyone enjoys being in love, but for Leo it's not just a question of enjoyment − it's something which is essential to her well-being, her inner core. A Leo without love in her life doesn't feel completely fulfilled and will search continuously to find the perfect partner.

At first you might feel you've given yourself an unnecessarily hard time when you became captivated by a Leo partner. She may have seemed almost too strong for you, a little bit too bossy and domineering. But weren't you flattered to think she found you so desirable? Didn't you enjoy being with someone who possessed such an independent air? Weren't you proud to be seen with her, enjoying the admiring glances she received from all your friends?

Yet this Leo woman who conveys the impression of being so tough and unbeatable is never quite so tough as she seems. Deep down she has her vulnerable moments, times when she wonders how she's going to cope. Her tears will be as real as any other star-sign when sadness enters her life. The trouble is that so much that has been written about your Leo partner conveys the impression that she is always dominant and bossy, craving the spotlight for herself and wanting to keep it that way. It's true that she's unlikely to relish a life where she never has the opportunity to be the centre of attraction – but you'd be surprised just what a Leo woman will accept when love enters her life.

This creative, vital sparkling woman might give the impression that having a captive audience is the most important thing to her. But if her captive audience is the man she loves, that's going to be good enough for her. Besides, deep down that fiery lioness knows that what she is really searching for is the one man who can tame her. That doesn't mean she wants anyone who wishes to turn her into a meek submissive little woman who quakes at the sound of his voice. No, she wants someone she can look up to and respect, someone whose advice is constructive, whose ideas are worth following, and who understands that her toughness can sometimes be a cover-up for the softness lurking in her heart.

She may appear to be totally self-sufficient and able to rule the world, but she's more than willing to share her throne with a man she respects. She has probably imagined herself in love many times, only to discover with sadness that the man she cared for was happy to put her on a pedestal and worship her but somehow didn't possess the strength of character necessary to tame her too. She doesn't want to sail through life as the dominant partner all the time, even if she did happen to be born under a Masculine sign.

You might think you have a few problems coming up – a woman who wants to be worshipped, flattered, complimented, yet refuses to think of herself as the weaker sex; can you cope with this fiery dynamo? Have you the strong shoulder she needs but doesn't always admit? Would she really turn out to be your perfect partner?

Just because she's such a shining star it doesn't mean she can't make you happy. If you've chosen a Leo woman to be your partner you will soon discover that you embarked on one of the happiest voyages of your life. Once she is convinced that she doesn't have to lose her independence, that you don't resent her need to know exactly how much she is appreciated, and she realizes that the last thing in the world you're prepared to be is the sort of hen-pecked partner she would never respect, you're half-way to establishing a relationship which will go from strength to strength.

Her sunny, sparkling personality shines even more when she is in love. She is not as impulsive and headstrong as Aries but she is just as keen to be in love. In fact, sex without love doesn't usually mean a lot to this woman. But you will have to remember that she can be very demanding in both these areas. She's a very physical lady and needs a man who is as deeply emotional and passionate as she is. With a partner whose sex drive is as strong as hers — or preferably even stronger — and who has proved just how much he loves her in a myriad of different ways, she lets down her defences and the fiery lioness soon becomes the playful lion club, though she definitely won't tolerate a selfish lover who thinks only of his own satisfaction and forgets all about hers. Not when she is such an unselfish mate herself.

Living with a Leo partner can be a real joy. She has such a wonderfully optimistic and delightful approach to life, that once you've got over the barrier of understanding that a little taming never goes amiss, you will see that you've found a real woman who is determined to ensure that your world will be as bright as hers.

But you'd better be warned that the Leo woman does like to have the best in every possible way, and she might be one of the most extravagant women you've ever known. It's not that she's selfish with her spending, for she is one of the most generous people around. And she would never want to take anyone for a ride over money, or expect lavish gifts if the man in her life couldn't afford them. However, it really could be a problem if she decided to settle down with someone whose financial prospects didn't look too rosy, and it's always best for both of you to know this from the start.

She's perfectly prepared to work to bring in some extra money, as long as it's not just for that reason. She has to be fulfilled in her work, and is often at the top of her career. She's definitely not too great at taking second place in that area of her life, and if you have her as a business partner she'd better be an equal one.

Your Leo partner will brighten up your life. She knows to her cost how her bossy ways can sometimes be too much, but she'll never let you down when there is any organizing necessary. She'll also work day and night to turn your home into a castle fit for any king or queen. She will be one of the most marvellous hostesses you've ever known. Entertaining is her forte, and the world is truly her stage. As a mother she will set a shining example to her children, she will be lovable but firm, wanting only the best for them in every possible way, and always being there when she's needed. However, she might start to get a little jealous if she has teenage daughters who suddenly start to receive more compliments than her! Even if she still holds down a job she will be sure her children never lack for anything, and of course she might still be very extravagant at times.

She isn't usually the sort of woman who will want to play around with other men once she's settled into a happy relationship with you. But 'happy' is definitely the operative word. Before she met you she was sure to have had lots of admirers, and if you betray her trust it certainly won't be difficult for her to find some more. She's definitely not a woman who likes to be put down in any way, and if you flirt with other women, watch out for those lion's claws. She also hates to think of other people being hurt because of love, and wouldn't go lightly into any kind of triangle relationship. She has a very strong sense of fair play. Even so she does enjoy light-hearted flirtations when she knows they are harmless. It's all back to being flattered and enjoying the limelight. It's just that she's definitely not so keen when you do the same sort of thing!

However, twisting a Leo woman around your little finger so that she remains by your side forever is often so much easier than it appears. It won't take you long to master the technique of showing her that she doesn't have to lose her independence to have a strong, willing partner in her life. And that while you're not prepared to be bossed around you have nothing against letting her be your equal in almost every way. Let her see that you'll be there when she needs you, that you won't betray her love, and that you've recognised her for what she truly is — one of the most loving and generous partners you could have ever hoped to meet.

It's worth doing all you can to make the high spots of your relationship outweigh the low spots — for they really will if you try. Just remember to respect her always and she'll happily share her centre-stage spot with you for ever more.

High spots with your Leo woman
She will
★ Be the sunniest, most sparkling partner you've ever known.
★ Be as generous as only a Leo can be.
★ Be affectionate, tender and humorous in bed, and incredibly passionate too.
★ Fulfil your dreams of finding the perfect soulmate.
★ Spoil you with the extravagant gifts you've yearned for in the past.
★ Help you to understand the power of love and show you how to keep its flames burning on.

Danger zones with your Leo woman
Never
★ Become a hen-pecked husband.
★ Let her spend *too* much.
★ Ever let her feel neglected.
★ Let her feel that she isn't the most important person in your life.
★ Forget the importance of her sexual fulfilment.
★ Forget that she becomes even more alive when the sun shines.
★ Injure her pride, or injure her vanity either!

The Virgo Partner

★ The Virgo Man ★

The perfect partner – does such a creature truly exist? Or is he fated to be a figment of your imagination for ever more?

Perhaps you need look no further than the Virgo man, who often thinks he can do no wrong. But that is rather unfair, for in many ways this Zodiacal sign of service who is so often accused of being such a perfectionist – so critical and analytical of everyone and everything around him – is actually equally critical of his own flaws as long as he's a truly evolved Virgo who has been around long enough to know that flaws and blemishes can exist, without causing too many problems! Nonetheless it's true that this man is looking for perfection, and is often prepared to leave no stone unturned until he finds a partner who fits the bill, as he perceives it.

And it's also usually true that he is searching for a permanent relationship. He isn't a man who wants to flit from partner to partner. He doesn't rush headlong into relationships without thinking about the morrow. He's fully aware that a good relationship needs to develop step by step. He's seen too many failed marriages and partnerships among his friends, listened to their woes calmly and patiently, helping where he could, to underestimate the importance of getting to know someone really well.

He can't help being a perfectionist and he's also well aware that he does sometimes set himself a difficult task in finding his ideal mate. But if you've begun to think that a Virgo man might be one of the most irritable and critical men you've ever had the misfortune to meet, please don't think that his negative points outweigh the positive ones. In many ways this man can fulfil your ideals of what a perfect partner is all about. Although, of course, if you're another Virgo, you might be more analytical than the rest and worry too much about it anyway!

However, if you feel you've had more than your fair share of men who've left you with a broken heart because they were so difficult, demanding or just downright undependable, you could definitely do a great deal worse than Mr Virgo — and learn to appreciate the blessings of being involved with this sign of service as you get to know him more and more each day. He's certainly not a fly-by-night character who would leave you by the wayside once he's found you. Not if you truly understand that when he loves someone, it is with devotion, not an instant passion which can disappear overnight into apathy.

Ruled by Mercury, planet of communication, Virgo is a Mutable Negative Feminine Earth sign — and your Virgo partner needs a woman with whom he can communicate just as much as Gemini, that other Mercury-ruled sign. But he's more down-to-earth than your average Gemini man and while he might sometimes appear cool on the surface, there is sure to be a passionate heart beating away below.

While the faults possessed by some star-signs might not be immediately apparent, at least you are usually far more aware of your Virgo partner's defects right from the start, even if you dont know very much about Astrology. You can also sense his sizing you up in every possible way, and you know it's not just that he's wondering whether you'd be good in bed. He might not be as psychic as Scorpio or Pisces, but he certainly has perfected the art of sensing what makes a person tick. He's definitely the nit-picker of the Zodiac, and you'll probably find him person-ally restless, even though he is incredibly organized too. If on one of your first dates he took you out to eat you'll soon have discovered that he's amazingly fussy about his diet — and he might go on a little too long about the importance of good health and moan about a headache or a cough he can't shake off.

If you haven't encountered many people born under his sign, you might start to wonder if you'd be in for a dull time if you embarked on a permanent relationship with him. But give him a chance. The Virgo partner has a wonderful sense of humour which surely has not escaped your notice, except perhaps on one of his bad days when worries and negative thoughts were clouding over him. And isn't it wonderful to know you've met a man you can truly rely on, who says what he means and does what he says? Even if your relationship does take off slowly, surely it's better for you as well? It will give you more time to size him up the way he has you.

It is important to remember that his sense of duty is paramount; he is quite content with his tag of 'the sign of service'; he will do anything in the world to make the people he cares about feel loved and secure. And he'll demand the same amount of loyalty from his partner too.

Though born under a Feminine sign, this man is masculine in all senses of the word. He is as forceful as Leo, as determined as Taurus, and just as passionate as Scorpio when love is in the air. Sometimes it may not be immediately apparent that he is a very sexy man indeed. He seems to be so concerned with working hard and providing for the future, worrying about the problems that tomorrow could bring, making personal sacrifices to make life better for others and sometimes seeming to miss out on the fun of life himself.

But just because he isn't so openly sensual as some other men, your Virgo partner will enjoy the bliss of sexual fulfilment as much as anyone else, and probably teach you a few tricks along the way! You have to remember he's probably striving for perfection in sexual ecstasy the way he strives for it in everything else. Sex is not simply one of his Virgo duties he feels compelled to undertake − it's something he wants to enjoy and to make sure you enjoy it too. You won't usually find a selfish lover when you have a Virgo man as your partner, although if he's been doing his overworking bit for far too long you should be understanding if he complains he's feeling tired or 'has a headache'.

191

Once you've started to live with a Virgo man you'll want to help him worry less and appreciate life more. You'll learn to let him see how much you appreciate his honest and direct approach. You'll even enjoy allowing him to organize you to make your life better too. You'll love his attention, the way he never forgets birthdays and anniversaries, and his obvious devotion to his family and friends.

In a business relationship with Virgo, no one could ask for a better partner, for this man would never let you down in any way. But equally he will expect from others the same sense of duty and hard work that he puts into every single day. The Virgo man cannot put up with any kind of shirking, it's almost like a sin to him. He's managed to discipline himself to cope with working hard, and sees no reason why everyone else cannot do the same.

Whether it's an emotional relationship or a work situation, he always needs someone to respect his views and listen to his advice. Sometimes he may seem to criticize you a great deal, but deep down you will probably recognize that so much of what he tells you is genuine constructive advice.

He's never as secure as he sometimes seems – those self-critical ways are not something he asked to be born with. In a love relationship he will do everything possible to ensure that you *don't* find too much you don't like about him. He yearns for someone to share his dreams, for just because he isn't as outwardly romantic and idealistic as his opposite sign of Pisces, on the inside he can just as easily be a true romantic too.

Every star-sign contains something of its opposite, and inside many a Virgo man is lurking that same desire to see the world in rose-coloured spectacles as Pisces; and that self-same dream of the perfect soulmate. So if your Virgo partner does not necessarily appear to be a romantic dreamer never forget that he may be. He can be bitterly hurt if he's perceived as a critical worrier and little else besides – it's unfair and it's so hard for him to accept anything which isn't fair.

But while this man will do anything for other people, he would also hate to think you were only doing things for him out of duty. He needs to believe totally in your love for him, and wants to share his life with someone he *can* sometimes fuss over and who will fuss over him *without* accusing him of being the fusspot of all time. He also hates to be called a hypochondriac just because he's concerned about his health, and to be criticized for his analytical views.

He may seem like a hard taskmaster, expecting so much from you, from life, from everyone he meets. But you need to know it's not really an expectation, just a hope that things will always work out the way he would like them to, if this was a perfect world. Meanwhile he's more than content to do his part to be a perfect partner if you'll do yours in learning to understand him even more.

He'll be a really responsible father when children come along, taking a keen interest in their education, guiding them along the way, although he'll sometimes need to learn to relax more and not worry about them quite so much.

His attitude to money might sometimes worry you. You would probably like it if he occasionally forgot about tomorrow and the need to save for those rainy days. He's usually much too practical ever to be a really big spender. He'll ensure you never want for anything important, but he will soon become very irritable if you always expect him to spend a fortune on entertainment and having fun. It's okay to celebrate on special occasions and well-deserved holidays, but he'll definitely be worse than a bear with a sore head if he sees his bank balance go into the red too often.

One of the most important things to remember if you want to twist your Virgo man around your little finger and keep him there is to let him see that you're just as dependable as he is. Virgo is not a philanderer and is much too busy to waste precious time flirting when he probably has work to do. He needs a woman who is as faithful and loving as he's prepared to be and problems will arise if you don't accept this from the very start.

If he has been badly hurt in the past it might be hard for him to believe that love can last for ever. He hates the idea of break-ups and divorce, and will do everything he can to avoid such things taking place in his life, yet still worry about it.

Once you understand your Virgo partner even better, you will do everything you can to make him enjoy the lighter side of life a little more. His feet are always so firmly on the ground that he almost seems to feel it's a crime to spend too much time with the woman he loves. But once he's realized the pure bliss of finding a partner who understands his strengths and weaknesses, and doesn't try to change him overnight, he'll try a little harder to be less analytical and will then start to relax and love you even more.

Of course there will still be some high spots and danger zones in your relationship. But you'll be so glad you have a partner who will stand by you rain or shine that you won't search for any other sign to be your ideal man.

High spots with your Virgo man
He will

★ Be one of the most devoted partners you could ever find.

★ Work hard to help make your life even easier.

★ Always remember every single anniversary.

★ Amaze you with his eye for detail.

★ Delight you with his witty sense of humour.

★ Look after you tenderly if ever you don't feel well.

★ Be a perfectionist at making love.

★ Do everything possible to make your relationship grow from strength to strength.

Danger zones with your Virgo man
Never

★ Criticize him *too much* about anything.

★ Be too much of a spendthrift.

★ Be too lazy about the house.

★ Moan because he works so hard.

★ Accuse him of setting too much store by duty and responsibilities.

★ Cook him meals you know he hates.

★ Lock the medicine cabinet when he needs an aspirin.

★ Forget he's sexier than he might sometimes seem.

★ The Virgo Woman ★

Just like her male counterpart the Virgo woman is searching for perfection in her life. The planetary symbol of this Feminine Earth sign is the Virgin with her sheaf of corn. She symbolizes purity in its deepest sense, and indeed the Virgo woman, with her strong sense of responsibility and duty, is extremely pure, but she can also be one of the most tender loving and caring women you have ever known. Her search for perfection doesn't mean that she doesn't expect you to have any faults. She is well aware that she's been tagged as the critic and analyst of the Zodiac, but she is as critical about herself as anyone else. It's not necessarily a characteristic she likes, but she's learning to live with it and to turn it into more of a positive aspect than a negative one.

Of course at first you may wonder what you've got yourself into when you become involved with her. She is obviously summing you up, noticing every little thing about you. It may almost be unnerving, especially if you start to wonder what she is thinking. But you'll soon discover that this warm and honest woman knows herself very well. She knows not only what she wants in a partner, but usually what she needs as well, and if the two don't match up, which sometimes they don't, she is determined not to waste any time.

That doesn't mean she won't work at making a relationship grow into something worthwhile, for she will often put more effort than many other women into doing just that. But because she is looking for permanence in her life, she often sees things in a more realistic way. She will give everything she's got if she's sure you have something going for the two of you.

If you're simply looking for a brief flirtation, it might be better for you to stop right here. Unless your Virgo woman has her reasons for not wanting to settle down, or unless her own personal horoscope contains aspects which conflict with her basic Virgo personality, she won't be out for a fling. On the surface she may sometimes be headstrong, flirtatious and provocatively sensual, giving you as good a come-hither look as anyone else can do, but deep down it's something else.

Your Virgo woman wants more than anything to have a

peaceful and calm life. She yearns for balance as much as Libra, the sign which follows hers. Astrologically Virgo is known as 'the sign of service', and a Virgo partner is willing to prove in every possible way that she will definitely live up to that. Discriminating, cool, analytical Virgo – she will create a challenge in your life you may never have known before.

If you want a woman who will agree wholeheartedly with everything you say or do with hardly an opinion of her own; someone who doesn't care if she loses her own identity because she's so involved with you; someone who will turn a blind eye if you flirt with anyone else, you may be in for a surprise, for a Virgo partner, who sometimes appears to be so shy and unassuming, will soon display the other side of her personality.

Because she does sometimes come over as so cool and detached, it doesn't mean she's lacking in emotion. It's just that she doesn't like to fly off the handle the way an Aries or Leo might do; but she knows exactly what she's thinking and it won't be long before you know too. Because she is ruled by Mercury, she is brilliantly adept at communicating her thoughts and ideas. She is equally clever at waiting for the right moment to come out with them. She would never want to upset you in public, she'd rather wait till you were alone to tell you what is on her mind.

You cannot fool your Virgo woman. Along with her analytical ability there often seems to be a sort of sixth sense which enables her to know just what is going on. But she also tends to worry a great deal, something which has been with her all her life, but she also yearns for the perfect partner who can help her to worry less. She needs someone who will make her relax a little more. She is so busy being that 'sign of service' for other people that she leaves not enough time for herself.

You probably won't sweep her off her feet by overpowering her with passionate declarations of love. She knows that some people find it far too easy to rush headlong into an affair. It's often easier for her to accept you as a friend at first, letting your relationship grow into something deeper in its own time and in its own way. The Virgo woman doesn't like to be rushed into anything. She has her feet very firmly on the Earth.

But if this loyal and loving partner is suddenly beginning to seem as though she is lacking in romance, you really don't have to worry. She can be just as romantic as her opposite sign of Pisces and just as idealistic too. However she often has a harder time because she knows all about those flaws and imperfections which sadly exist in romance too.

She will have to be convinced that you're not going to let her down in any way, especially if she has been hurt before by not listening to her inner voice. She also needs to be sure that you won't want her to give up her independence, for she's not the sort of woman who always finds that running a home is enough in her life. She enjoys working hard and puts a great deal of effort into everything she does, and is marvellous at coping with a strenuous career as well as looking after her partner, and in time children too.

The sexual side of your relationship is sure to be important, and she can probably be critical here as well, because she's very aware that while sexual compatibility is incredibly important in sustaining the perfect relationship, it doesn't always happen overnight. She's not going to deflate your ego if you don't totally fulfil her every single time you make love. But she'll expect you to be able to talk over any problems with her so that you learn more about each other's needs and desires, and are able to fulfil them. She may not necessarily think of sex as *the* most important part of your relationship but it will definitely have its place.

Living with a Virgo woman can be wonderful. She will genuinely do everything in her power to make your life together as emotionally contented and fulfilling as possible, and that isn't just from her sense of duty. She is usually extremely tidy and well-organized at home, and quite likely to moan if she has to go around picking up things after you. You will always be proud of her appearance for she hates sloppiness in any way at all. And even if she does sometimes complain about all the housework she has to do, she's not the sort of woman who will leave the washing-up overnight or let your dirty shirts pile up in the laundry basket. She is also careful with money and hates to be in the red. She'll manage to work long hours and still give a marvellous dinner party; be a strict but loving mother, and be your very own Florence Nightingale if you're down with flu.

Your Virgo partner isn't the sort of woman who is usually unfaithful, especially as it's hard for her to think of hurting other people by having to tell lies. And she'll set the same high standards for you as she does for herself, so remember that before you start to flirt with anyone else. She may not look as if she is the sort of woman who can be wildly jealous – but she can. And if she is badly let down, she also has the strength of mind which gives her the ability to break up a relationship if she feels it cannot go on in the same way as before. This isn't to imply she would leave you without a great deal of thought, but she has a very logical mind which, in addition to its ability to recognize mistakes almost the minute they occur, enables her to plan more realistically than many other signs.

You might think she could never be 'the other woman' in a triangle situation, but 'never' is too strong a word. The Virgo woman falls in love just like other women, and if she was totally convinced that something permanent would arise without creating too many hurts for others, she would be able to cope.

In a business relationship with a Virgo woman, you have one of the most dependable and supportive partners you could ask for. But just because she is prepared to put in extra long hours, way beyond the call of duty even for a Virgo, that should be no reason to take advantage of her. Admire her for her strict work ethic, but don't let her see *you* slacking.

Twisting a Virgo woman around your little finger to ensure she will stick by you for ever is not as difficult as it might seem. You will have to let her see that while you can't prevent her from worrying ever again, you will certainly do your utmost to see that you don't give her any new problems; you will make her understand that you appreciate her for what she is – a quiet, peaceful and loving woman with a gentle disposition who is prepared to do everything she possibly can to create a perfect relationship with the man she loves. Of course you'll have to overlook *some* of her critical ways, but you'll enjoy her honesty, her faithfulness, her caring and tender attitude.

And perhaps you can learn how to make her have more fun, to laugh more and use her warm and witty sense of humour. She needs a man who is her equal, but who can also make her feel like a young girl in love for the very first time. She has always had her own special romantic dreams hidden in her heart, but has probably filed them away meticulously in a compartment which she never has time to unlock.

Your Virgo woman is so busy being of service to others, she needs a partner who will appreciate her for herself. Just remember that she is definitely not as self-confident as she might appear. Sometimes she can be incredibly shy under her efficient manner, and on occasion she is so busy analysing her own negative points that she forgets about the many good ones which help to make her one of the most perfect partners you could ever meet.

There will inevitably be some danger zones, times when her preoccupation with her health or her diet, and probably yours too, irritate you beyond belief. Moments when you simply don't want to hear her opinion of what you're doing wrong. But the high spots of your relationship can far outweigh the low points so that you won't want to be with anyone but her.

High spots with your Virgo woman
She will
★ Be one of the most devoted women you've ever met.
★ Help to make your worries fade away.
★ Work as hard as you to make the future brighter.
★ Always make sure there is money in the bank.
★ Create the perfect home surroundings.
★ Nurse your pains away.
★ Bring you greater emotional security.
★ Be as warm and loving in bed as out of it.

Danger zones with your Virgo woman
Never
★ Pick too many faults in *her*.
★ Accuse her of being extravagant − it can't be true!
★ Tell her any lies.
★ Embarrass her in public.
★ Let her think you've been unfaithful.
★ Fail to pull your weight in making your relationship grow stronger.
★ Be *too* untidy around the house.
★ Accuse her of being a hypochondriac.

The Libra Partner

★ The Libra Man ★

If you long for a man who has no qualms about letting you see how sensitive he can be, as well as possessing an abundance of strength; who knows all about the importance of having the right balance of mental stimulation and sexual compatibility to create the perfect relationship; who is charming, diplomatic, and invariably a pleasure to be with, then you will certainly appreciate Mr Libra. Those positive characteristics of this sign will enable him to fulfil many of your dreams, and make you believe that the remaining ones will soon come true as well.

The Libra man is definitely an interesting partner. Born under a Masculine, Cardinal, Positive, Air sign, he seems to have a flair for getting what he wants, for being able to communicate his ideas with ease, to analyse almost as well as Virgo, and to be as forceful as any Leo when he wants to lead. Everything is inevitably carried out with great charm. He's almost irresistible.

But your Libra man doesn't find it very easy to make up his mind even when he does think he's found what he wants. You may have decided from the outset that he was the perfect partner for you, but it's not always that easy to convince him to see it that way too. And he can't be pushed. Libra is symbolized by the Scales, and your Libra man is going to spend a great deal of time weighing things up. It's often true that when it comes to love he can rush into something almost as fast as his opposite sign of

Aries without doing too much rationalizing at the time. But that's also because he is ruled by Venus, and you can't have forgotten that Venus is the Goddess of Love. Is it any wonder that a world without love and romance would make Libra feel the same way as Leo? It's impossible to imagine such a disaster. Love makes his world go round and his scales dip far too low if he feels lonely and neglected.

But the trouble starts if he realizes that he's embarked on something which he knows can't last, for then he can suffer agonies of indecision over the best way to get out of it. He finds it so hard to hurt anyone's feelings. So if you ever have a relationship with a Libra man and sense you love him more than he can ever love you, it's much better to be the one who faces up to the facts and try to end it all as painlessly as possible.

Because he can be quite a womanizer in his search for the perfect partner, you might be slightly wary when you first meet him. Sometimes that charm seems almost overdone; the lazy indolent way he sums you up, the compliments he knows you'll love to hear. He's almost childlike in the way he obviously wants to impress you, and it can be very hard to resist.

One of the most relevant things to remember about this man is that he truly is searching for the perfect partner. He knows how much he needs the right person to share his life. The sign of Libra relates to partnerships, and even if he knows nothing about astrology he will instinctively know that the perfect partnership will help balance his scales as nothing else will do.

Your feminine wiles will help to attract him to your side, but you'll need a lot more than that to convince him that you belong there for ever. He's an idealist with a highly logical mind too. He probably yearns for security, but he won't be blinded by the heat of passion into thinking that you're the one person who can be a permanent fixture in his life until he's got to know you really well, and recognizes there is mental compatibility too.

But days can turn into weeks, weeks into months, and perhaps longer, before your Libra man will decide if he's prepared to settle into a permanent relationship, unless his Ascendant or Moon sign, or various other planetary aspects in his chart, influence his Libran personality to such an extent that he makes an instant decision that he never wants to live without you. He's usually quite prepared to argue the pros and cons of the whole situation from morning to night; he'll see the good and the bad sides of everything, he'll drive you crazy with the way he rationalizes every single thing. He has a deep-rooted sense of fair play and so you won't feel inadequate in any way, he's more than willing to point out all the reasons he feels he might make *you* unhappy.

So by now you're probably gathering that a relationship with a Libra man can be incredibly frustrating if you don't know exactly where you stand. And it will be up to you to decide whether you're prepared to wait or not. But when your feminine intuition has convinced you that it is really only a question of time; that your relationship is growing stronger every day, and you sense you truly have something so special with your Libra man that he'd have to go a long way to find it again, you can start to relax a little, and perhaps do a little subtle leading, but still never pushing, to bring up those words you've been longing to hear − like 'let's move in together' or 'get married' or 'put this on a more permanent basis'.

A Libra partner can bring balance into your own life too. He has a marvellous understanding of what makes you happy. He's not the argumentative sort of man who criticizes you unreasonably, who expects you to be at his beck and call from morning to night. And he would hate you to be like that with him. He is invariably a kind and gentle lover who knows just how to bring you to the heights of ecstasy. But don't start wondering about how many women he might have known before you, or even worse start grilling him about them. If he has decided to make a firm commitment to you then it's the present and future which is important − not the past. So leave it be.

It's often said that Libra is a lazy sign, and certainly after long periods of excessive activity your Libran man might suddenly decide he needs a good rest. But again that's all down to balancing those scales. Too much of anything is bad for him, as well he knows, for since Libra rules the kidneys, Librans who indulge in excessive drinking can often give themselves unwanted problems.

However when it comes to making love, you're unlikely to find your Libran partner a lazy lover. He's a highly sensual man who is one of the most unselfish partners you could have. It's very rare for him to put his needs before yours. He wants to share the ecstasies of a totally blissful relationship in every way he can. But since he's often been a philanderer in the past, he just might start to wander again if you let him think that the physical side of your relationship isn't quite so important to you. To the Libra partner, that idyllic blending of mind, body and soul is what a true relationship is all about. He doesn't want to put up with anything less. It took him long enough to make up his mind that he's found his ideal woman, so don't let him start wondering if he has made a mistake by failing to share his ideals or ever letting him think you're bored.

Once you have started to live with a Libra man his indecision will sometimes irritate you beyond belief. He might consider it balancing his ideas, seeing both sides of the situation, call it what he will – you see it as plain old indecisiveness and a certain weakness. But somehow his appealing charm will always win you over and you'll learn to accept this facet of his personality. He has so many other good points to make up for it, for he is basically such a lovable man. Just don't be too indecisive yourself.

A business relationship with a Libra man is better when it's a partnership than in any other way. He invariably enjoys working with someone else far more than on his own. Even if he is the boss of a company he will probably treat his most trusted employees as equals anyway, especially if their knowledge and experience can make his life even easier when important decisions have to be reached. The Libra man is always much happier when he has someone around who believes in him. Solitude is not for him on any permanent basis.

His love of beauty combined with his desire for peace and tranquillity mean he hates to live in an untidy home. He might not be as critical as Virgo, but he'll certainly give you a hard time if there is always a mess around when he comes home, even though he might be the first to admit that he isn't particularly tidy himself. But he won't expect you to give up your own career to look after him and be a perfect housekeeper. He admires a woman who makes her own way in the world — just as long as he remains as important as ever in your life.

Problems in a relationship can sometimes arise where money is concerned. Your Libra partner can be incredibly extravagant. He is happy to take you out to expensive restaurants, see you in lovely clothes, but he doesn't always think realistically about where the money is coming from. If you don't work yourself and are not therefore helping financially, it is sometimes difficult to make him realize the importance of keeping a realistic budget. It's one of those areas where his scales tilt and he is off on his extremes again, and you'd be wise to help him see the error of his ways — but never nag him.

His relationship with his family and friends is usually a very friendly one. He enjoys keeping in touch and seeing them. And as a father he is loving and affectionate, always fair, but firm and marvellous at keeping the peace when arguments flare up. He is a man who tries hard to be tolerant in every way, hating the injustice he sees around him. So try never to be intolerant with him. He needs a mate who will share his love of beauty, enjoy his taste in music, the art which appeals to him; someone who doesn't insist on decision-making every other moment of the day.

He may not seem especially jealous on the surface, but although he loves to flirt himself, he won't be at all happy if you're the sort of woman who mentally indulges her sexual fantasies whilst being chatted up by anyone but him!

As he gets older he will realize even more just how much he relies on having the perfect partner in his life. You see, once his mind *was* made up, he hated to think of ever going through that particular time of indecision ever again.

Sex will always be an important part of your relationship together, and will always go hand in hand with his need for the inner contentment that stems from being with a woman who has shared his strengths and weaknesses and helped him to balance those finely tuned scales.

Of course his procrastination will sometimes infuriate you still, and you might hate it when you've just had a big argument with someone and yet he feels they are as much in the right as you. But would you change your Libran partner for anyone else? A relationship with this man is definitely one in which you're part of a team. He needs someone to share with him in every possible sense. Don't expect him to be too much of a dominant force or a weakling you can push around. Always remember he needs to hear you tell him how wonderful he is, how great he looks. His ego is never quite as strong as it might sometimes appear. In return he will help you to appreciate the joy of feeling fulfilled on every possible level.

And if he still enjoys receiving those admiring glances from other women, and giving a few in return, surely you can cope with that when you've managed to convince him that he could never have made a better choice of partner than you. Think what an exhilarating challenge it can be to keep his Libran scales from tilting too high or too low so that he stays by your side for ever.

Of course there will be high spots and danger zones, those moments when your kind and gentle Libran partner becomes indecisive about something once again, or an argument will flare up unexpectedly and his logic cuts no ice with you. But by then you will have learnt to balance your own personality to work side-by-side with his. And therefore how could you have chosen anyone but your sentimental and sensitive Libran to be your perfect soulmate? Not since you've experienced the joy of watching your relationship grow stronger day by day.

High spots with your Libra man
He will

★ Brighten your days with tender loving care.

★ Fulfil your dreams of romantic bliss.

★ Find a thousand ways to tell you that you're his perfect woman.

★ Make you understand what total empathy is all about.

★ Always delight you with his tastefully chosen gifts.

★ Perfectly match sensuality with sensitivity.

★ Balance your own life with his Libran scales and show you just how beautiful everything can be when you're together.

Danger zones with your Libra man
Never

★ Deflate his ego by telling him he doesn't look good.

★ Nag him into making up his mind − he has to take his time.

★ Neglect him too much or his eyes could start to wander.

★ Go on continually about his being lazy or go on about him being wildly extravagant (the subtle approach works much better).

★ Accuse him of being a bad lover or accuse him of being too much of a flirt either.

★ Let your own appearance slip.

★ The Libra Woman ★

One of the first things to learn about the Libra woman is that while she is one of the most feminine women in the entire Zodiac, she's not as soft and unassuming as you might first think. Libra is one of the Cardinal signs, and so your Libra partner will possess all those Cardinal qualities of leadership shared by Aries, Cancer and Capricorn. It is also a Masculine sign and she will have an abundance of male logic alongside her feminine intuition. But then, of course, she is ruled by Venus, Goddess of Love, and so being in love is definitely what life is all about to the Libran woman.

When you first become involved with a Libra partner you will wonder how you've managed to get on for so long without her. She seems to fit the bill of your ideal woman in every way. Bright, witty, sentimental, affectionate, you find her irresistible and only hope she feels the same way about you. But don't expect her to rush into your arms without a second thought, promising to love and obey you for the rest of your life. This woman spends a great deal of time weighing up the pros and cons of everything. If you didn't know that the planetary ruler of Libra was the Scales, it's something you must definitely remember from now on. That Libran balancing act is renowned to anyone who has ever been involved with this woman. She doesn't simply weigh things up once and then decide on her plan of action: that would be far too simple. She can spend a great deal of time procrastinating before her Libran mind is satisfied and she can go ahead. Then it all becomes perfectly easy. She's made her decision and that's that.

You might already be thinking that you could be in for a hard time if you have to prove yourself in a myriad of different ways before you're going to be accepted as the ideal man by Ms Libra, but one thing will help to make it easier. This woman is not someone who really wants to be alone. Libra is the sign of partnership, and her greatest desire in life is to find the right person to share her hopes and aspirations and be a permanent part of her life.

It's not that she's incapable of creating a good life for herself on her own. She is a highly versatile woman who has a great deal of inner strength and the ability to achieve. It's just that she is so much happier being part of a team, planning for the future with the man she loves. She is a woman who will do everything in her power to help the man in her life move onward and upwards, but don't expect her to subjugate her own personality in the process. Being part of a team means she will expect you to help her as well.

And perhaps this is the moment to remind you that if you'd imagined a quiet and peaceful life for ever more just because you've read that Librans need harmony and tranquillity in their lives, you will soon discover that your Libran woman is prepared to defend to the bitter end anything she believes in strongly. It's definitely a misconception to think of her as being weak. Think of Margaret Thatcher and you'll see what I mean, for can you imagine her giving in on anything when she is convinced she is right?

To understand your Libra partner totally, you will have to realize that she is a mixture of masculine strength and feminine sensitivity; that she is searching for perfection in a world which seems to become more imbalanced every day. She also some-times finds it hard to imagine finding a man who will help her balance her scales because she realizes she can set herself incredibly high standards.

If you can accept that inside every star-sign is something of its opposite, then perhaps it will make it easier for you to imagine that inside every seemingly soft and pliable Libran is a tough and determined Aries. Your Libran woman will be a tower of strength, possessing so much energy and vitality you'll wonder how on earth anyone could describe Librans as being lazy. And yet they seem to go through life having to fight against that description. However, what you will discover is that your Libra partner seems to possess a sixth sense as powerful as a Scorpio for she knows that if she does let herself go to extremes in any way her health could suffer. She might work like a Trojan for an inestimably long time but she knows when to rest and replenish her energy. So when she does take a break it's not laziness but simply common sense − of which she possesses a great deal. She also believes strongly in fair play. Just like her male counterpart she hates injustice and intolerance and will fight against it in every way she can. When she gives her heart she wants it to be for ever. But since you already know that she isn't likely to fall headlong into a relationship at the drop of a hat, you will have to work hard at convincing her that you're searching for perfection as much as she is. She is far too astute to think that physical compatibility alone is enough to make a good relationship, important as it is. She needs a man who is sentimental as well as sensual, someone whose love-making is combined with the ability to whisper soft words in her ear. Perfect sex needs to be that perfect balance yet again, the ideal blend of mental, physical and spiritual which makes her feel completely fulfilled even though a passionate sex life on its own might be exciting for a while.

Living with a Libra partner can be a truly wonderful experience because once she has the right male by her side this woman seems to become even more alive. She has such a basically positive attitude that even if she sometimes irritates you beyond belief when she falls into one of her indecisive moods, you know that she will always do everything possible to help your relationship grow from strength to strength.

I know many Libran women who hold down highly successful careers, and look after husbands and children brilliantly, doing their own housework and managing to give marvellous dinner parties, so you will always feel proud of her. Your Libran partner will also have the amazing ability to look far younger than her years throughout her life, and she will always appreciate being complimented and flattered on her appearance.

In a business relationship with a Libra woman you'll enjoy having someone who is so fair-minded and able to see both sides of every situation. You will know you can always depend on her intelligent approach, her tactful and diplomatic manner when any problems do arise. Like her male counterpart she doesn't usually enjoy working on her own and feels much more fulfilled in a partnership or at least where she has the right kind of rapport with her boss and colleagues.

Your Libra partner loves company, and will not expect to give up her friends or neglect her family once she's settled into a permanent relationship, so even though she will be one of the most devoted and loving women you could ever meet, don't try to control her life in any way, for she can turn into quite a rebel. She may not appear to be so independent but you'll soon realize that she is. She will make immeasurable sacrifices for someone she loves, her courage in the face of adversity is remarkable and once you've embarked on a relationship with her you'll find it hard to envisage how you survived so long without her.

Never let her feel neglected for any length of time. She's not the sort of woman who will have affairs with other men to spite you, but she definitely always needs love and romance in her life. That's not something which lessens as the years go by. There will start to be a danger if the compatibility between you starts to slip in any way and neither of you are prepared to work at repairing it. However with that innate sense of fair play which was instilled in her from the moment she was born she is not the sort of woman to walk out on a relationship without making every possible effort to improve it even if sometimes the problems seemed almost insurmountable.

Like the Libran male, problems can arise if your Libran woman is extravagant with money – and an awful lot of people born under this sign do possess this fault to extremes. You have to remember that Venus endows Libra with a great love of beauty in all its shapes and forms. Your Libran partner will always want to look wonderful for you, which might mean spending far too much on her wardrobe; your home must also look perfect, she will want to buy you gifts she knows you have always yearned for. It's important for both of you to ensure that this doesn't create any real difficulties in your relationship, and therefore if your Libran woman is determined to keep up her own career, you don't have to be the sort of macho male who prefers her to stay at home all day.

Twisting a Libra woman around your little finger to keep her close to you for ever will be one of the most pleasant tasks you've ever known. It's really simply a question of mentally visualizing those Libran scales and learning the best way to keep them balanced; to ensure that she trusts you and that you're mentally in tune with each other's hopes and aspirations, that she understands you'd rather be with her than anyone else you've ever known.

Sharing the good times and the bad ones too will make you realize that teamwork is definitely what life is all about – and who could convince you of the validity of this better than your Libran partner? Resolve that you will never take her for granted, undermine her confidence in any way, or be too irritated if she seems to take an eternity to make a decision yet again. Would you really want a partner who wasn't absolutely sure that she was doing the right thing in the end? One who didn't realize the importance of taking time to have the right soulmate in her life?

The high spots of your relationship can always be greater than the low points if *you're* not too lazy to practise a spot of balancing yourself.

High spots with your Libra Woman
She will
⊛ Be one of the most delightfully seductive partners you could ever meet.
★ Do everything in her power to make you happy with her.
★ Enable you to see there are always two sides to everything.
★ Be fair-minded and tolerant.
★ Bring peace and harmony into your life.

★ Give you the mental stimulation you've always yearned for.
★ Be a perfect lover in every way.
★ Use her Libran scales to create the right balancing act between you.

Danger zones with your Libra woman
Never

★ Force her into anything before she's made up her mind.
★ Underestimate her need for that total blending of mind, body and soul.
★ Expect passion alone to keep her by your side.
★ Expect her to be too practical where money is concerned.
★ Forget to compliment her when she's looking wonderful.
★ Let her see you flirting too much with anyone else.
✪ Expect to win too many arguments.
★ Let her think you could be intolerant in any way.

Of course I will!

The Scorpio Partner

★ The Scorpio Man ★

It's strange but true that many women are frightened at the thought of embarking on a relationship with a Scorpio man. Perhaps it's because there always seems to be an air of mystery surrounding him; you sense the magnetic hypnotism of his personality, his inner strength and powerful ego. Is he saint or sinner? Perhaps you've read too much about the 'sting in the Scorpion's tail' or have been burnt in the past by going with a man who even if he wasn't actually a Scorpio had strong Scorpio influences in his chart, and mainly negative ones at that!

If you're only going to think about the negative aspects of his character it's probably best for you to choose a different sign. However, you'd be doing your Scorpio man a great disservice by not finding out a little more about him, and losing out on the chance of a great deal of happiness too, once you understood him better. If you've never known a Scorpio before, and also know very little about astrology it may make your life a lot easier to learn a few more facts. For instance, any faults possessed by a Scorpio partner will not be staring you right in the face at the start of your relationship, because that is just where his magnetism comes in. He will overwhelm you with the intensity of his feelings and leave no stone unturned to persuade you to get to know him better. Youll be swept off your feet and inevitably adore the attention and flattery you receive.

Seldom have you known a man quite so determined to win you by fair means or foul; for Mr Scorpio often has no qualms about setting his hat at someone who is already half-heartedly involved with someone else. If he believes you to be right in his eyes, you're right. Regardless of his age, the Scorpio man is determined to have what he wants and is therefore often described as 'being a law unto himself'. And while he may not be as pushy as Leo, he is often as optimistic as Sagittarius in chancing his luck that you'll recognize him as your perfect partner in the same way that he has decided that you are for him.

If there is one word in the dictionary which describes a Scorpio partner completely it is 'invincible'. He is possessed with so much courage and inner strength that you will feel absolutely protected when he is around. But he does have quite a reputation as a womanizer; for from a very early age his desire to seek out all the mysteries of life inevitably grew as strong as his passionate yearning for the perfect soulmate to share them with.

However, because he does place so much importance on sex, he has also inevitably made some mistakes too. He's sure to have been swept off *his* feet very often by someone who fulfilled his physical desires, only to discover that the person in question had little else in common with him. One of the important things to remember with this man is that while everyone always goes on about his being the 'sex symbol' of the Zodiac, and while he might even be able to add a few extra passages to the *Kama Sutra*, he definitely needs a partner to be mentally compatible, for Scorpio is not only passionately intense about sex, and about life, he is also highly intelligent with a very inquiring mind, and he needs a partner who is as intensely interested in the world as he is.

Your Scorpio man belongs to the Water element, though you could be forgiven for thinking he is a Fire sign. Scorpio is a Fixed Negative Feminine sign and possesses two ruling planets — Mars, God of War, and Pluto, Lord of the Underworld, who in Greek mythology was known as Hades. And while his planetary symbol is commonly recognized as the Scorpion, it can also be the Eagle, representing the Higher Self. Scorpio relates to birth and death, reincarnation and regeneration. Not only does he have incredibly strong emotions, but he also has a habit of keeping them bottled up inside him far too long.

In some ways he treats life rather like a battlefield, which is the influence of Mars. However, he is very different from an Aries man, and often more self-confident too. The patient side of his personality comes not only from his being a Fixed sign, but also from the opposite sign, within him, of Taurus. Another Taurean characteristic which your Scorpio man has in abundance, although people are often so busy maligning him they dismiss it from their minds, is a concomitant deep-abiding loyalty. It's certainly true that he finds it incredibly hard to either forgive or forget, and that taking revenge is something he sometimes finds almost too easy. But his loyalty to the people he cares for can never be underestimated and is one of his greatest attributes.

A relationship with a Scorpio man definitely doesn't have to be a frightening experience, making you tremble with trepidation at its very thought. It can be one of the most exciting and mind-blowing happenings in your life. However, if you're expecting peace and tranquillity every minute of every day, you'd be barking up the wrong tree with this man since there are sure to be fireworks at times.

It's not as if your Scorpio man is lacking in the tender loving care stakes. He is a Water sign, and there is plenty of sensitivity and sentimentality lurking below the surface. He can be as emotionally vulnerable as any other man, although he's an absolute master at hiding it. It doesn't necessarily mean he considers it a weakness, just that from the time he was a tiny child he knew he needed his privacy — his own little space to retreat into where he could collect his thoughts, and charge up his batteries to give the extra supplies of the vital life-force he thrives on. So never accuse him of being cold and unfeeling for he'd be bitterly hurt.

A Scorpio man in good form will ensure you want for no one else. You'll learn to love his passion for life, if you don't already. You'll thrive on his devotion and thrill when you're transported to those heights of sexual ecstasy which you've never known with any other man.

This leads to a very important point. While your Scorpio partner doesn't expect you to still be a virgin in this liberated world of ours, he is intensely jealous – and always will be. He will inevitably try to prise out of you every secret you have. When it comes to the previous men in your life, the knowledge won't necessarily make him happy! Scorpio always feels the urge to play with fire, even though his high intelligence tells him he is sure to get burned.

You have to understand that this man's insatiable curiosity about everything means that he cannot contemplate living with someone who has secrets from him.

When you have settled into a relationship with him, there are two very important things to remember. The first is that *his* jealous prying nature is one thing; the second is that it definitely is not allowed for you to be jealous and possessive with him. He is a law unto himself. He knows that this can sometimes make him very difficult to live with – but I'm afraid he is unlikely to change now.

This is when you must remember about his loyalty, and have sufficient confidence in your own ability to keep him by your side to turn a blind eye if he flirts with someone else. Anyway, he might only be testing your reaction in order to check if you can live up to his high ideals!

He wants a woman who has strength of mind and strength of character, but who will never try to boss him around too much. He expects to be in charge for he genuinely believes that it is up to the man to look after his woman. But he certainly doesn't want a little mouse who would never say boo to a goose, or someone who gaily lets him go on his merry way with never a word of complaint.

He won't ask you to give up your own career for him; but he will certainly expect his needs to be of paramount importance in your life. Because he has incredibly strong instinct and intuition, he will invariably know what you are thinking, and if you have any worries on your mind. This man can be so psychic he will be miles away and pick up your thoughts.

Learning more about how to enjoy the good parts of a relationship with a Scorpio man and also how to overcome any bad times will definitely never be boring. There are bound to be some stormy moments, some times when his jealousy infuriates you, and the urge to go through his pockets to check if he has taken any other woman's phone number becomes almost irresistible. But why should he be the playboy of all time if he's settled into a fulfilling partnership with you? Just as long as it *is* fulfilling in every sense there is no reason why he should want to roam no matter how often he has in the past. When he is accused unjustly of something you will soon see on the surface the burning rage he hides away inside. Anger is a part of himself he doesn't necessarily like, but he knows and accepts that it is there, so you will have to accept it too.

Twisting your Scorpio man around your little finger to make your relationship last means that you will definitely have to enjoy making love to him for the rest of your life. His physical desires don't diminish with the passing years. There will always need to be plenty of excitement combined with sexual grati-fication. Perhaps you'd better check up on the *Kama Sutra* yourself. The Scorpio man isn't usually a selfish lover just because he has such strong sexual needs and high hopes of what love and living together is all about. But he can't cope with frigidity or someone who veers more towards a platonic relation-ship even if she loves him. He has to have your mind, body *and* soul, and the 'body' part must never slip.

Because he sets himself such high standards, he is probably determined that material security will never be a problem in your relationship together. Of course he can be extravagant at times, but then his instinct invariably enables him to overcome any real financial problems. Besides, you can't have forgotten that he is invincible.

A business relationship with a Scorpio will soon prepare you for the knowledge that in work as in everything else this man has to win. He is absolutely determined to achieve power and success which means that he's invariably much better as a boss than an employee, and as an equal partner rather than one who only holds 40 per cent.

Perhaps on the surface it looks as though this man is so intent on being such a powerful force in every way that living with him could be an unnecessarily exhausting time, a battle of strength in which he simply has to be the victor. But he can be such a devoted husband, so loving with his children, so sensitive and, yes, so vulnerable too.

He's not such a ruthless egomaniac as he's sometimes made out to be or the sex maniac of all time. He's just a passionate believer in life and what it has to offer, and with the right partner by his side he can soar to the heights of happiness. Once you learn to understand him more, to recognize his good points and to realize that often the so-called bad ones are nowhere near as bad as they seem, your relationship with your Scorpio partner will climb from strength to strength.

The art of seduction is something this man knows all about and it's importance can never be understated for you as well. Life with him will be like being on a voyage of discovery which can last for ever more. And since he is always so fascinated by mystery, try to retain a little part of yourself that he never truly knows. It's sure to be difficult – but it's sure to be worthwhile.

High points and lows will invariably occur in your relationship, as they will in any other. But life with a Scorpio man will never be dull. The magnetic charisma of his personality will never lessen; what other man could sweep you off your feet time and time again with just one look from his eyes? Who else could yearn so much for the world to be a better place and do all in his power to try and make it so, and combine so much passion with so much tenderness too? The Eagle soaring to the heights or the Scorpion with its sting – this man's deep-rooted convictions and belief in himself will ensure that your own life would definitely not be the same without him; as if you could ever envision such a thing!

High spots with your Scorpio man
He will

★ Be the dream lover you yearned for all your life.

★ Possess a charisma you've never known before.

★ Help you to learn everything you needed to know about sexual fulfilment.

★ Show you passion with a capital P.

★ Captivate you, mind, body and soul.

217

★ Share his search for the meaning of life with you.
★ Be sensual and sensitive too.
★ Be irresistible for evermore.

Danger zones with your Scorpio man
Never
★ Pry too much.
★ Be too jealous.
★ Be too domineering.
★ Be too tired to make love.
★ Give him any reason to be jealous of you.
★ Find faults in his sexuality.
★ Talk too much about a past lover!
★ Destroy his belief in past and future lives.

★ The Scorpio Woman ★

The Scorpio woman is often sick and tired of being referred to as the 'femme fatale' or Mata Hari of the Zodiac. Lots of women born under this sign are also resentful of being described as sex symbols, refusing to accept it as a compliment and turning it into something negative, when it's not meant that way. However, the Scorpio woman may indeed be incredibly sexy, but she's also a lot more than than, and wants *everything* about her to be recognized.

Scorpio is an extremely strong Feminine Water sign. Your Scorpio woman has two exceedingly powerful planetary rulers, Mars and Pluto, so that exactly like her male counterpart she has a powerful desire to succeed in everything she aims for.

This doesn't mean that she is going to be any less feminine than other women you have known; she is highly sensitive and needs the right man in her life. But like the Scorpio man, deep down she knows that she is invincible and is not going to settle for anything less than the best, no matter how many hurdles she has to overcome in the process.

At first you may have felt as though you were being drawn into the clutches of a spider's web, or pulled like a moth to a flame, when you initially became involved with a Scorpio partner. One look from her eyes and you feel yourself drawn deep inside them. You sensed her mysterious power, drawing you ever closer and perhaps you even became a little frightened. But it's unlikely that you drew away.

The Scorpio woman knows her own power, but it sometimes frightens her a little too. She often feels she has been given an unnecessarily hard time, not just because of those descriptions of her sign, but because she sometimes yearns to be not so strong and so intimidating when she meets a man. She might wonder why she couldn't have been born under one of the other Water signs – Cancer or Pisces, who don't seem to frighten quite so many men away when they tell their star-signs.

Of course if you're genuinely interested in getting to know her better you will soon realize that this woman, who appears to be cool as ice and hard as steel, will be one of the most adorably feminine women you've ever known if she thinks you're the perfect partner for her. Perhaps 'thinks' is the wrong word. The Scorpio woman is so amazingly psychic that she often knows before you do that you fit the bill. The only problem is that because, like the men of her sign, her sexual needs are so important, the sheer sexual chemistry can be so overpowering that she forgets to consider anything else. But if you assume I'm implying that a Scorpio woman is only looking for sexual excitement, and will be content to indulge in lots of quick flings rather than search for a permanent relationship you will have to think again, although she does need sexual fulfilment and would hate to think of a life without it.

Although she may appear to be so strong, she hopes to find her perfect partner just as much as everyone else. She needs someone who appreciates her for what she is, a brave courageous woman who can survive the greatest adversities and still come out on top; someone who can share her deep desire to fathom out all the mysteries as to why we're here and where we're going. She has depths of emotions that she is longing to reveal to the man who can unlock the key to her heart and prove to her that he is the kindred spirit she has been searching for all her life.

Your Scorpio partner can be one of the most amazingly life-enhancing partners in the Zodiac, once she trusts you enough to let herself go. She certainly needs to be convinced that you can see a great deal more than the sex-symbol image with which she's been tagged for far too long, and that you'll be able to have long intelligent conversations with each other far into the night.

Like her male counterpart the Scorpio woman can be exceedingly jealous and possessive. Surely 'Hell hath no vengeance like a woman scorned' can only have been written about a Scorpio! She truly can't cope with the thought that you would betray her by giving yourself to another woman. And if she does have to cope you can be sure she will manage to wreak her own particular vengeance in one way or another. However, since she is not usually the sort of woman you would want to two-time this problem will hopefully not arise.

When she embarks on a relationship which is a perfect blending of mind, body and soul, she definitely wants it to last for ever, and will do everything in her power to ensure that it does. The physical side of your relationship will always be highly important. It's definitely not something which begins to burn itself out as the years go by. She's usually as highly skilled in the art of sexual seduction as everything else, but you would be wise not to ask her too many questions about how she managed to be such a fantastic lover. While she tends to be extremely curious about your own past escapades, she feels she retains the right to keep her own past secrets to herself.

Secrecy is something which could drive you wild about your Scorpio partner until you learn to accept that she has been secretive since she was a little child. Only she doesn't call it secrecy, it's privacy to her. She's always needed those quiet moments to retreat into her own private space, and keeping certain things to herself is an integral part of her nature. But if you're beginning to worry that your Scorpio partner is the sort of woman who is going to be unfaithful and tell you a hundred and one lies, you can forget about that instantly. She is one of the most loyal star-signs in the entire Zodiac just as long as that loyalty is not betrayed in any way. And don't forget that because she is so psychic she would know in a flash if it is!

However, because the sexual side of your relationship *is* so vital to Scorpio, you hopefully won't ever be one of those men who after working all day want to do nothing more than put your feet up in front of the television after she's cooked you an appetizing meal. That's fine on occasion, and she's certainly not going to force you into the bedroom against your will, but her physical desires must not be neglected for too long or she will even begin to believe you don't love her any more.

Living with a Scorpio partner may not always be smooth, and if you want a woman who will never argue with you or make a single criticism, who will do everything you ask without a second thought, you might be asking for more than she can give. Yet deep down she is quite prepared to let herself be dominated by a man she respects in every possible way. Well, perhaps dominated is too strong — but she'll follow you to the ends of the earth if she truly believes you're right. Haven't you yet learned that this woman will never give up on *anything* she feels is right?

You will discover that she sets great store by creating a perfect home for the man in her life. She doesn't like second-best in anything. She will never let you want for a thing if it's in her power to do something about it. She can be extremely good with money until she suddenly decides it's the moment for an extravagant shopping spree, but her instinct usually enables her to know just when to stop, even if she hasn't checked her bank balance first. And while she may not be as outwardly affectionate to her relatives, friends and children, they will never have cause to doubt that she cares about them. But don't expect her to mix too often with people she really cannot stand — she'll never forgive you! And forgiveness is something that is truly hard for her. Both forgiving and forgetting are not easy for the typical Scorpio of either sex, no matter how much they try. And that is definitely something to remember when lovers' tiffs arise between you too.

In a business relationship with a Scorpio woman, her determination to suceed is immediately apparent, and again it can be almost frightening the way she seems to have such a power complex, determined to climb to the top, and she can of course be jealous if she feels anyone is unfairly promoted over her. But again, she'll be extremely loyal and dependable as a colleague, and her intuition will always prove invaluable when important decisions need to be made.

Twisting a Scorpio woman around your little finger to ensure she remains by your side forever will invariably be an impossibility unless *she* has decided that's where she wants to be. But once you have learnt how to convince her that you can be the strong and understanding soulmate she has always searched for – that you, and you alone, can provide her with that blissful blend of mental and physical compatibility on every conceivable level (and once she's aware that she can let herself be a truly feminine woman and not just a sex symbol in your eyes) you will find it amazingly easy to make your relationship become stronger day by day.

Always try to remember her need for passion in her life and let her feel that you admire her strengths and can cope with any weaknesses she may suddenly display. Sometimes you'll think she is a woman who will always be one of life's true mysteries – but what a wonderful time you'll have getting to know her more and more. As long as you remain a winner in her eyes, you'll be one of the luckiest men around, and any low spots in your relationship will be more than compensated for by the high spots you enjoy together.

High spots with your Scorpio woman
She will

★ Be the most seductive woman you've ever known.
★ Help you to fight to achieve your highest hopes.
★ Be passionately interested in every aspect of life.
★ Amaze you with her ability to overcome problems.
★ Make physical and mental compatibility seem impossible with anyone but her.
★ Inspire you with her loyalty.
★ Delight you with her emotions.
★ Let you finally understand what ecstasy really means.

Danger zones with your Scorpio woman
Never

★ Play around with anyone else.

★ Unjustly accuse her of doing the same.
★ Push her too far.
★ Expect her to tell you *everything*.
★ Forget she can't forgive or forget easily.
★ Try to dominate her totally.
★ Show too many signs of weakness.
★ Go on too much about that 'sex symbol' description!

The Sagittarius Partner

★ The Sagittarius Man ★

If you're looking for a partner who will be the best friend you ever had in your life, you don't have to look any further than Mr Sagittarius.

However, convincing him to spend the rest of his life with you is not always the easiest task in the world. Indeed, for him to contemplate spending the rest of his life with *anyone* is sometimes almost impossible for him to imagine.

This lovable, happy-go-lucky man can be perfectly capable of bouncing into your life one minute and bouncing out again without even realizing the impact he has made. He will bowl you over with his charm, delight you with his sense of humour — his ability play the fool one minute and philosophize the next. It's not just Librans and Geminis who can charm the birds down from the trees — your Sagittarian man can teach even them a few tricks. He might even remind you of that boy next door you always hoped would stop treating you like someone's kid sister and let you tag along with him and his pals who always seemed to have such a great time while you toiled through your homework (and naturally he still passed all his exams).

And yet if he has decided he wants to know you better, you'll discover it fast. This man doesn't like to take no for an answer and he won't be put off by any apparent lack of interest. Besides, he can't *imagine* that you wouldn't want to be with him.

He won't sulk if you always appear to be busy and you don't answer the phone messages right away. Things like that don't bother the Sagittarius man − he's an incurable optimist and he's quite prepared to take the gamble that you'll see the error of your ways by not spending some time in his company.

Sagittarius is a Masculine Positive Mutable Fire sign − the explorer of the Zodiac, sign of the higher mind, the long-distance traveller. Ruled by the lucky planet Jupiter, his planetary symbol is the Centaur half-man/half-horse, aiming his arrow as far as it can reach. Your Sagittarius man was born with insatiable curiosity, a need to search for truth in all its forms, however long it takes.

It's best to warn you from the beginning that the Sagittarian man is one of the most restless of men. His wanderlust doesn't diminish with the passing years; Sagittarians can't imagine getting older anyway, and they seem to retain their youthful image long after many of the other star-signs. But this doesn't mean that he's going to be a womanizer, the sort of playboy you had always warned your friends to keep away from; and had steered very clear of yourself. What you have to remember from the start of any relationship with a Sagittarius man is that he loves people, *all* people, and the more the merrier. He is one of the friendliest, most open characters around. He loves to communicate, that's what being born under a Mutable sign is all about. You also have to keep in mind that within his personality is something of his opposite sign of Gemini, that other master of communication. And it's surely no coincidence that both Gemini and Sagittarius are dual signs − the Twins and that half-man/half-horse Centaur. What may seem like flirting doesn't have to mean anything more than the fact that he enjoys talking with a pretty woman and listening to what she has to say. That's the way he sees it, and that's probably the way it is. So you don't have to get yourself into a state by reading it all a whole different way. Of course, if you're a Taurus or Scorpio you will have to learn to control your jealous feelings a little better if you're involved with a Sagittarius man.

You can't usually force him into anything against his will. It's not that he is averse to listening to all the reasons as to why it might be best for him to do something a different way, but he has such an infallible faith in himself that he truly believes he knows all the right answers. He loves to give advice, and is often described as 'The Sage' or 'Counsellor' of the Zodiac, but that's quite a different thing to taking it! So never push him too hard.

It might seem that a relationship with a Sagittarian man will have more than its normal share of ups and downs, that he sounds as though he's much too selfish or self-centred to ever be a perfect partner, but that is wrong. It's true that he seems to know exactly what he wants – and doesn't want; and that his free-and-easy attitude to life could perhaps make it impossible for him ever to settle down. But think of all the Sagittarian men who are blissfully happy in permanent relationships. Perhaps some of them have had previous long-term involvements or marriages before their current ones but you may not know the reasons they had failed.

A relationship with a lovable Sagittarian can bring you everything you ever dreamed of. Do you honestly think he isn't searching for that ideal soulmate as hopefully as everyone else? And do you really think that once he found her he'd want to roam off searching for someone new? So be as optimistic as he can be – it really does work.

He's well aware that he needs a woman who has an independent spirit, someone who will understand that the way to keep him by her side is to let him feel inwardly free and never trapped, someone who will share his enthusiasm for the good things in life, and never quench his optimistic spirits by being a pessimist. Nothing is guaranteed to depress your Sagittarian man more than being with someone who has a *constantly* bleak viewpoint on life.

He won't try to interfere with your career, your family, your friends in any way at all and equally he won't expect you to interfere in his. Of course he will expect you to be able to get along with everyone he likes, and he probably won't understand at all if you find reasons for disliking anyone whom he had chosen to be a friend, but never fake your feelings. Furthermore, he is totally honest about everything. Sometimes you'll be more

inclined to call it downright tactlessness and be hurt by yet
another of his outspoken remarks just when you were expecting
to receive a compliment. But surely you'd rather have things this
way than be with a man you subconsciously suspected of lying
through his teeth. At least with your Sagittarian partner you will
always be able to discuss any problems openly and frankly, and
it's surely better to put up with a few hurts than go through
endless worries if difficulties do arise.

Once you have embarked on a relationship with a Sagittarian
you will discover that his 'I want to be free' ideal doesn't mean
that he doesn't fall as passionately in love as anyone else. He's
a Fire sign, remember, and can be as headstrong and impulsive
as any Aries where his heart is involved.

He is also not quite so convinced as it might appear that 'till
death us do part' are words he doesn't want to hear. Once the
Sagittarian man is happily involved in a relationship with a
woman with whom he can really communicate on a mental and
physical level, who can be *his* best friend the way he wants to be
yours, so many of his fears will disappear.

You will also have to remember that Sagittarius will probably
expect you to have a suitcase permanently packed so that you
can take off on a sudden trip together, typical of one of his spur-
of-the-moment ideas; to make sure that sport or an outdoor sort
of life isn't something you view with total horror; and that
though he might not be the strictest father in the world he always
has an ability to get on famously with his children and obtain
their total trust.

Problems in a relationship with Sagittarius can arise over
money. He's not only extremely generous, but extremely
extravagant too. Invariably he tends to have his blind faith that
everything will always come out in the wash, and consequently
he will sometimes take risks and gambles that terrify you, unless
you're born under his same lucky star.

Try to encourage his aims and ambitions, but don't be afraid
to speak out if there really is a serious issue and too many bills
start to remain unpaid, especially as he probably hasn't noticed
them anyway, and even if he has they often slip his mind. He
certainly doesn't want a woman who is frightened to speak her

mind, not when he is so open about everything he feels himself. But neither does he want someone who thinks she can boss him around from morning to night. He needs to feel that you are his equal if your partnership is to be a strong one.

And although he puts such great store on being the best of friends, you definitely mustn't take this to mean that sex isn't important to your Sagittarius man, even if your relationship did start off in such a casual friendly way. He will display plenty of fiery passion when it comes to making love, and he'll be as optimistic as he is about everything else about sex becoming more and more satisfying to you both as time goes on. He'll always delight you with his tender amusing little stories as you curl up in bed. Sex is one more searching quest for adventure in his book, and he might well be one of the most inventive lovers you've ever met. Never be shy about experimenting as you get to know each other better. Sex will be not only passionate with your Sagittarian partner but it can also be great fun too.

Physical compatibility alone will never satisfy him completely, for he is searching for a soulmate. Perhaps that's why he sometimes takes so long to be convinced it's time for him to put down roots. You see, he really can't see settling for anything but the best. It's the gambling instinct he was born with, aiming for the highest stakes, convinced he's going to win, maybe not today or even tomorrow, but some day not too far away.

A business relationship with Sagittarius will inevitably instil you with as much optimism as he possesses himself. You might sometimes wonder if you will be able to pin him down long enough ever to get anything done – but you will. He will be an enthusiastic, fair and extremely loyal colleague. But his enthusiasm will sometimes outweigh his instinct, or perhaps it's just that he's so determined to reach for the top that he will gamble yet again even if the odds are impossible. He needs a partner who will temper this with logic, passed on in a really tactful way, of course.

If you're still wondering how to twist this man around your little finger so that he can be yours for ever more, without his Sagittarian wanderlust burning too bright in his heart, just remember to be always yourself. Any forms of pretence or hypocrisy, lies (even the whitest ones) will upset him more than you would ever believe.

Never be too possessive or clinging, or forget to show sufficient interest in the things in which he believes. And always let him realize that you will continue to be his best friend as well as being the woman he loves. If he has been hurt in the past by women who tried to possess his body without bothering to understand his inner needs, it is even more important to let him see that you would never act that way. Show that you are quite prepared to be a loving and devoted wife and mother as long as he's willing to work equally hard at preserving the perfect relationship as you are.

Best friends and perfect partners — could you really want for anything more?

High spots with your Sagittarius man
He will

★   Always be your best friend as well as your lover.
★   Be the most positive and optimistic man you've ever met.
★   Make your life a constant adventure.
★   Take you off on trips to places you've always yearned to visit.
★   Help you to see the funny side of life.
★   Always let you retain your independence.
★   Give you masses of moral support and encouragement.
★   Always be honest with you.

Danger zones with your Sagittarius man
Never

★   Let him think you can be too negative.
★   Try to fence him in too much — he needs to feel inwardly free!
★   Boss him around.
★   Be too lazy — he likes an energetic life.
★   Encourage him to gamble — it could become a habit!
★   Tell him you know better than him — even if you do.
★   Ever expect too many effusive declarations of love, unless he has a Pisces Ascendant!
★   Live in too small a space with him — he cannot bear to feel confined.

★ The Sagittarius Woman ★

The Sagittarian woman can probably do a great many things better than you − or at least that's the way she sees it.

It's not that she sets herself up to be as much of a perfectionist as a Virgo, or that she has always considered men to be the weaker sex − simply that just like her male counterpart she has an unquenchable optimism and total faith in herself and her beliefs.

It's true that she is born under a Masculine sign but that doesn't mean she's not a real woman. Independent and high-spirited, capable of tackling any adversities which come her way with amazing strength, she is quite prepared to be submissive sometimes when the perfect partner is part of her life. But never forget that word 'sometimes' for you're not likely to get her agreeing to anything which is totally against her will.

In the beginning you may have wondered if she was ever the slightest bit interested in you when you first met your Sagittarian woman. She seemed to be just as friendly with all the other men around as she was with you. Or did you sense that she perhaps glanced your way more than once when she thought you weren't looking? And did her smile seem even brighter when you began to have an interesting chat?

You will learn to realize that Ms Sagittarius is almost always friendly and bright, that she enjoys meeting new people, and learning more about them, for friendship is definitely one of the most important parts of life to her. She isn't usually the sort of woman who can be swept off her feet, although naturally that must also depend on her own particular horoscope too. But deep down she is also searching for a soulmate, someone who is going to appreciate her enthusiasm, her optimistic views and her honesty.

However, perhaps more than many other woman she is totally capable of living on her own and getting the maximum enjoyment out of life. She isn't someone who will give up her freedom just for the sake of having a man in her life, until she's sure he really is the right man. When she's young this isn't always so. Love and romance excite her as much as anyone else. But a

Sagittarian woman who has been through a difficult relationship or marriage which ended because it was wrong in the very beginning won't be in too much of a hurry to settle down again.

Perhaps you're already thinking you're in for a hard time, having decided that your perfect partner is a Sagittarian woman. And if you don't understand that she really does need her inner freedom to be at her best, then it might have been best to cut your losses and search for a different star-sign.

To understand your Sagittarian partner totally you need to realize that she is well aware that her independence can sometimes put men off; that they think she's going to boss them around far too much, and that her sense of humour can be just a little too risqué. But the nonchalant devil-may-care attitude with which she appears to prance through life doesn't have to mean that there haven't been times when she's been lonely too. Just because she attracts people to her side it doesn't always mean they've been people she wanted to be with, but this friendly warm-hearted woman would never want to hurt anyone's feelings, so make sure you never deliberately hurt hers.

The third, and last, of the Fire signs, your Sagittarian woman has such a fantastic zest for life that it won't take long before you wonder how you managed to enjoy anything without her. But if you want her to enjoy being with you on a permanent basis you will have to convince her that you won't try hard to pin her down from the very start. Flattery might delight her but she'll see through you in a shot if you overdo it. Bossing her around will infuriate her if she's in one of her 'I can do it better myself' moods, and simply assuming that good sex is sufficient to keep her interested in you will only mean you're in for a shock.

You have to remember that the Sagittarian personality has two distinct parts – the fun-loving side and the far more philosophical one. Your Sagittarian woman can switch from one to another just as easily as a Gemini woman can switch her roles. But which ever part she's playing she is still the explorer discovering new aspects of life.

Perhaps one of the reasons that she sets so much store by friendship is that she knows that love can be blind, certainly in the heat of passion. She won't rush into a relationship until you've proved you *will* be her friend as well as her lover so that the two go hand in hand. But you don't have to think that she doesn't set too much store by the sexual side of your relationship, for she can be as passionate a partner as any other woman. It's just that seduction also needs to be fun as well. Since she is usually the proud possessor of a great sense of humour, a man who is intensely emotional but unable to laugh at himself if she pokes fun at him for coming on too strong might not share her bed for very long. So vow to yourself that you'll never let your own sense of humour slip.

But don't start to worry that your Sagittarian woman thinks that sex is only a game. Remember that she is a Fire sign, and her sexual fulfilment is highly important to her. She also wants you to feel as emotionally fulfilled as possible and for you to share some wonderfully passionate moments together.

This cheerful, optimistic and adventurous woman often gambles for high stakes in love in much the same way as she is prepared to gamble with other things in her life. Just like her male counterpart, she's not frightened to take risks. And knowing that she has such an independent spirit you may be concerned that she is more likely to play around with other men. But then you don't know her very well yet. She is much too open and honest to want to hurt anyone she loves by fooling around. A friendly flirtation, which is really just a game of verbal dexterity, is one thing. But the sort of 'triangle' situation where she has to play the 'other woman' is never one she finds very easy.

It's not as difficult as it may seem to tame her restless spirit so that she never wants to leave you. Just because she's often so used to sailing through life with a great deal of ease it doesn't mean she wouldn't be happier with the perfect partner by her side. And if she truly believes you're the right man, she won't worry too much about your financial prospects, or what is going to happen in the future. Her optimism shines through and enables her to see beyond any immediate problems which could arise; and she won't show much patience if you're the one who starts showing too many doubts. If she thinks something is going to work out well, she's sure to have the ability to persuade you to think the same way.

Living with a Sagittarian partner is a definite bonus. Her delight in life will inspire you, and the wonderful atmosphere of equality will make you feel totally at ease. Sometimes she will be incredibly serious about life, sometimes she'll make you laugh more than anyone has ever done before. But she will never bore you.

She may not appear to be the sort of woman who enjoys housework – but she'll surprise you on every count. She will probably be better at DIY jobs than you are; be able to entertain a dozen people to a *haute cuisine* meal at the shortest possible notice, and boost your spirits any time you feel down. But she'll definitely want to keep up with her own interests too. And she will expect you to get along with her family and friends in the same relaxed and easy way that she does.

Just like her male counterpart she often thrives on a sporty outdoor sort of life. She will usually be a marvellous mother, with the ability to stay young at heart and have a great communication with her children, even if she is sometimes a little too convinced that her advice is always right.

In a business relationship with a Sagittarius woman you have someone who will always get things done no matter how long they take. The words 'it can't be done' simply don't exist in her vocabulary. She will put the same optimism and enthusiasm into a career that she puts into every other aspect of her life. She's a true go-getter and thrives on challenges. She will also relate well to her fellow-workers. She is the sort of partner everyone needs, provided that her tendency to take risks is tactfully curbed from time to time.

Sagittarius is a strong sign, the Archer aiming his arrows out into the world isn't just aiming them anywhere. Discovery and exploration are what Sagittarius is all about, searching for truth. Sagittarius is also the sign of the 'higher mind' and your Sagittarian partner will always be interested in learning more about life.

Twisting a Sagittarian woman around your little finger to keep her there for ever might have seemed impossible at first, knowing how restless she can be, so always remember to indulge the wanderlust in her spirit. Plan exciting holidays together as often as possible, and the further afield the better. Keep the fires of passion burning but remember how much she needs to think of you as her friend too. This intelligent and honest woman needs to be convinced that she is with a man who really does want a soulmate in every way, a perfect companion who is also a perfect lover. Then she can be yours for ever.

She may give the impression of wanting things to be done *her* way an awful lot of the time, but since she was born under a Mutable sign you'll soon find she's actually very adaptable, as long as you don't boss her around too much. But just like her male counterpart she can sometimes be a little too extravagant with money. It's not that she's the sort of person who will want to spend a fortune on herself. She's just amazingly generous and warm-hearted, and her gambling instinct might sometimes lead her astray too. Difficulties can obviously arise if this ever gets out of hand, but she is invariably much too bright and intelligent to let this happen.

Life is definitely meant to be for living as far as your Sagittarius partner is concerned. And she is determined that problems can always be resolved if they're worked at in the right way. So it really shouldn't be hard to make the high spots of your relationship outweigh any low points, if you're as positive and honest as she will always be.

High spots with your Sagittarius woman
She will

★ Always be your equal in every possible way.

★ Bring you excitement, mental stimulation and fantastic friendship.

★ Always be honest with you.

★ Be romantic, sexy and have a great sense of humour too.

★ Be wonderfully free-spirited and independent.

★ Be eternally optimistic.

★ Accept your friends as her friends too.

★ Be loyal, loving and lovable.

Danger zones with your Sagittarius woman
Never

★ Refuse her the independence which she allows you.

★ Accuse her of neglecting you for her friends — she needs you all.
★ Let her think you don't trust her.
★ Forget to stimulate her mind as well as her body.
★ Question the love she feels for you.
★ Try to quench her wanderlust spirit.
★ Let her be too extravagant too often.
★ Ever lose your sense of the absurd.

The Capricorn Partner

★ The Capricorn Man ★

Have you always dreamed of having a perfect relationship with a man you will always be able to rely on? Someone who realizes the importance of emotional fulfilment and material security too. Someone who doesn't indulge in idle flirtations and doesn't underestimate the seriousness of life in these troubled days? Are you prepared to wait perhaps longer than you've ever waited before to convince the man of your dreams that if he's searching for a perfect partner he needs to look no further than you?

Of course if you're expecting instant gratification; for someone to be so bowled over by your sexy body or your scintillating conversation that he proposes almost on the spot, you'd really better concentrate on a different star-sign − for unless your Capricorn man has lots of Fire signs in his chart, or a Scorpio Ascendant, he's much too staid and laid-back ever to behave like that.

Saturn is the planetary ruler of this sign. Poor old Saturn, always maligned for giving everyone problems when he passes through their birthsigns. The truth of the matter is that Saturn, known as the Taskmaster of the Zodiac, is concerned greatly with time. In Greek mythology he was known as Cronus − old Father Time himself − but Saturn, while often giving us some hard lessons to learn, also brings the greatest rewards in the end.

The point of all this is to help you understand your Capricorn partner a little better; for Saturn's transit through the Zodiac takes between 28 and 30 years to return to its original place and no matter where it was placed in your partner's natal horoscope, you can almost bet your life that the first 28 − 30 years of *his* life will not have always been the best he could have wished for. Then suddenly things will start to improve − those rewards start to come flowing in, and your Capricorn partner will discover his life gets better and better all the way along.

Are you beginning to understand why your Capricorn man sometimes seems to have such a serious view on life? Why he doesn't always find it so easy to relax and have as much fun as some of the star-signs you have known before?

And there's more to come. Capricorn is a Cardinal sign, just like Aries, Cancer and Libra. Your Capricorn man is born to be a leader − and there is one thing you will soon discover − he doesn't care how long it takes him to succeed in his aims and ambitions, as long as he gets there in the end. His planetary symbol is the Mountain Goat − and just think about the way this animal manages to surmount the obstacles of nature to reach that mountain peak − just like your Capricorn man.

Material success is highly important to this Earth sign, especially if he had a difficult childhood; and even if he didn't he'll be determined to scale his own mountain top. Sometimes he can be such a workaholic that it's hard for him to find a woman he can relate to who will truly understand his disciplined approach to life. He seems to be so self-sufficient. Or are you beginning to realize that it might appear that way because he's become so used to hiding his deepest feelings for so long that he's now scared to let them show at all?

You should remember that he is a total believer in tradition and conformity. Love leads to marriage, children, and growing old together, in his book. He's not out for one night stands, holiday romances, and the chance to change partners from one month to another (unless his personal chart has definite reasons to contradict this!) − apart from anything else he simply doesn't have time for all that. Life is a very serious business for your Capricorn partner, as you must have begun to see by now. But if you're also beginning to wonder if romantic tenderness will be sadly lacking in a relationship with this man, you really don't have to worry, for you'll learn to bring it out.

The opposite sign to Capricorn is Cancer, and beneath the Goat's somewhat stern exterior lurks a man who is just as sentimental as any Crab. He doesn't necessarily want to admit it, but that's another thing. You also have to remember that if his first thirty years were indeed more demanding than he'd have chosen, it's equally possible that his first experiences in love didn't live up to his expectations; that his heart was badly burnt, and that he's vowed to be more discriminating in his search for the perfect partner.

Discriminating — does that sound an awful word to use about your Capricorn man? Is he really as critical as Virgo? Is he going to sum up every aspect of your character and give you points from one to ten? Saturn is his personal Taskmaster but are you about to have a Taskmaster in your life too? (For if *you're* also a Capricorn you'll know just what that means.) Don't start getting into a panic. It's not like an exam you have to pass before you can move on into the next class. Your Capricorn partner simply has to be practical — he's been like that all his life. He knows that a relationship has to work on all levels to be truly successful — and isn't that what you want it to be too? Just like that other Earth sign Taurus, your Capricorn man needs to feel incredibly sure about you before he can contemplate a blissful life together for ever more. He doesn't want to take any risks and love is definitely not a game for him.

But once this man has reached the conclusion that the two of you could make a wonderful team, he's not going to take a 'no' from you. His courtship might not be the most exciting you've ever known, and you will probably have to cope with phone calls from his place of work telling you he has to finish some important tasks before he can get away (and that's one thing which will never change once you're involved with the No. 1 workaholic in the entire Zodiac). But isn't it a wonderful feeling to know that you've met a man who really is reliable and will never wittingly do anything to hurt you?

Just because he may not outwardly seem to be the exceptionally passionate type, you'd be surprised how quickly he can let himself go when he wants you to enjoy sexual fulfilment. It's often said that Capricorns seem to get younger as the years creep on – and his physical desires and ability to be the perfect lover will probably be your confirmation of that!

If you're wondering just what he'd be like to live with, you surely must have gained more than a few inklings by now. You'll have to show him that you're quite prepared to respect and trust him, accept his constructive advice, and live up to his expectations of what his perfect partner should be.

Is it beginning to seem unequal? Are his expectations going to mean that you'd be tied to a life which only revolved around him? You'd be getting him wrong if that's what you think. He believes in duty and responsibility but he would never ask anyone to give up their own independence completely for him. Just show him you're quite prepared to love, cherish and obey him in principle, retaining your rights to disagree when his Saturnine personality makes that 'taskmaster' personality too much to bear, and you'll be on the right track to convince him even more that he's found the woman who can be his ideal mate.

Of course there are bound to be problems if you're the spendthrift of all time; even if you only occasionally slip and allow yourself to spend extravagantly you're sure to be in his bad books. More than almost any other sign he knows how money problems can create real problems in a relationship no matter how perfect it might seem in other ways. He also knows how long it can take to build up the material security for which all Capricorns yearn.

You'll always have to remember that this man is invariably born with a pessimistic approach to life, even though he probably would tell you that it's realism – not pessimism. Call it what you will, but you'll never get him to trust to luck (unless he has a Sagittarius Ascendant), and hopefully you'll learn to ensure that the housekeeping budget never goes way over the top.

He certainly won't expect you to give up your own career just because you're living with him. He will support and encourage you to achieve your own ambitions in the same way that he'll want you to do for him. However, there can be a selfish, almost ruthless, side to the Capricorn man. He sometimes does set such

239

store by material security and the right social background that relationships and marriages can founder if there is little else to bind them together.

He sometimes doesn't realize that the power of love is incredibly important, and it's a lesson he needs to learn. In a working relationship with a Capricorn you certainly don't ever have to fear that the workload will be too heavy for him. But remember that he will be determined to climb to the top and you could be left out on a limb if you're not prepared to put as much effort into everything as he does. In business, just like in every other aspect of his life, he's cautious, highly organized, and a hundred per cent realistic. And when it comes to raising a family, he'll have very definite ideas of where the children must go to school and be a loving but often stern disciplinarian.

Loyal and devoted, calm and understanding, your Capricorn man has his wonderfully dependable personality which will make you realize just how marvellous it can be to watch a relationship grow from strength; to learn from each other's vulnerabilities, to accept each other's idiosyncracies and plan for a better world together.

To twist this partner round your little finger so that he will be yours for ever means you must try never to let him down in any way at all. Show him that his pessimism can be forgotten – you will teach him the joys of a more optimistic approach to life. Don't give him any reasons to feel jealous about you, for jealousy is not something he's comfortable with; it's far too much of a weakness in his book. And always realize that he's not quite as self-sufficient as he seems. He's only learnt to make himself that way in his journey up that ladder to success.

Just because your Capricorn man is such a strong shoulder for others to lean on it doesn't mean that he's not vulnerable as well. It doesn't matter how long it might take you to make him see you as his perfect partner, for the happiness you can bring each other by enjoying total trust and watching your relationship become more and more idyllic is something which can never be under valued.

If he sometimes infuriates you by being too materialistic, by having such exceptionally high standards – do you really think that's so bad? His purpose in life is to make things succeed in the best possible way — and that's surely a good maxim to remember when embarking on a relationship with him!

Of course you're not going to have a charmed life just because you've become involved with a Capricorn man. But you wouldn't have that with any other sign either! And isn't it fantastic to know that emotional insecurity is something you're never likely to experience with your Capricorn partner — unless he lets his work take over his life. For with you beside him he can be convinced for ever more that a totally fulfilling relationship means searching for that perfect balance of mind, body and soul, and watching it grow.

High spots with your Capricorn man
He will
★ Be a loyal, dependable tower of strength.
★ Ensure you never want for anything.
★ Be a tender and considerate lover.
★ Be determined to succeed at his chosen profession to bring you greater security than ever.
★ Do everything possible to ensure that your relationship grows from strength to strength.
★ Be a supportive partner, full of constructive advice.
★ Be realistic, with his feet firmly on the ground.
★ Stick by your side through thick and thin.

Danger zones with your Capricorn man
Never
★ Embarrass him by being too sexy in public.
★ Be dishonest with him.
★ Let him think that you could be a spendthrift.
★ Criticize any of the other people in his life.
★ Try to pry him away from his workaholic ways.
★ Ever accuse him of being a snob — even if he is sometimes!
★ Be too disorganized.
★ Put him down in front of anyone.

★ The Capricorn Woman ★

Capricorn is a Cardinal Negative Feminine sign, and while your Capricorn woman can be just as feminine as anyone else, she has a steely strength about her, an icy determination to make her way through life that sometimes makes men fear that embarking on a relationship with her could be a daunting experience.

So perhaps the first thing to be aware of is that, just like her male counterpart, your Capricorn woman is firmly under the influence of her ruling planet Saturn. Saturn's negative qualities are gloom and pessimism. But this planet truly can bring great rewards for those who are determined that its limitations will not get them down. And there aren't many people more determined than Capricorns!

Even if the first part of your Capricorn woman's life did seem to have more pitfalls than high spots, she's sure to have sailed through them all with flying colours. But remember that she sets very high standards for everything, and that includes finding the perfect partner.

Becoming involved with a Capricorn partner is not usually something which happens overnight. She won't rush into your arms, convinced you're the be all and end all of her life even if the sexual chemistry between you is sizzling wildly. Besides, if she's a typical Capricorn she won't allow her physical feelings to show until she's got to know you a lot better. And that's not going to happen until she knows more about who you are, where you're from and where you intend to go in life.

At this point she might even lose out on the chance of meeting the perfect partner by appearing to be, sorry Capricorn, snobbish and calculating. It's all down to those high standards which sometimes do give her a harder time than most women in finding emotional contentment with the man of their dreams. But the whole point of learning more about her is to discover that this might be an important facet of her personality but it's definitely not the only one. Once you have started to know her better, you'll soon see that the Capricorn woman can be one of the most lovable and loyal partners you could ever hope to meet. It's simply that she takes the same serious view of life as her male counterpart. She knows the value of security and consequently the knowledge of just what that entails.

Very often the Capricorn woman (but this will also depend on her own personal horoscope) is drawn to men older than herself. It could be that she is searching for a father figure, perhaps because of her childhood experiences, or that she feels an older man will be more likely to provide her with the security she needs. A failed relationship in her life is often more likely to have failed because of serious financial problems than almost any other reason.

Although it isn't money *per se* which is her ultimate criteria in life, she understands the value of it for future security – and more than most of the other star-signs. Certainly she doesn't want to indulge herself extravagantly. With a Capricorn woman, that building for the future together can be one of the most rewarding experiences you've ever known. She's not looking for a part-time relationship, an idle fling to satisfy herself that she's capable of attracting any man she wants; her morals are invariably strict, and being part of a triangle relationship is never something she could take very easily.

And you don't have to worry that she's the sort of woman who is going to start bossing you around from morning to night, urging you to work harder, get another promotion, buy a bigger house. She certainly doesn't want a hen-pecked man around her side, and while she has a shoulder big enough for both of you to lean on, deep down she needs a partner who will enable her to let her defences slip just a little and be as emotionally sentimental as Cancer or Pisces without it seeming that she's allowed herself to be weak.

With her deep-rooted belief in the sanctity of marriage, and her strong allegiance to traditional ties, she will not only be an incredibly devoted and supportive partner, but will display those same characteristics to her family and friends as well.

With a Capricorn woman by your side you will soar to greater heights, knowing that you have someone who totally believes in you in every way, for how could she be with you otherwise? Equally she will demand from you the same support and allegiance; the same encouragement with her own particular aims and ambitions. She doesn't want a 'yes' man as a partner, and she definitely doesn't expect to be treated as a glorified housekeeper by you. But of course you've already realized that for yourself!

Your Capricorn partner will manage to hold down a strenuous working life and still ensure that your domestic situation doesn't suffer one bit. She probably won't even have anyone to help her with the housework. She's practical, extremely well-organized and is never going to waste any precious time when she knows there is work to be done. That's something Saturn taught her long ago when she was still a child.

Besides, even when she *was* a child your Capricorn woman probably related better to adults than playmates of her own age. It's almost as though Capricorns become adults earlier than any other signs. And just like the male Goats, the Capricorn woman seems to become younger as the years go by, especially after she's reached the age of thirty. And she'll enjoy hearing you tell her this.

Calm, practical and serious − are there no erotic yearnings deep below the surface of this feminine Earth sign? Is friendship more important in her life than sexual fulfilment? Will she sometimes turn over and yawn when your desires are crying out to be satisfied? Will she insist on discussing the economic instability in the world when you're longing for her to cuddle up close beside you and give you a passionate kiss? Just because she can be brilliantly adept at disciplining herself in the strongest possible way, you don't have to worry that she might have sublimated her sexual desires in her search for material security. It might take more time for your Capricorn partner to become as uninhibited in the art of love-making as some of the more outwardly passionate signs, but when she knows she's with the right partner she's quite prepared to let herself go and enjoy the delights of making love.

In a business relationship with a Capricorn woman you'll have a lot to live up to. She will probably be the dominant one in any partnership, and her purpose in life is quite definitely to climb right to the top. But there is no way she will ever gamble − not when her security is at sake! And she will also fight to the bitter end to protect the security of her loved ones. Sometimes people sarcastically describe the Capricorn woman as a social climber, who will leave no stone unclimbed to get to the top just like the Mountain Goat which is the planetary symbol of her sign. But every sign has its positive and negative qualities – and Capricorn has no more or less than anyone else.

Being part of the right social set and living in the right part of town might be important on the surface to your Capricorn woman, and being able to send her children to a good school where they receive the best possible education will certainly be one of her priorities – but she isn't usually the sort of woman who would sell her soul for material security without any love involved. Her puritanical morals would stop her from doing that. But then half the battle of getting what you really want out of life is actually knowing what that is and then putting out the positive thoughts to attract it. Your Capricorn woman is perfectly capable of sending out her own positive thoughts to attract a partner who is as financially secure as he is emotionally appealing. Anyone is – but then she has the patience and determination to wait, knowing that long-term security is what life is all about to her.

So if you want to twist your Capricorn partner around your little finger to keep her there on a long-term basis, you'll have to let her see that she doesn't have to worry about the future with you around; that you'll do everything in your power to keep her respect and love; will always understand her need to keep her own identity and achieve her own personal successes, and will never ever be a spendthrift. Let her realize that she can start to relax and enjoy life more and always remember to bring a little more romance into her life too.

Growing up was probably a serious business for your Capricorn woman, but deep inside her personality there is still a little girl longing to believe that she's found the perfect partner who can make her happier than she's ever been before. She wants the high spots of your relationship to far outweigh any low ones – so do everything you can to keep them that way.

High spots with your Capricorn woman
She will

★ Be totally dedicated to the people she loves.

★ The wisest woman you've ever known.

★ Always have her priorities right.

★ Help you keep your own feet on terra firma.

★ Work hard to create a perfect lasting relationship.

★ Manage to combine a successful career with a successful home life too.

★ Always impress you with her ability to do *everything* so well.

★ Become even more wonderful as the years go by.

Danger zones with your Capricorn woman
Never

★ Complain about feeling neglected if she's working hard to help bring in extra money.

★ Criticize her for being 'cold' just because she finds it hard to let herself go sexually.

★ Underestimate her need for security in every possible form.

★ Let her down by breaking a promise.

★ Be too serious — she's serious enough for both of you and needs to laugh a little more.

★ Accuse her of flirting with anyone else.

★ Criticize her dress sense — she's usually elegance personified.

The Aquarius Partner

★ The Aquarius Man ★

Are you ready for a relationship with the most original man in the Zodiac? That's how I like to think of Aquarius, for 'unpredictable' and 'unconventional' are descriptions given to him with good reason. Your Aquarian man never will conform to any preconceived pattern. He is a complete individualist, and that's the way he wants it to be.

If your idea of bliss is a life which tends to go on in the same way from day to day, and your perfect partner must never have moods which can change without a moment's warning, Aquarius is not the man for you (unless his personal horoscope reassures you otherwise!).

At the start of a relationship with an Aquarian man you'll warm to his friendly enthusiastic manner, and be thrilled to discover how brilliantly adept he is at the art of conversation. You'll love the little twinkle in his clear blue eyes (yes, they often are!) when they catch yours, and you'll long to get to know him better. But, you may have to wait a while to get to know him really well; or, for that platonic friendship with him to develop into something deeper.

However, it's not that the Aquarian man likes playing hard to get — or has a Libran Ascendant, making him indecisive — for him friendship is one thing and a love relationship is something totally different. For Aquarius *is* the sign of friendship, and

Aquarians love to be everybody's friend. Some of them are actually much better at being friends to the world in general than coping with their closest ties. It's not that they're selfish and avoid deep involvement with anyone. It's just that, in general, they sometimes seem to find it hard to communicate on an intensely personal one-to-one basis. So if you're in a relationship with an Aquarian man, it's best for you to know from the start that even if he is madly in love with you it can often be hard for him to express his innermost feelings. Therefore remember to reassure him that you understand this, and don't accuse him of loving you any less. Besides, just when you've given up expecting to hear those few sentimental words from his lips, your Aquarian man – demonstrating again just how unpredictable he is – will whisper wonderful words of sincere devotion!

Sometimes, Aquarians are accused of being cold and unfeeling – but that is so unfair. You have to understand that he has to rationalize everything he says and does – but isn't that often better than rushing headlong into situations without thought? If you want to have a perfect relationship with your Aquarius man it will help to be a 'people' person just like him. But while he will love to meet your friends and be curious about your interests, he will soon start to sulk if they take over to the extent that he feels left out in the cold. Once he's given his heart to you, he needs to feel he's as important to you as you are to him, yet it can take quite a long time before he totally believes he has found the one woman in the world who can be his soulmate on every level. You'll discover along the way that he can often be more vulnerable than he appears; although he'd probably be horrified to know that he's given this away; so remember always to be subtle – and tactful too!

Aquarius is a Fixed Positive Masculine Air sign, and this man doesn't like to follow anyone else's path. He is an idealist, a visionary, hoping for a better world in every possible sense. Aquarius is the sign of the humanitarian, and your Aquarius partner is sure to have very strong leanings to 'good' causes, politics, science and education.

But although he's an idealist, he's also a man with his feet firmly on terra firma when it comes to love. If you think you can sweep him off balance with seductively feminine wiles alone, you will definitely be barking up the wrong tree. The best way to develop a relationship with your Aquarian man is to let him totally believe that you are a wonderful friend, and for a while, maybe leave it like that. It could be frustrating if you're longing for a little more passion because you were convinced from the moment you met him that he was the most perfect partner you could ever meet. However, it could definitely work out in your favour if you'll stick at it for a while.

Your Aquarian man doesn't like to feel he's being pushed into anything. He wants to feel totally in charge. Remember, his opposite sign of the Zodiac is Leo, and Leos are famed for often being bossy. Inside your Aquarian man is something of that Leo personality, and while he doesn't necessarily roar like a lion when he doesn't get his own way, he can certainly make quite a squeak!

He also doesn't necessarily put as much importance on sexuality as many of the other signs. Of course, he knows it's a highly desirable part of being in love and there is no way he's going to negate it's importance to keep a love relationship properly balanced. He enjoys sexual fulfilment with the right partner as much as anyone else, so you don't have to worry whether or not your Aquarian might not be the red-hot lover of your dreams. He knows the true value of having a partner who is on his mental wavelength too.

Your Aquarian man puts great store on the intellect. It's not that he's an intellectual snob who insists that you have a university degree, but he does yearn for someone who can talk his language, understand his ideals and ideas, and be as interested in life as much as he is. There might easily be moments when you're not quite sure whether you have a genius to contend with or someone whose ideas are so over the top they're totally unfathomable! But, you can be sure that there won't be many times that you can accuse your Aquarian man of being a bore. True he might discourse for hours on one of his favourite sub-jects when you're longing to put out the lights and cuddle up to go to sleep. But you'll have to admit that in the end he always manages to fascinate you one way or another.

Now you may be thinking, that to have a really good relation-ship with an Aquarian man, you have a great deal to live up to. But since in every relationship there has to be a great deal of give and take for both partners it's unnecessary nonsense to think that things are going to be any more difficult with this man than any other. If he has decided that you *are* perfect for *him*, his fixed ideas of what is right will mean he isn't going to change his mind, even if it does seem to take a long time for him to commit himself. So think what a marvellous time you can have getting to know each other better; don't you enjoy having a wonderful friend around? Someone who is loyal, devoted and attentive, but allows you to enjoy your own freedom too?

Freedom is highly important to Aquarius. Never ever try to fence him in by being too possessive or demanding. He is ruled by the dynamic planet Uranus – which can be inspirational but also disruptive. If an Aquarian is locked into a claustrophobic relationship, he can't cope with it for long – and somehow something *will* have to change. Be his understanding friend as well as his lover, and you'll have learnt one of the tricks to keep him by your side for ever. But, become a nagging partner and you'll soon see how cold and stubborn he can be.

One thing is for sure: although he's not going to be the most uncomplicated man you could have met, he's amazingly percep-tive and intuitive, and he'll know almost before you do if there are problems you need to discuss between you. He'll read your mind like a book. He will also expect there to be total trust between you. Since he took his time to get to know you well, he won't worry that you could be the sort of woman to play around with other men. He places far too much faith on his instinct for that. And equally he doesn't expect you to feel jealous where he is concerned. Although you'd better be prepared for him sometimes to arrive home hours late because he's been discussing the problems of the world with his friends, or to turn up on the doorstep with all of them just when you were hoping for a quiet night.

An Aquarius man in good form will live up to everything you've ever dreamed of in a partner; he will be good natured, kind, funny and totally unselfish. On a bad day he will be a rebel in every way, unwilling to concede that anyone could be right but him. However, he really does believe in equality for all, moreover he doesn't want a woman who loses her identity just because she's living with him. Always retain your own individuality – he'll appreciate you so much more for that. He won't expect you to give up your career for him; he will support and encourage you and be one of the most understanding men you could find if you need support and encouragement. He has a flair for being creative and recognizing creativity in others. He's a true inventor.

You'll sometimes find it hard to understand how he can switch moods so suddenly, and turn from being a fun-loving extrovert to someone who wants to cut off from the world. But this is simply down to his unpredictability. It won't usually have anything to do with you. He simply knows he needs his moments to switch off from what is going on around him and to display that detached side of his personality. He knows that he is not always easy to live with – but he's as aware as you that no one else is either all the time. And once you've started to live with him you'll realize that he wants to make your relationship work just as much as you do. He's not a man who is looking for lots of different partners, especially if he took a long time to build things up with you. He might have been unbearably elusive in the early stages, but he's a man who commits himself deeply when he recognizes his true soulmate.

A business relationship with an Aquarius man can be fantastic as long as he isn't tied down to a humdrum routine situation. With that he simply cannot cope. He's as unconventional and unpredictable about his working life as he is about everything else. And he is sure to invent new ways of doing things rather than to stick to tried-and-true methods. Give him a worthwhile goal to aim for and he'll never let anyone down.

He's no different with his family and friends than he is with anyone else. He wants everyone to be happy with each other. But he doesn't want to be pinned down as to when and where he's going to be at any given time. Don't commit your Aquarian man to a family gathering two months ahead of time – how can he know what will be happening then? He probably doesn't even know all his commitments for tomorrow.

He may not be the stereotype parent that some children have, but he'll enjoy helping them to grow up learning the meaning of life, and he'll be doing everything in his power to encourage them along the way.

Problems could arise in your relationship if both of you are extravagant. Your Aquarian man will either be a genius at making money — or it will fall so far down on his list of ideals that he doesn't consider it a major issue. But since he's always so concerned about helping humanity in general, you'll have to impress on him the necessity of taking good care of the people at home too! And let him see that you're equally willing to do the same, for he certainly won't relish the idea of having a spend-thrift around when there are so many worthy causes needing help.

In any relationship with an Aquarian man it won't take you long before you realize you've found a real original — no other man would be able to live up to him. Even on his down days you will soon discover why you were attracted to him in the first place. He's a will-o'-the-wisp, a rebel, a truth-seeker, a man who has high morals and high ideals, and he streaks ahead of everyone else. Discoveries and inventions are what Aquarius is all about. You can almost bet he'll be one of the first passengers to fly to the Moon when space buses gear up for operation. You now know that he's more vulnerable than he seems where love is concerned, so if you want to twist him round your little finger so that he will be yours for ever, don't ever let him feel insecure in any way. Be as optimistic about the future as he is; let him see that you value having him as a wonderful friend as much as you enjoy having him as the love of your life for ever more.

High spots with your Aquarius man
He will

★ Always fascinate you with the different facets of his person-
   ality.
★ Never ever bore you.
★ Seduce your mind as well as your body.
★ Delight you with his witty sense of humour.
★ Make your life more exciting than it's ever been.

★ Surprise you in a myriad of different ways.
★ Be a marvellous friend and a romantic idealist too.
★ Want to share his visions of the future with you.

Danger zones with your Aquarius man
Never

★ Expect him to stop being unpredictable just because of you.
★ Expect him to be a great time-keeper.
★ Demand passionate embraces when he's not in the mood.
★ Criticize his favourite 'cause' or political leanings.
★ Try to tie him down too much – he must feel inwardly free.
★ Destroy his idealistic view of what life should be all about.
★ Expect him to lead a routine humdrum life.
★ Try to change him!

★ The Aquarius Woman ★

Aquarius – the Water Carrier – is ruled by Uranus, planet of change. A Masculine Positive Fixed Air sign – it's the change-ability of Aquarius which perhaps fascinates and infuriates other people more than anything else.

One of the first things you'll discover about the Aquarian woman is that, just like her male counterpart, she can be incredibly elusive. You might almost think she's a Gemini, playing a dual role in your life. That's if you've managed to feel that you are truly part of her life since for her telling someone 'I love you' could be to allow a weakness to show in her character.

No sign of the Zodiac is quite so cool and detached as Aquarius. But when the Aquarian woman is happily involved with her perfect partner she will enjoy a blissfully fulfilling sexual relationship just as much as any other woman. It's just that she may take much longer to reach the point where she's prepared to commit herself to something as deeply emotional as love. Friendship yes – but love?

Are you beginning to think you've found the original Ice Maiden? A woman who will take so long to thaw out that you've lost interest in her before you've even got to know her very well?

Does it appear that sexuality is something which shouldn't even be discussed with her? You will be doing your Aquarian woman a great injustice if you start thinking along those lines, and you'd certainly never see her again if she learnt of your thoughts; remember that Aquarians are highly intuitive!

First of all you'd be wise to get one thing straight from the start. The Aquarius woman is never going to be your doting 'yes' woman who stays at home minding her own business and thinking of nothing else but you. If that's what you're hoping for as the perfect partner — you'll be butting your head against a brick wall if you think she can play this part. Even the very rare Aquarian, whose personal horoscope gave her all sorts of contradictory facets to her personality, would deep down still rebel against the conventional, run-of-the-mill mould.

Tell an Aquarian woman she's moody and she won't understand what you're talking about. It's not really that she's moody in the true sense of the word. It's just that her moods are always changing, not necessarily from good to bad, high to low, but changing. She doesn't stick to the same ideas, she'll sometimes say one thing and mean something completely different. You think she's going to be feeling wonderful because everything is going so well between you, and yet she screams at you as though you're the meanest man in the world. Yet when you expect things to be bad — she gives you the biggest smile you've ever seen and showers you with praise.

Two of the characteristics most frequently used to describe this sign are 'unconventional' and 'unpredictable' — and both male and female Aquarians live up to these most of the time. At first you may wonder what you're involved with when you first begin a relationship with an Aquarian woman. She obviously liked you, stuck by your side, listening to everything you said, and seemed delighted that you were interested in so many of the things she had to discuss. She seemed to want to see more of you, but she suddenly became totally non-committal when you suggested meeting again. When you called her up a few days later it was almost as though she'd forgotten who you were.

You have to remember that the Aquarian woman always has so much on her mind, always so many people to see, that she can totally cut off from a situation when something else takes precedence. It wasn't necessarily that she didn't want to see you again — just that the moment of close contact had slipped. And of course you were fascinated enough to persuade her to see you again! For one of the delights of having an Aquarian woman as your partner is that you will never have a boring life. You will never have to worry about putting up with too much routine — she hates it with an overpowering passion.

You will also find out early on in your relationship that mental compatibility at the highest possible level is a total necessity for the Aquarian woman. If you can't communicate easily it will be almost impossible for her to envision a relationship growing from strength to strength. She is not the sort of woman who will embark on an intimate physical involvement unless she's also intimately involved with your mind. Make sure you have a good sense of humour too: it always helps to bring you even closer together and she may be one of the wittiest women you've ever known.

She is an idealist, a humanitarian, someone who would do everything in her power to make the world a happier place for everyone. But sometimes it seems to be the hardest thing in the world for her to reflect on just what she needs in her own life to make her feel totally fulfilled. It's as though deep down she is fearful of a total commitment because she knows how hard it is for her to reveal her innermost feelings to anyone. That might be one of the reasons she feels so much safer when the only thing involved is friendship. Love is something different, a totally consuming mind-body-and-soul experience which is very different. She wants and needs to let herself go and experience it all, but something holds her back. But never hurt her by criticizing her for this — she knows about it already.

Always let your Aquarius woman feel that she can trust you as a friend as deeply as she can enjoy you as a lover. Once she can do that it will be much easier for her to unleash her physical feelings and let herself go totally. Remember she can be quite a liberated woman when she really wants. Sexual freedom is something she believes in when the time and place is right, although you don't have to worry about her playing around with other men once she's committed to you. The Aquarius woman is amazingly loyal and devoted to the man in her life and would also never try to make him jealous just to create a scene. But make sure you're not a philanderer yourself because since she has amazing powers of intuition she will always know if she has any cause for jealousy and definitely sparks will fly if she has. However once you've discovered what a wonderful soulmate your Aquarian partner makes – especially when you fear her unpredictable personality could mean you'd lose her! – you will be careful not to let this happen.

It may seem as though she is completely independent, a fun-loving, freedom-seeking New Age woman with fixed opinions and fixed goals in her mind. But when she is happily settled in a relationship with a man she can truly respect, she will be the equal you've dreamed of. She'll encourage you about your own goals, encourage *your* hopes and aspirations and help to plan a better life for the two of you together. She's a very determined lady, your Aquarian woman – there's definitely something of her opposite sign, of Leo, in her personality, and although she may sometimes be a little domineering, it's simply that she knows exactly what she wants – and her Aquarian intuition often means she knows rightly what's best for you as well.

Don't try to force her into anything against her will – she can be more stubborn than Taurus. And don't expect your home life to be smooth-running one hundred per cent of the time. She has an awful lot of other things going on in her life too, and punctuality is not always one of her strong points. She's also much more of a night person than an early riser!

When she becomes a mother, her children will always know they have a wonderful friend they can rely on; even if it is sometimes hard for her to tell them how much she loves them, just as she finds it so hard to tell you. But there'll be a depth of understanding between this woman and her loved ones which is one of the firmest bonds there is, even if words are sometimes lacking it will be impossible to miss the deep feeling which is intrinsically there.

In a working relationship with the Aquarian woman you'll soon realize that she has to feel totally committed to her profession in the same way she has to feel about everything else. But she can switch careers almost at a moment's notice if she is no longer creatively inspired and starts to feel tied down by too much routine. She is used to erratic hours quite often and might not be too concerned about financial rewards if she feels she is doing something really worthwhile to help others. Every Aquarian must have a cause to believe in.

Do you think you can cope with the unpredictability of your Aquarian woman and learn to enjoy to the full the pleasure of having this unique and idealistic partner for your very own? It might sometimes seem that twisting her round your little finger to keep her by your side for ever could be quite a difficult task, so always let her see how much you admire her independent ways, resolve to try and understand her goals and share them with her, and be happy that she has taught you the value of having a loving partner who is also the best of all possible friends.

Sometimes she may seem almost eccentric with some of her far-out ideas, sometimes you'll want to scream when the house is full of all her friends and you've come home exhausted, hoping to find her on her own; but far more times than not you'll thank your lucky stars that you've met a woman who truly understands that the most perfect of all relationships is one which contains a wonderful balance of mind, body and soul. And, where you both share the same visions of your future the high spots in your relationship will become even more wonderful – and the danger zones will diminish.

High spots with your Aquarius woman
She will

★ Be everything you ever wanted, and never the same way twice!
★ Be a wonderfully supportive helpmate as well as soulmate.
★ Be a romantic idealist, a visionary, a true free spirit.
★ Will make life exhilarating and exciting too.
★ Be mentally stimulating and unconventional too.
★ Be totally honest ... always.
★ Inspire you to turn your dreams into realities.
★ Always be tolerant – and never try to change you.

Danger zones with your Aquarius woman
Never

★ Criticize her for being 'different'.

★ Find fault with her ideals.

★ Object to any of her friends.

★ Expect her to fit in with any preconceived ideas of what the perfect partner might be!

★ Expect her to be too intimate when other people are around.

★ Criticize her taste for ethnic clothes.

★ Destroy her trust in human nature — and especially in you!

★ Risk losing her respect.

The Pisces Partner

★ The Pisces Man ★

If you long for some good old-fashioned romance in your life; for a man who will whisper sweet nothings into your ear, buy you red roses every time he feels you need cheering up and write you the most beautiful poems you've read in your life, then you're well prepared for being hooked by a Pisces man. But to have a perfect relationship it's going to take a whole lot more than the trimmings of love. Although it would be wonderful to think you could survive on romance alone for ever more, life isn't quite so simple.

I'm certainly not trying to put you off a relationship with a Pisces man; far from it, we all need a bit more romance in our lives. But you need to get to know a little more about him before you picture spending the rest of your life with him. And he can be absolutely irresistible when he's out to charm the woman of *his* choice! If you'd always thought it was signs like Aries and Scorpio who led the field in sweeping women off their feet, it's time you found out differently. Every Pisces man doesn't come across exactly as a roving Casanova. Nonetheless it probably won't take you long to fall under his seductive spell.

At the start of a relationship with a Pisces man he'll be the sweetness and light you've always yearned for; the heart throb you dreamed of as a child. He'll be the most sensitive, understanding man you've ever met and you'll enjoy every minute you spend together. He will willingly bare his heart and soul to you. And you will long to share his dreams with him and help him turn them into realities.

But be forewarned that a great many Pisces men have dreams which never do become realities, no matter who is by their side. The trouble with this charming romantic dreamer is that so often he is too busy looking at the world though his rose-coloured spectacles and forgets that it can all look very different when he takes them off. Of course, there may be thousands of Pisces men who will totally disagree with this, but obviously their personal horoscopes will show the reason for the disparity, and I can only generalize here.

But don't start getting worried, for perhaps if your Pisces man fits the bill as one of these romantic dreamers, you can help him to become a little more realistic without his having to lose sight of his dreams. And he's the sort of man who is always a great deal happier about life when he has the right partner by his side. Perhaps you can be one of the first people in his life who brings romance *and* realism; for he often has difficulty in believing that the two can go together.

Pisces is ruled by the inspirational planet Neptune, perfect for helping him with all his creative and artistic aspirations. But Neptune also creates illusion and deception, which will help you to understand why your Pisces man likes to see the world his way even if deep down he knows it's not supposed to be that way.

A Mutable Negative Feminine sign, the symbol of Pisces is those two fish swimming in opposite directions – upstream and down – what better description could there be for this, the last of the Water signs? But is he just a two-faced charmer going his two different ways, a man who lies through his teeth yet actually believes everything he says, a smooth talker who can't resist a pretty face – time and time again? You'd be doing your Pisces man an incredible disservice if you really believed that. And even if you've ever nursed a broken heart because of a romance with a Pisces man, I'm sure you will have some wonderful moments to treasure too.

A Pisces man knows he's right on one point. Romance *is* one of the great necessities of life, and if you're a woman who sets more store on more materialistic matters it could be asking for trouble to consider this man as your perfect partner. It almost sounds as though his negative qualities outweigh his positive ones, which is very unfair. But it's surely better to put all the cards on the table and let you see what you're getting yourself into.

Sensitive, compassionate, emotional Pisces, he'd do anything in the world for the woman he loves, and for a whole lot more people who probably come to him for help as well. You couldn't ask for a kinder man, who sometimes finds it much harder to do the right things for himself. Depending on his age, your Pisces man may have suffered from quite a few failed relationships or even marriages. He needs a woman who fulfils his romantic dreams but isn't just going to follow in his footsteps, losing her own identity in the process. If she's too strong she could accuse him of being weak, it's inevitably happened before that way and he is wary of this imbalance. He needs encouragement and support, but never bossiness; praise and adulation when he deserves it, and constructive criticism too. He knows he's an idealist, but wouldn't you rather have *him* than a pessimistic partner who sees gloom and despondency around every corner?

The Pisces man wants to settle down with a woman who can understand him on every level, physical, mental and spiritual. And the spiritual is often very important to him. His perfect partner really is his soulmate but sometimes he is too easily deluded into thinking he's found her. A sensitive Pisces isn't always very good at accepting the fact that he's failed, and sometimes his idealistic optimism falters and he seems to wallow in despair rather than to rationalize that his perfect partner could still be just ahead.

But don't get the idea that a relationship with a Pisces man could turn into a wishy-washy affair and that he would always be wondering if you are really right for him. Your Pisces man is also one of the most intuitive people around, so that if he has been deluded once or twice he is far more aware of what it takes to make a good relationship. In fact when he was very young he imagined that it was possible to 'live on love' . . . that money didn't matter when two people cared for one another. He could never imagine a life without a partner who shared his romantic ideals; however, he does tend to become more practical as the years go by, though not completely, for that would be far too much to ask of him. Nonetheless, although living in a garret up five flights of stairs might have seemed wonderful once upon a time, he does learn to like his creature comforts as much as everyone else does.

Problems can arise, however, in a relationship with your Pisces man if he does have difficulty making ends meet. One problem is that because he has such a kind heart he tends to be the 'soft touch' for anyone and everyone who could do with a loan. Pisces is always trying to help other people, and at home he will always want to surprise you with little unexpected gifts. But if he's the sole breadwinner in the relationship things can sometimes get tough. Of course there are Pisceans who, through their optimism, climb to the heights of success and become millionaires too, but your average sensitive fish is happy to swim along without too much attention to his material assets.

Since many Pisceans often veer towards the artistic field, this could also mean that they work in freelance occupations, and if you're a woman who sets too much store by financial stability, you could have a few headaches from time to time. However, at least you know you have a man who will always protect you in every way he can, making all sorts of sacrifices to ensure that you never suffer.

You'll be very aware that your Pisces partner needs a great deal of love; not the smothering possessive kind, but love which is based on total trust and understanding. Always remember he's a very receptive Water sign, but he's sometimes very shy about showing just *how* sensitive he is. There is a little-boy-lost quality about him which is so appealing that you'll always want to look after him: but he certainly doesn't want to be mothered by his partner: he wants someone to help him achieve his unfulfilled dreams, who won't laugh when he unleashes his secret fears and insecurities.

The sexual side of your relationship can be more magical than you ever imagined. This man is a poet and will be one of the most tender and sentimental lovers you have ever known. If you've yearned for true romance which you previously thought existed only in movies or novels, you will be in for a delightful surprise with Mr Pisces. It's not simply that he gets such great pleasure from whispering all those wonderful words of love in your ear; but he really does put his own mind, body and soul into bringing you to sexual fulfilment. The art of making love is never underestimated by your Pisces. And it's the snuggling up together and waking up so close in the mornings which will bring you so much happiness too. He's not the sort of man who will be too tired to make love at the end of a busy day. And he'll never forget any anniversaries which mean something special to you both.

He can be very jealous if he feels someone else is competing for your attention and he'd hate to be involved with someone who liked to flirt. But he won't like it quite so much if you show too much of a jealous streak yourself, for he does enjoy talking to other women without having someone leaning over his shoulder.

A business relationship with a Pisces can soar to the heights if he doesn't always live in his dreams. He can be a great achiever but he needs someone to bring him down to earth from time to time and temper his idealistic aspirations with constructive common sense. In his family relationships he will always be there when he's needed, willing to listen to anyone's problems and he's exactly the same way with his friends. As a father he might not always be the most practical of parents but his children will never want for love and affection and a sympathetic ear.

Pisces needs to have beauty in his life. He needs peace and harmony just as much as any Libran; and cares about humanity in the same way as Aquarians do. He doesn't like to live in a disorderly home although he'd probably be the first to admit he's not exactly the tidiest of men. But he doesn't expect you to devote your life to cleaning up after him! Giving him lots of tender, loving care is essential though, and letting him enjoy the happiness of seeing his world become more perfect because of you.

Sometimes people accuse Pisceans of being weak, pointing out that when this sign gets low and depressed they are more likely than many other people to seek solace in drink. It's true that there is a negative quality which can turn Pisceans into escapists, but you certainly don't have to fear your Pisces man will suddenly hit the bottle just because he's had a bad day. Always remember that security to this man means having a woman who loves him for himself, not because of how much he has in the bank. If along the way you can help him to become more conscious of the material side of life without making him think you're losing faith in him, it can work wonders in making your relationship become even better.

Sometimes he doesn't believe in himself as much as he should, and a little extra loving encouragement will be a wonderful boost to his confidence. Of course there are sure to be both good and bad times; moments when you wonder why you chose such an emotional dreamer to share your life. But isn't it marvellous to know that you can have one of the most warm and loving relationships imaginable when you have this man by your side?

High spots with your Pisces man
He will

★ Be the most romantic tender lover you've ever known.
★ Read your mind even if you're far away.
★ Be sentimental, sensitive and compassionate too.
★ Turn your dreams of everlasting love into reality.
★ Whisper sweet nothings into your ear − time and time again.
★ Build castles in the air for you to share together ever more.
★ Help you see the beauty in the world by seeing it through his eyes.
★ Show you what being a true soulmate is all about.

Danger zones with your Pisces man
Never

★ Expect him to be too brilliant where money is concerned (unless you know his personal horoscope!).
★ Destroy his ideals.
★ Nag him because he's not the most practical man you've ever known.
★ Hurt him by being uncommunicative or failing to understand what he's about.

★ Run him down in front of anyone.
★ Let him brood on any problems — be a sounding board.
★ Forget that he's highly intuitive and can read your mind!

★ The Pisces Woman ★

In case you didn't already know, Pisces is the most romantic sign of the entire Zodiac, and your Pisces woman will be one of the most feminine women you have ever met. Even if she comes across as the go-getter of all time (probably due to an Aries or Leo Ascendant), since she was a little girl she's been dreaming of growing up and living happily every after with the perfect man.

You see, dreaming is what life is all about for the Pisces woman. Dreams to her are like strong intakes of caffeine to lots of other people. Just like her male counterpart, she much prefers to see the outside world through a pair of rose-coloured spectacles, for too much disillusionment sets in when she puts them away. But if you are beginning to think you may have come across a totally irresponsible woman who doesn't have a single sensible thought in her mind, how wrong you'd be.

In fact, your Pisces woman is probably one of the most creative and artistic women you know. She isn't an empty-headed romantic — simply a wise and wonderful, mystical and magical woman who knows that a relationship without enough romance will be very hard to sustain for very long. And just because she appears to be so shy and sensitive, it doesn't have to mean she is weak. Your Pisces partner will be a tower of strength when necessary, especially when other people are relying upon her in one way or another. And yet she loves to have someone to depend on, a partner with a shoulder big enough on which to lean when the worries of the world become too much to bear, but it definitely won't be one-sided.

A Feminine Negative Mutable Water sign, Pisces is the last sign of the Zodiac, and its ruler is the inspirational planet Neptune. But the most important factor affecting your Pisces partner is that her planetary symbol is the two fish, swimming upstream and down, simultaneously. She needs to learn to take the positive road in life, and avoid the negative pitfalls. But time and time again she is torn in both directions, confusing herself and everyone else.

Sometimes life is too much of an illusion for your Pisces woman and when she has to cope with its reality she suffers from the hardships she may have to encounter. Failed love affairs are not something she likes to contemplate, but because of her continual search for the partner of her dreams who so often cannot live up to her expectations, she may have sometimes had her heart broken.

Soft, sensitive, compassionate Pisces – her feminine mystique will over power you as you become closer to her. You long to convince her that you'll do everything in the world to protect her from her fears, to make her feel secure for ever more. When she gazes soulfully into your eyes you want to melt away and you feel your perfect partner can be no one but her.

So isn't it wonderful to know you've met a woman who will almost always concede that the man in her life is the boss? Who will never try to dominate you, argue with you in front of your friends, forget your birthday or moan when she has to cook your favourite meal? However since every star-sign has its positive and negative sides, you'd also better be prepared for a partner who sometimes seems to think that money really does grow on trees. It's not that she sets out to be wildly extravagant, although at times she can be that too. It's just that she doesn't always set sufficient store on having enough money in the bank to pay all the bills, not after she's lent some to her best friends, bought you a shirt in your favourite colour as a surprise gift, and sent off a cheque to her favourite charity. Hopefully, you won't be one of the last of the big-time spenders yourself, since unless your financial assets give no cause for concern – this could definitely lead to problems in your relationship with a Pisces woman.

Because your Pisces partner is so disinterested in money *per se,* you won't have to worry that she's the sort of woman who could suddenly decide to leave you if things did get really bad. When she loves a man it's for good and bad; she'll support you through thick and thin, and even if she's never worked before she won't worry about having to take on a job to help. She's the sort of woman who loves to be needed. There is something of her opposite sign of the Zodiac, Virgo, within her, which also makes her long to be of service to others, but you need not worry that your Pisces partner will be as critical and analytical as the typical Virgo; far from it, for in her eyes the man she loves is almost always perfect!

She is a woman who is in love with love, but then you're sure to have discovered this very early on. To be able to express her innermost feelings to that someone who can fulfil her in every way is pure joy to her. That's why it's so difficult for her if she ever finds her trust has been misplaced. For just like her male counterpart the Pisces woman can be prone to depressions and insecurities which lead her to search for an escape, and just like him this can lead her to drink too much. So always understand her need to believe in you. She wants true love to last for ever, not to be a fleeting passage in her life.

She is often amazingly psychic, so if you start to behave like a philanderer behind her back, it won't take long before she will discover it, and she can be incredibly jealous. But she's not averse to a little gentle flirting herself, often simply to gauge your reaction and to make sure you love her enough to care about it! Sometimes she's accused of being devious and avoiding the truth, but the truth is simply that she hates to think of ever hurting people, and sometimes feels it's best to colour a story slightly to avoid doing this. She doesn't deliberately set out to tell a lie!

She is usually quite prepared to give up her independence when she starts living with you. She doesn't feel the need to have a career outside her home when she is with the man of her dreams. However, since so many Pisceans are involved in the arts, she is unlikely to forego something she finds really fulfilling if she can combine it with everything else. Generally she has no trouble being on the right wavelength with her family and friends, for they too know she will always be on hand when she's needed. And although she might not always give her children the firm discipline they need, at least they will know they have one of the most loving signs of the Zodiac as their mother, who will instinctively understand their needs even before they do.

The sexual side of your relationship will be yet another magical mysterious part of living with your Pisces woman. She seems to be so deep and unfathomable; her passion is mixed with a sweet innocence which is wonderfully exciting. She's not a brazen, brash lover who sets out to make all the overtures. She wants the man in her life to awaken the deep feelings lying inside her by tenderness and with soft whispered affirmations of his love, and because she is such a sensitive soul she cannot envision a perfect relationship which isn't on the mind, body and spiritual level. Sex alone will never make her happy for very long. It's that intimate sense of belonging in every possible sense which she craves and needs.

In a business relationship with a Pisces woman, her lack of interest in the financial stakes often means she needs the right back-up around her to protect her interests. In a partnership, it is to be hoped that you're the possessor of immense practicality which will counterbalance this.

Living with a Pisces woman will help you to understand just why she sets so much store by having lots of romance in life. You'll wonder why you never realized it before. Twisting her around your little finger to keep her by your side for ever doesn't have to be at all difficult. For as long as she knows she can believe in you she'll never want to roam. Just don't forget how quickly she can become hurt if she feels misunderstood, and let her see that she doesn't need to wear those rose-coloured spectacles to view the world when you're around — for you'll do all you can to help make it a better place.

The charisma of your Pisces partner is something which grows stronger day by day. Her femininity will always delight you and before too long you'll enjoy sharing more and more in her dreams.

High spots with your Pisces woman
She will
★ When she feels truly loved and protected, be the most life-enhancing partner you could meet.
★ Be a real mind/body/soul mate!

★   Encourage you to build your special rainbows in the sky and help you achieve miracles.
★   Be the most tender sentimental partner in the world.
★   Be totally receptive to all your needs and desires.
★   Be artistic, creative, sensitive − a joy to be with!
★   Follow you to the end of the earth when she believes in you.
★   Believe in true love and romance like no one else you've ever met.

Danger zones with your Pisces woman
Never
★   Destroy her belief in rainbows in the sky.
★   Expect her to be totally practical.
★   Rely on her to be too materially minded.
★   Think that sex alone will keep her by your side.
★   Hurt her by making sarcastic jokes about her desirability − she'll take them too much to heart.
★   Drive her to drink!
★   Think of her as weak even if she sometimes does appear that way!
★   Think of love and romance as being 'sloppy'.

Conclusion:
Never ever give up

There is no pre-ordained time-span with relationships. A perfect partner can appear during your twenties, thirties, forties, fifties and even later. People today are so preoccupied with age, with years passing them by. But your age is simply a number; what is important is *you,* and what you're about. That's why learning to love yourself more and being honest with yourself about your innermost needs, desires – and insecurities too – is invaluable in this endless quest to have and hold the perfect relationship.

Every experience has its benefits. Even if you had bad relationships in the past, you will have gained something from them. If you have fallen for someone who is married, or whose lifestyle makes it impossible for you to contemplate a permanent relationship perhaps this is also because you have purposely chosen the unattainable through your own fears and insecurities of becoming totally committed. But it's wonderful to know that love can strike at any time. However, you must never play with love, treating it totally as a game. Always be honest; so much unnecessary time and negative energy is expended when people are not truthful with each other.

Relationships are real – not mythical situations dreamed up by romantic novelists and cinema moguls. But one of the saddest things I heard whilst writing this book was about a mother with thirteen children who constantly replenished her huge stock of romantic novels because she adored reading about love and romance with the perfect partner. When it was pointed out to her that, since she had thirteen children, surely she knew all about love, she replied 'Oh, is that love?'

I don't believe that sort of experience needs to be part of your lives. But I do believe you must apply a positive attitude to *all* your relationships in order to achieve the very best for yourself and the other people around you.

Once you've learned more about yourself, your foibles and idiosyncracies, your strengths and weaknesses, you will be in a much better position to build and maintain every relationship in your life. You will also realize why you have such perfect communication with some members of your family, yet so often end up at cross purposes with others; how certain working relationships are perfect on one level, but frustrating on another; how you can love someone in a platonic way but find it impossible to contemplate a sexual relationship with them; and how it can be equally possible to have a sexually fulfilling relationship with someone else and yet be poles apart on a mental and spiritual plane.

Understanding yourself and your partner even better will prove to you beyond all doubt that astral compatibility is not simply something dreamed up by an idealistic astrologer, and that jealousy, possessiveness, bitterness and envy do not exist in a perfect relationship – while empathy does.

Greater self-awareness, plus the ability to give and receive love will enable *all* your relationships to grow stronger day by day.

Believe in yourself – use your instinct, your common sense, your new-found astrological knowledge – and you'll never look back!